Paradise Lost

An Annotated Bibliography

THE MAGILL BIBLIOGRAPHIES

The American Presidents, by Norman S. Cohen, 1989
Black American Women Novelists, by Craig Werner, 1989
Classical Greek and Roman Drama, by Robert J. Forman, 1989
Contemporary Latin American Fiction, by Keith H. Brower, 1989
Masters of Mystery and Detective Fiction, by J. Randolph Cox, 1989
Nineteenth Century American Poetry, by Philip K. Jason, 1989
Restoration Drama, by Thomas J. Taylor, 1989
Twentieth Century European Short Story, by Charles E. May, 1989
The Victorian Novel, by Laurence W. Mazzeno, 1989
Women's Issues, by Laura Stempel Mumford, 1989
America in Space, by Russell R. Tobias, 1991
The American Constitution, by Robert J. Janosik, 1991
The Classic Epic, by Thomas J. Sienkewicz, 1991
English Romantic Poetry, by Brian Aubrey, 1991
Ethics, by John K. Roth, 1991
The Immigrant Experience, by Paul D. Mageli, 1991
The Modern American Novel, by Steven G. Kellman, 1991
Native Americans, by Frederick E. Hoxie and Harvey Markowitz,
    1991
American Drama: 1918-1960, by R. Baird Shuman, 1992
American Ethnic Literatures, by David R. Peck, 1992
American Theater History, by Thomas J. Taylor, 1992
The Atomic Bomb, by Hans G. Graetzer and Larry M. Browning, 1992
Biography, by Carl Rollyson, 1992
The History of Science, by Gordon L. Miller, 1992
The Origin and Evolution of Life on Earth, by David W. Hollar, Jr.,
    1992
Pan-Africanism, by Michael W. Williams, 1992
Resources for Writers, by R. Baird Shuman, 1992
Shakespeare, by Joseph Rosenblum, 1992
The Vietnam War in Literature, by Philip K. Jason, 1992
Contemporary Southern Women Fiction Writers, by Rosemary M.
    Canfield Reisman and Christopher J. Canfield, 1994
Cycles in Humans and Nature, by John T. Burns, 1994
Environmental Studies, by Diane M. Fortner, 1994
Poverty in America, by Steven Pressman, 1994
The Short Story in English: Britain and North America, by Dean

Paradise Lost

An Annotated Bibliography

P. J. Klemp

Magill Bibliographies

The Scarecrow Press, Inc.
Lanham, Md., and London
and
Salem Press
Pasadena, Calif. and Englewood Cliffs, N.J.

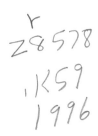

SCARECROW PRESS, INC.

Published in the United States of America
by Scarecrow Press, Inc.
4720 Boston Way
Lanham, Maryland 20706

4 Pleydell Gardens, Folkestone
Kent CT20 2DN, England

British Cataloguing-in-Publication Information Available

Library of Congress Cataloging-in-Publication Data

Klemp, P. J.
Paradise lost : an annotated bibliography / by P.J. Klemp.
p. cm. — (Magill bibliographies)
Includes index.
1. Milton, John, 1608–1674. Paradise lost—Bibliography.
2. Fall of man in literature—Bibliography. 3. Epic poetry,
English—Bibliography. I. Title. II. Series.
Z8578.K59 1996 [PR356?] 016.821'4—dc20 96-671 CIP

ISBN 0–8108–3152–x (cloth : alk. paper)

♾™ The paper used in this publication meets the minimum requirements of
American National Standard for Information Sciences—Permanence of
Paper for Printed Library Materials, ANSI Z39.48–1984.
Manufactured in the United States of America.

CONTENTS

ACKNOWLEDGMENTS

While working on this volume, I incurred a number of debts that I am glad to acknowledge here. Professor Roy C. Flannagan kept me well informed about current publications on *Paradise Lost* that I was in danger of overlooking; Professor Edward Jones found some elusive studies. In addition to typing most of the bibliography, Heidi M. Heidenreich brought her organizational abilities and attention to detail to the project. She invested a great deal in this bibliography. My gratitude goes to Heidi and Edward because they provided motivation and encouragement at key times. I am particularly indebted to Mr. A. J. Sobczak, who edited this volume and patiently taught me so much about the editorial process. Randy Haasl diligently proofread the manuscript, worked on the indexes, and located some important scholarly works. Stephen Beers made a large contribution to many aspects of this bibliography, including work on the annotations and the indexes.

INTRODUCTION

The tradition of Milton scholarship is long and diverse. Commentary on the man and his writings started to appear even during his lifetime,[1] and it remains vital after more than three centuries.[2] Of all his works, *Paradise Lost* has received by far the most attention, for writers in each succeeding age define critical issues and themselves by turning to the epic. As Stanley Fish cautions, however, prevailing ideological conditions determine which questions literary critics find meaningful and which answers they consider convincing.[3] Thus broad patterns of cultural change and approaches to literary analysis, especially in England and America, are clearly reflected in the phases in Milton scholarship, which moves from the biographical and political concerns of his contemporaries[4] to the application of neoclassical standards during the Restoration and eighteenth century,[5] from the emphasis on Satan's heroism in the Romantic age[6] to the revival of interest in political and biographical matters in early America,[7] the Victorian age,[8] and the beginning of the twentieth century. From the 1930s to the 1970s, two divergent approaches to *Paradise Lost* dominate: historical scholarship investigates the poem's biographical, political, literary, and theological contexts and traditions, usually through sources and analogues,[9] while the New Criticism explores ironies and ambiguities in context-free, ahistorical analyses.[10] Each stage of Milton scholarship not only articulates the prevailing ideological conditions of its age but also reflects the emphases of Anglo-American literary criticism in general.

During the past twenty years, critical approaches have multiplied, and one cannot identify a consensus about any interpretive method or major literary work, including *Paradise Lost*. No longer focusing almost exclusively on Milton's biography, literary-theological traditions, or poetic style, the current age may be considered a period of great diversity in which traditional historical critics coexist, though not always amicably, with such post-structuralists as new historical, feminist, and Marxist critics. The high quality of recent commentary on *Paradise Lost*, particularly its originality and provocativeness, is in some measure the result of these varied approaches. Though some critics see diversity as an invitation to ignore the work of others, particularly if they have different theoretical orientations, the tolerance and practice of multiple approaches have helped to define pluralism—"the bringing to bear on a subject of diverse points of view, with diverse results"[11]—and to continue the scholarly tradition of combativeness, always a sign of good health, as Milton recognizes in *Areopagitica*: "Where there is much desire to learn, there of necessity will be much arguing, much writing, many opinions; for opinion in good men is but knowledge in the making."[12]

Unfortunately, this atmosphere of productive, respectful quarreling among critical schools is threatened by the narrow-mindedness of some engaged in the growing practice of deconstruction, a provocative literary theory that has yielded fascinating results in scholarship about *Paradise Lost*. Some practitioners of deconstruction claim, in effect, that its radically destabilizing methodology deserves to have a monopoly on analytic approach and results. In other words, this theory, which uses binary oppositions and the play of signification to describe how a text is always already divided against itself, privileges itself as an interpretive method.[13] Many literary theories implicitly do just this, of course, and some even claim to provide unique access to a text's true meaning. While critics using other theories usually leave room for a range of different approaches and respectfully engage them in fruitful debate, however, many practitioners of deconstruction have established themselves as literary theory's new forcers of conscience. Just as the New Criticism's domination of academic discourse for more than a generation led to a certain predictability in explications of ironies and ambiguities, so deconstruction's privileged status during the next generation has led to analysis after analysis that practices destabilization and explores the thematics of contradiction with weary regularity. The problem is not deconstruction, but the predictability of its results and the intolerance of many of its advocates. The notion of practicing a tolerant pluralism when searching for valuable insights, which may, like the figure of Truth in *Areopagitica*, "have more shapes then one,"[14] needs to be taken seriously, particularly because the alternative, conforming to one critical method, is so obviously opposed to the central values of Milton's life and the scholarly tradition about *Paradise Lost*. Tolerance is precisely what Milton recommends "if all cannot be of one mind, as who looks they should be?"[15] The strength of Milton scholarship lies in disagreement and diversity, two qualities that are well worth maintaining and that suggest the important role of deconstruction and feminist criticism, the most stimulating approaches of recent decades.

So much is written about *Paradise Lost*, an average of about one hundred books and articles in each year of the twentieth century, and so much of it is important, that Milton's readers at all levels—advanced undergraduates, graduate students, professors, and scholars whose works are represented in the following pages—may profit from a selective annotated bibliography that draws attention to many crucial works. This bibliography focuses on the most significant scholarship on *Paradise Lost* of this century, emphasizing material published during the period of great diversity from about 1967, when Fish's *Surprised by Sin* appeared, to 1995 (though coverage of the final year is necessarily not complete). That a book, chapter, or article is cited here implies a positive judgment about its contribution to the study of *Paradise Lost* in terms of methodology, provocativeness, originality, insight, or resolute common sense. Some of the works summarized in this bibliography are introductory in nature, some far more advanced, and the vast majority somewhere in between, as the annotations suggest. This bibliography does not include works that are highly specialized or narrowly focused, even if they are of high quality, and it omits dissertations and studies in which *Paradise Lost* plays a minor role. More than one-third of the entries do not appear in my previous bibliography, *The Essential Milton: An Annotated Bibliography of Major Modern Studies* (1989): I added them to bring the present work up to date and to make amends for some oversights and wrong-headed judgments.

Whenever possible, the citations include reprint information, though it can never be complete, to increase a reader's opportunities to find a scholarly work. If a book contains only one chapter on *Paradise Lost*, I maintained this bibliography's focus by citing and summarizing just that chapter; if a few chapters of a book, but not all of it, discuss the epic, they may be treated individually or as a group in one entry, depending on how much material needs to be summarized; if a study devoted largely to *Paradise Lost* includes some pages about, say, *Samson Agonistes* or *Comus*, for reasons of space I focus on the main points about Milton's epic. Though some of the citations here also appear in *The Essential Milton*, when reading books and articles for this bibliography I steadfastly refused to look at my earlier annotations, so the ones contained in this volume are all new. The annotations describe the contents of reference texts or editions, while they summarize the main points of the arguments of analytical works. The annotations are written almost exclusively in the historical present tense, and everything

in them—including conclusions about *Paradise Lost* or temporal references (such as "current Milton scholarship")—should be considered as
coming from the original critic's perspective.

This bibliography is organized in three main sections: scholarly
tools, or works that are important for reading and pursuing the study
of *Paradise Lost*; subjects, or some of the main areas scholars have in-
vestigated; and, using the narrator, his invocations, and his muses as
a preface, the epic's main divisions as reflected in the following group-
ing of the poem's books:

> —Books 1-2 (hell; Satan and the devils; the demonic
> council; Sin, Death, chaos)
> —Book 3 (heaven; God and the Son; the divine coun-
> cil; the limbo of vanity)
> —Book 4 (paradise; Adam and Eve; Eve tells of her
> first moments of existence)
> —Books 5-8 (Eve's dream; Raphael tells of the scale
> of nature, the Son's exaltation, Abdiel's confrontation
> with Satan, the war in heaven, creation, and astron-
> omy; Adam tells of his first moments of existence)
> —Books 9-10 (Adam and Eve's separation; the temp-
> tation; the fall; Adam and Eve's repentance; the judg-
> ment; Satan's return to hell)
> —Books 11-12 (Michael tells of future history)

Since some characters play a key role in many books of the epic, I
placed studies of them in the most logical subsection, the one that deals
with the book where they are introduced. Thus, discussions of Satan
appear in the subsection that deals with Books 1-2, and those that focus
on Adam, Eve, and gender relations in *Paradise Lost* appear in the subsection on Book 4. Because brief annotations can provide only a limited
amount of information, the cross references at the end of some entries
indicate studies with similar interests or conflicting conclusions. This
bibliography closes with two indexes: an Index of Scholars that focuses
on authors and editors, and an Index of Subjects that offers additional
guidance by referring to the main issues raised in each annotation as
well as some others for which there was no space.

Notes

[1] See John T. Shawcross, ed., *Milton: The Critical Heritage* (London: Routledge and Kegan Paul, 1970) and *Milton, 1732-1801: The Critical Heritage* (London: Routledge and Kegan Paul, 1972).

[2] See Logan Pearsall Smith, *Milton and His Modern Critics* (London: Oxford University Press, 1940); James Thorpe, ed., *Milton Criticism: Selections from Four Centuries* (New York: Rinehart and Co., 1950); John Peter, "Reflections on the Milton Controversy," *Scrutiny* 19 (1952): 2-15; Patrick Murray, *Milton: The Modern Phase. A Study of Twentieth-Century Criticism* (London: Longmans, 1967); and Paul J. Alpers, "The Milton Controversy," in *Twentieth-Century Literature in Retrospect*, ed. Reuben A. Brower (Cambridge, MA: Harvard University Press, 1971), 269-98.

[3] Stanley Fish, "Transmuting the Lump: *Paradise Lost*, 1942-1982," in *Literature and History: Theoretical Problems and Russian Case Studies*, ed. Gary Saul Morson (Stanford, CA: Stanford University Press, 1986), 36.

[4] See William Riley Parker, *Milton's Contemporary Reputation: An Essay, Together with a Tentative List of Printed Allusions to Milton, 1641-1674* (Columbus: Ohio State University Press, 1940).

[5] See Edward Dowden, "Milton in the Eighteenth Century (1701-1750)," *Proceedings of the British Academy* 3 (1907-08): 275-93; J. G. Robertson, "Milton's Fame on the Continent," *Proceedings of the British Academy* 3 (1907-08): 319-40; Arthur Barker, "'. . . And on His Crest Sat Horror': Eighteenth-Century Interpretations of Milton's Sublimity and His Satan," *University of Toronto Quarterly* 11 (1942): 421-36; and Dustin Griffin, *Regaining Paradise: Milton and the Eighteenth Century* (Cambridge: Cambridge University Press, 1986).

[6] See Joseph Anthony Wittreich, Jr., ed., *The Romantics on Milton: Formal Essays and Critical Asides* (Cleveland, OH: Press of Case Western Reserve University, 1970); and Lucy Newlyn, *"Paradise Lost" and the Romantic Reader* (Oxford: Clarendon Press, 1993).

[7] See George F. Sensabaugh, *Milton in Early America* (Princeton, NJ: Princeton University Press, 1964); Keith W. F. Stavely, *Puritan Legacies: "Paradise Lost" and the New England Tradition, 1630-1890* (Ithaca, NY: Cornell University Press, 1987); and Lydia Dittler Schulman, *"Paradise Lost" and the Rise of the American Republic* (Boston, MA: Northeastern University Press, 1992).

[8] See James G. Nelson, *The Sublime Puritan: Milton and the Victorians* (Madison: University of Wisconsin Press, 1963).

[9] See A. S. P. Woodhouse, "The Historical Criticism of Milton," *PMLA* 66 (1951): 1033-44.

[10] See Cleanth Brooks, "Milton and the New Criticism," *Sewanee Review* 59 (1951): 1-22.

[11] M. H. Abrams, "The Deconstructive Angel," *Critical Inquiry* 3 (1977): 425.

[12] *Areopagitica*, ed. Ernest Sirluck, in vol. 2 of *Complete Prose Works of John Milton*, gen. ed. Don M. Wolfe (New Haven, CT: Yale University Press, 1953-82), 554.

[13] M. H. Abrams raises a similar objection when he refers to "the conviction that Derrida's theory, which deconstructs the possibility of philosophical truth, is itself the truth about philosophy" ("Construing and Deconstructing," in *Romanticism and Contemporary Criticism*, edited by Morris Eaves and Michael Fischer [Ithaca, NY: Cornell University Press, 1986], 155). See also John M. Ellis, *Against Deconstruction* (Princeton, NJ: Princeton University Press, 1989), viii-ix, 144-45.

[14] *Complete Prose Works* 2: 563.

[15] *Complete Prose Works* 2: 565.

PART I:

SCHOLARLY TOOLS

1. EDITIONS

1   Bush, Douglas, ed. *Paradise Lost*. In *The Complete Poetical Works of John Milton*, 201-459. Boston, MA: Houghton Mifflin Co., 1965.

Bush provides a short introduction and brief annotations for his modern-spelling edition of *Paradise Lost*.

2   Darbishire, Helen, ed. *Paradise Lost*. In *The Poetical Works of John Milton*, vol. 1. Oxford: Clarendon Press, 1952. xxxviii + 326 pp.

With extensive textual commentary but no annotations, Darbishire's edition presents a "reformed text" of *Paradise Lost* according to Milton's principles of spelling and punctuation, which are discussed in detail. This text is based on the 1667 edition, with corrections taken from the manuscript of Book 1 and from the 1674 edition when it shows signs of Milton's deliberate revisions. See entries 9, 11-12, and 126.

3   Elledge, Scott, ed. *Paradise Lost*. New York: W. W. Norton and Co., 1975. xxix + 546 pp.

Elledge's modern-spelling edition of the 1674 text follows the original punctuation. Footnotes are thorough, and half of this volume is devoted to sections on Backgrounds and Sources and on Criticism. A Selected Bibliography lists editions, reference works, biographies, background studies, collections of critical essays, and studies of *Paradise Lost*.

4   Flannagan, Roy, ed. *John Milton: "Paradise Lost."* New York: Macmillan, 1993. vii + 686 pp.

A thorough introduction discusses the epic genre, Milton's theology and *Paradise Lost*, the fable (including Milton's outlines for a drama on the fall), rhetorical strategies (including prosody and style), the epic poem and architecture and painting, Milton and his poem, key critical questions, the text, and editions. This old-spelling, original punctuation text contains an extensive bibliography, a chronology of the principal events in Milton's life, and thorough annotations for *Paradise Lost*.

5   Fletcher, Harris Francis, ed. *Paradise Lost*. In *John Milton's Complete Poetical Works*, vols. 2-3. Urbana: University of Illinois Press, 1945-48. 634 pp.; 455 pp.
          The subject of volume 2 is the first edition of *Paradise Lost*, while volume 3 deals with the second edition. Each volume contains a long essay on the composition, printing, and publication of the edition and a facsimile of it. Volume 2 includes reproductions of Milton's portraits that appear in a number of his works.

6   Fowler, Alastair, ed. *Paradise Lost*. In *The Poems of John Milton*, edited by John Carey and Alastair Fowler, 417-1060. London: Longmans, 1968.
          A modern-spelling text, Fowler's edition has an extensive introduction and thorough annotations.

7   Hughes, Merritt Y., ed. *Paradise Lost*. In *John Milton: Complete Poems and Major Prose*, 173-469. Indianapolis, IN: Odyssey Press, 1957.
          Hughes's modern-spelling text includes an extensive introduction and full annotations.

8   Patterson, Frank Allen, ed. *Paradise Lost*. In *The Works of John Milton*, vol. 2, parts 1-2. New York: Columbia University Press, 1931. ix + 258 pp.; 547 pp.
          The Columbia Edition contains an unannotated, old-spelling text of the 1674 edition of *Paradise Lost*, including a collation of manuscript readings from Book 1 and a list of variants from the 1667, 1668, and 1669 printings.

For a study that examines Milton's editors and commentators, see entry 95.

2. TEXTUAL STUDIES

9   Adams, Robert Martin. "The Text of *Paradise Lost*." In *Ikon: John Milton and the Modern Critics*, 60-111. Ithaca, NY: Cornell University Press, 1955. Reprinted 1966.

There is no contemporary evidence that Milton diligently proofreads the printed text of *Paradise Lost* or follows clear principles of spelling, italicizing, and capitalizing. Printers tend to such details, with Edward Phillips or Milton reading proof carefully (by their standards). Because of its actual merits, the second edition (1674) generally provides a superior text. To gain fuller meanings and effects, Milton sometimes misspells words or distorts grammar; by remaining alert to large, imaginative effects, editors should avoid emendation in these instances. Milton primarily aims at broad effects and, because of his blindness or indifference, is careless about minor matters of correctness. See entries 2, 11-12, and 126.

10   Darbishire, Helen, ed. *The Manuscript of Milton's "Paradise Lost," Book I*. Oxford: Clarendon Press, 1931. xlvii + 74 pp.

Darbishire's facsimile and transcript are preceded by a discussion of the manuscript's history, corrections, relationship to the printed text, spelling, and punctuation.

11   Moyles, R. G. *The Text of "Paradise Lost": A Study in Editorial Procedure*. Toronto: University of Toronto Press, 1985. x + 188 pp. 11 illustrations.

Although five different title pages and about one hundred variants appear in *Paradise Lost*'s first edition, it is in fact a single edition, printed in mid-1667. Of the alterations, only two are substantive, while some of the rest represent improvements, some are in error, and many are indifferent. None is beyond the capacity of a proof-corrector or printing-house master, who may have been standardizing the manuscript's spelling, but not very diligently. Nothing suggests Milton's serious concern about the minutiae of his text or close supervision of its printing. He has no orthographic system to indicate unemphatic and emphatic forms of words, he does not use apostrophes to signal elisions in a consistent way, and his spelling is not based on phonetic principles to guide pronunciation. Practicing a reasoned eclecticism when dealing with substantives, an editor of *Paradise Lost* must not view either the 1667 or 1674 text as completely authoritative. For the accidentals, an editor should choose one of those editions as the copy-text (for neither is superior) and emend only when it is manifestly in error. See entries 2, 9, 12, and 126.

12   Shawcross, John T. "Orthography and the Text of *Paradise
         Lost.*" In *Language and Style in Milton: A Symposium in
         Honor of the Tercentenary of "Paradise Lost,"* edited by
         Ronald David Emma and John T. Shawcross, 120-53. New
         York: Frederick Ungar, 1967.
         As one of the proofreaders and correctors of *Paradise Lost*'s
manuscript, Edward Phillips is far from fastidious. The corrector for
the first edition (1667), perhaps Phillips or the compositor, works from
the manuscript but makes a few additional changes. There is no evidence that Milton is concerned about consistent spelling. Sometimes the
manuscript's scribe produces Miltonic spellings; the corrector or
compositor alters the spelling to normalized forms, sometimes in
agreement with Milton's practices; thus, the text of *Paradise Lost* does
not reproduce his spelling at all points. Having some but not full
authority over the first edition, the second edition (1674) is set from a
copy of the first that was inconsistently corrected by someone who
knew Milton's spelling. See entries 2, 9, 11, and 126.

Other works that discuss the text of *Paradise Lost* appear in entries 4-5
and 126.

3. BIBLIOGRAPHIES

13   Fletcher, Harris Francis. *Contributions to a Milton Bibliography 1800-1930, Being a List of Addenda to Stevens's "Reference Guide to Milton."* Urbana: University of Illinois Press, 1931. 166 pp. Reprinted New York: Russell and Russell, 1967.
     A supplement to Stevens's bibliography (see entry 18), Fletcher's is organized chronologically. Each entry includes a brief annotation, and the volume contains an index of authors and subjects.

14   Huckabay, Calvin. *John Milton: An Annotated Bibliography, 1929-1968.* Revised edition. Pittsburgh, PA: Duquesne University Press, 1969. xvii + 392 pp.
     Huckabay's bibliography includes an extensive section on *Paradise Lost* (items 1071-2047), very brief annotations for most entries, and an author index.

15   Klemp, P. J. *The Essential Milton: An Annotated Bibliography of Major Modern Studies.* Boston, MA: G. K. Hall, 1989. xiv + 474 pp.
     Many of the entries in this reference book are relevant to *Paradise Lost*, but items 435-802 identify books and articles that focus on Milton's epic. Including subsections on *Paradise Lost* and the biblical and epic traditions, style, and the narrator, this bibliography also contains a subject and author index.

16   Patrides, C. A. *An Annotated Critical Bibliography of John Milton.* New York: St. Martin's Press, 1987. xii + 200 pp.
     Though citations relevant to the study of *Paradise Lost* appear throughout Patrides's bibliography, entries 412-810 refer to books and articles that focus on the epic. This reference book includes a brief index of subjects and a complete index of authors.

17   Shawcross, John T. *Milton: A Bibliography for the Years 1624-1700*. Binghamton, NY: Medieval and Renaissance Texts and Studies, 1984. xiv + 452 pp. *Milton: A Bibliography for the Years 1624-1700. Addenda and Corrigenda*. Binghamton, NY: Medieval and Renaissance Texts and Studies, 1990. i + 34 pp.

Shawcross includes many citations relevant to *Paradise Lost*'s publishing history, contemporary reception, and imitators.

18   Stevens, David Harrison. *Reference Guide to Milton from 1800 to the Present Day*. Chicago, IL: University of Chicago Press, 1930. x + 302 pp. Reprinted New York: Russell and Russell, 1967.

In his coverage of *Paradise Lost* (items 654-1098), Stevens briefly annotates each entry. The index primarily lists authors, but a few subjects are included under Milton's name and the titles of his individual works. See entry 13.

4. REFERENCE WORKS

19   Hunter, William B., Jr., gen. ed. *A Milton Encyclopedia*. 9 vols. Lewisburg, PA: Bucknell University Press, 1978-83. 208 pp.; 206 pp.; 199 pp.; 218 pp.; 206 pp.; 216 pp.; 208 pp.; 205 pp.; 170 pp.

This encyclopedia contains articles about every significant aspect of *Paradise Lost*: characters, settings, versification, composition, and so forth.

20   Ingram, William, and Kathleen Swaim, eds. *A Concordance to Milton's English Poetry*. Oxford: Clarendon Press, 1972. xvii + 683 pp.

The concordance lists every word used in Milton's English poetry (except for some prepositions, conjunctions, and articles), including *Paradise Lost*'s variants and manuscript readings.

PART II:

SUBJECTS

5. PROSODY AND STYLE

21   Berek, Peter. "'Plain' and 'Ornate' Styles and the Structure of *Paradise Lost.*" *PMLA* 85 (1970): 237-46.

The unpoetic expositions of doctrine at the beginning of Book 3 provide linguistic standards that help the reader respond properly to the more attractive parts of *Paradise Lost*. As Satan's oratory indicates, Milton associates contrived verbal skills with depravity, while the narrator seeks inspired, unpremeditated verse and Adam and Eve use prompt, unmeditated eloquence. Satan treats words as things, entities with independent value and existence, leading him to define dignity as one's title or the Son's exaltation as a verbal misunderstanding. For Satan, language obscures truth by creating the appearance of a logical argument. God, on the other hand, repeats words to insist on their single, doctrinally correct meaning, his emotionless language acting as logic's slave by corresponding exactly to ideas and having no existence apart from them. The Son's speech, with its rhetorical questions, stylistic elaboration, and hints of ambiguity, mediates between the perfect Father and the fallen reader. Before the fall, Adam and Eve use language to reveal the facts of the world; when they fall, their language questions the relationship between words and reality. The language of *Paradise Lost* helps readers recognize characters' various fallen and unfallen states.

22   Bridges, Robert. "On the Prosody of *Paradise Lost.*" In *Milton's Prosody*, 1-45. Oxford: Clarendon Press, 1921. Revised edition 1965.

As a rule, each line of *Paradise Lost* is decasyllabic with five iambic feet, though Milton occasionally inverts the stress, usually in the first foot and rarely in the fifth. Most of the apparently extrametrical lines can be accounted for by elision, and the epic contains no lines with a deficient number of syllables. Milton uses the caesura in a variety of places to emphasize a line's meaning. See entry 40.

23   Broadbent, J. B. "Milton's 'Mortal Voice' and His 'Omnific
        Word.'" In *Approaches to "Paradise Lost,"* edited by C. A.
        Patrides, 99-117. London: Edward Arnold, 1968.

Man's mortal voice and God's omnific word illustrate two extremes of poetic language in *Paradise Lost*. With his mortal voice,
Milton uses colloquial rhythms and diction and a prosaic plainness that
can result in a special kind of definiteness, as in the account of the
creation. But his descriptions are analytic, appealing to the intellect
rather than the senses, because his words are signs for ideas. The
syntactic structure of his language also makes readers feel constricted,
though it offers some energy and freedom. If *Paradise Lost*'s rhythms
and diction are sometimes colloquial, flat and simple words frequently
gain force from their elevated context. The omnific word is a world-
making voice that functions best when acting most freely and in terms
of physical existence or action. This is Milton's authoritarian voice, the
voice of a parent speaking in adult language.

24   Broadbent, J. B. "Milton's Rhetoric." *Modern Philology* 56
        (1959): 224-42. Reprinted in *Milton: Modern Judgements*,
        edited by Alan Rudrum, 270-95. London: Macmillan, 1968.

That Books 3 and 9 contain no tropes but most of the iterative
and verbal figures in *Paradise Lost* indicates their relevance to a theological context in which issues are stated in an abstract, verbal treatment through debate and temptation. In these books, Milton constructs
a theodicy with a rational poetic that allows readers to think about theology. When characters speak lyrics or present soliloquies to express
misery, their speeches contain many rhetorical figures. Milton uses
rhetoric for "tonal coolness" and "intellectual freedom" (242), as well
as for ornament and musical delight. See entries 311 and 425.

25   Corns, Thomas N. *Milton's Language*. Oxford: Basil Black-
        well, 1990. xi + 143 pp.

Thoroughly English in syntax and diction, Milton's style does
not emphasize words used in their Latin sense or the Latinate periodic
construction by which syntactic elements are postponed. Very short
sentences, which have dramatic potential and usually contain short
words, appear far more frequently in those parts of *Paradise Lost* that
simulate speech than in the narrative sections, whose sentences have a
plurality of main clauses for the plain exposition of serial events linked
primarily by their chronological relationship. More distinctively Miltonic than the narrative parts, the epic's speeches, like his prose, are

sharply distinguished by subordinate clauses that depend on other subordinate material, a complex structure permitting the representation of
controversy. Sentences in *Paradise Lost* end at line endings and (like
clauses) begin at line beginnings less frequently than in analogous
contemporary poems. Milton thus redefines English poetry's lineation
conventions, increases syntactic options, and reshapes the reader's
expectations. That the epic contains relatively few neologisms may be
attributed to a movement toward neoclassical austerity and a shift in the
rate at which words were entering the language in general. Milton
does, however, alter or extend the semantic range of words already
used in English.

26   Davis, Walter R. "The Languages of Accommodation and the
        Styles of *Paradise Lost*." *Milton Studies* 18 (1983): 103-27.
        To help readers experience the movement of its plot as succes-
sive states of mind, *Paradise Lost*'s styles direct these mental actions
and heighten the attention readers give them. While Books 1 and 4 use
a visual approach and lyric definition to represent states of mind, Books
2 and 9 work with dramatic conflicts and Book 3 has an auditory style
that gives body to theological concepts. In Books 5 and 6, the epic's
language undergoes a great shift: divine and human languages intersect
as accommodation (and typology) dominates, with images acting not as
visible objects pointing to the truth but as analogues of it. The account
of the war in heaven conveys the tone of pain for day one and its
redefinition of heroism through analogy; irony and sarcasm accompany
the literal, moral style for day two and the denigration of false heroism;
and the progressive revelation of truth through typology is used for day
three and the concept of salvation through Jesus Christ. In the narrative
of the war, Raphael moves "from language as difficult striving for
expression to language as gradual satisfying revelation" (117). Milton
applies the four senses of scriptural exegesis—literal, analogical (using
allegory and accommodation), moral, and anagogical (or typological
and prophetic)—in Raphael's discourse in Books 5 and 6.

27   Di Cesare, Mario A. "Advent'rous Song: The Texture of
        Milton's Epic." In *Language and Style in Milton: A Sympo-
        sium in Honor of the Tercentenary of "Paradise Lost,"* edited
        by Ronald David Emma and John T. Shawcross, 1-29. New
        York: Frederick Ungar, 1967.
        Effects of the Virgilian style appear in the Latinate elements
of *Paradise Lost*'s syntax and diction. Containing allusions to Virgil

and Dante, some similes describing Satan stress his monstrous and static qualities while linking him to the war in heaven. Adam and Eve's relationship is defined from their perspective by the recurrent motifs of solace and sole (echoed in soul) and from the Satanic perspective by the contrasting use of muddled language, bad puns, and bitter irony. If Satan is associated with a labyrinth, Adam and Eve seem to be encircled and eventually constricted. *Paradise Lost*'s conclusion is transformed by the theme of triumph, as Adam and Eve once again hold hands and may achieve what Eden prefigured.

28   Eliot, T. S. "A Note on the Verse of John Milton." *Essays and Studies* 21 (1936): 32-40. Reprinted as "Milton I" in *On Poetry and Poets*, 156-64. London: Faber and Faber, 1957; reprinted in *The Modern Critical Spectrum*, edited by Gerald Jay Goldberg and Nancy Marmer Goldberg, 169-74. Englewood Cliffs, NJ: Prentice-Hall, 1962; reprinted in *Milton: "Paradise Lost," a Casebook*, edited by A. E. Dyson and Julian Lovelock, 77-84. London: Macmillan, 1973. Frequently reprinted.

Milton is a great poet whose work can exert only a harmful influence on other poets (see entry 80). Because his gifts are naturally aural and his sensuousness is withered by book-learning (and blindness), he lacks a visual imagination and the ability to convey particulars. Instead, he uses artificial and conventional language and complex syntax that only introduces sound patterns into simplified and abstract thoughts. His poetry is thus at its best where there is little to visualize and it can concentrate on sound. Because there is a division in his verse between the aural and the visual and tactile, just as Milton is himself divided between being a poet and a theologian, one must read *Paradise Lost* in two different ways—for sound and for sense. The English language has not recovered from the damage Milton did to it. See entries 31, 36, and 90-91.

29   Goldstein, Leonard. "The Good Old Cause and Milton's Blank Verse." *Zeitschrift für Anglistik und Amerikanistik* 23 (1975): 133-42.

By defending blank verse for epic poetry, Milton defies contemporary neoclassical aesthetic norms that communicate royalist or counterrevolutionary politics and view the closed couplet as the only appropriate form for poetic expression. The heroic couplet's emphasis on order and self-sufficiency makes it the perfect vehicle for retarding social change, while the refusal to use rhyme is a politically revolutionary act since it denies the closure that a couplet creates and suggests that a failed revolution can still lead to future victory. Like the developing bourgeois social structure it reflects in medieval Europe, rhyme gives a sense of a stable whole whose parts may change without affecting the whole. Milton, the poet of England's bourgeois revolution, rejects rhyme because the bourgeoisie no longer opposes the Restoration; blank verse thus aligns him with the exploited masses—artisans, day laborers, and the lower-class citizens—who resist Charles's return and seek freedom.

30   Leavis, F. R. "Milton's Verse." *Scrutiny* 2 (1933): 123-36. Reprinted in *Revaluation: Tradition and Development in English Poetry*, 42-67. London: Chatto and Windus, 1936; reprinted in *Milton's Epic Poetry: Essays on "Paradise Lost" and "Paradise Regained,"* edited by C. A. Patrides, 15-32. Harmondsworth: Penguin Books, 1967.

When readers study *Paradise Lost*, they must resist the verse's monotonous movement, but they cannot win, for the heavy rhythmic pattern inevitably leads to a foreseen thud. Because the verse functions like a ritual, however, its pattern takes on an unusually expressive function, though it remains hollow and suffers from sensuous poverty. Milton renounces the English language and writes a tyrannical style. The limitation in the range of his interests renders them inadequate to produce a sense of myth.

31   Leavis, F. R. "Mr. Eliot and Milton." *Sewanee Review* 57 (1949): 1-30. Reprinted in *The Common Pursuit*, 9-32. London: Chatto and Windus, 1952.

Contrary to T. S. Eliot's claims (see entry 28), *Paradise Lost* relaxes readers' attention to sense and encourages them to demand less force and consistent meaning from the poem. Milton's preoccupation with sound or music precludes the vivid use of images that depend on the language's body and action, but the Miltonic grand style is eloquent, made up of argument and strong rhetorical statement. In *Paradise Lost*, poor and inconsistent visual imagery is only a symptom of the author's weak realization of themes and conceptions, a condition that makes him unqualified to write about God's ways to men. Though he lacks such self-knowledge, Milton has enough pride and confidence to choose this subject. When his feeling and theory conflict, readers find certain matters, such as Satan's personality and the fall, presented one way but explained in another.

32   MacCabe, Colin. "'So Truth Be in the Field': Milton's Use of Language." In *Teaching the Text*, edited by Susanne Kappeler and Norman Bryson, 18-34. London: Routledge and Kegan Paul, 1983.

The twentieth-century debate about Milton's language, discussed in terms of syntax, grammar, and sense, vindicates it only by ignoring some of its most valuable aspects, including ambiguity and complexity. Milton believes certain figurative uses of language can provide glimpses of divine truth, a view that is being displaced when he writes *Paradise Lost*. By constantly pitting readers' linguistic performance (or use of language) against their linguistic competence (or knowledge of language), Milton's language insists on "those limits where syntactic patterns can no longer be held together" (30). He thus demonstrates the difficulty of searching for the truth.

33   Patrides, C. A. "*Paradise Lost* and the Language of Theology." In *Language and Style in Milton: A Symposium in Honor of the Tercentenary of "Paradise Lost,"* edited by Ronald David Emma and John T. Shawcross, 102-19. New York: Frederick Ungar, 1967. Reprinted in *Bright Essence: Studies in Milton's Theology*, by W. B. Hunter, C. A. Patrides, and J. H. Adamson, 165-78. Salt Lake City: University of Utah Press, 1971.

Theological language must combine an appropriate oddness with a certain logical behavior, a characteristic missing in *Christian Doctrine* but present in *Paradise Lost*, particularly in the metaphors of light used to explain the Godhead. While Milton refuses to face the implications of the metaphoric language of accommodation in *Christian Doctrine*, in *Paradise Lost* he resolves his problems with this issue by adopting a language whose center is the image, metaphor, or myth. The epic thus uses language that always points beyond itself to articulate an insight.

34   Prince, F. T. "Milton's Blank Verse: The Diction" and "Milton's Blank Verse: The Prosody." In *The Italian Element in*

Milton's Verse, 108-30 and 131-44. Oxford: Clarendon Press, 1954. Revised edition 1962; part reprinted in *Milton: A Collection of Critical Essays*, edited by Louis L. Martz, 56-60. Englewood Cliffs, NJ: Prentice-Hall, 1966; part reprinted in *On Milton's Poetry*, edited by Arnold Stein, 151-66. Greenwich, CT: Fawcett Publications, 1970.

Milton's continental journey shows him the tradition of epic magnificence in Italian, a style that changes his writing. In English verse, he develops the Italian epic tradition, with its blank verse, grandeur, and epic syntax. Though English is less capable than Italian of imitating Latin syntax, Milton's native tongue is more flexible, so it can sustain the Virgilian manner. He adapts the Italian style, particularly as Tasso practices it in terms of placement of adjectives, defying logical word order, and verbal conceits.

The prosody of *Paradise Lost* shows affinities with Tasso's recommendations, including such adaptations of his style as harsh consonants, elisions, and stress on a line's final syllable. Finding the English equivalent for Italian prosody, Milton creates a line with a theoretical ten syllables, the final syllable always receiving a stress (or having the possibility of being stressed) and another stress falling on the fourth or sixth one.

35   Rajan, Balachandra. *"Paradise Lost*: The Providence of Style."* In *The Lofty Rhyme: A Study of Milton's Major Poetry*, 100-12. Coral Gables, FL: University of Miami Press, 1970.

The elevation of *Paradise Lost*'s language creates the distance required to portray transcendent events and characters, while the poem's structure focuses on human concerns. Milton creates an interplay between grammatical and metrical forces that shapes the entire poem.

36   Ricks, Christopher. *Milton's Grand Style*. Oxford: Clarendon Press, 1963. vi + 154 pp. Frequently reprinted; part reprinted in *Milton's Epic Poetry: Essays on "Paradise Lost" and "Paradise Regained,"* edited by C. A. Patrides, 249-75. Harmondsworth: Penguin Books, 1967; part reprinted in *On Milton's Poetry*, edited by Arnold Stein, 167-82. Greenwich, CT: Fawcett Publications, 1970; part reprinted in *Milton: "Paradise Lost," a Casebook*, edited by A. E. Dyson and Julian

Lovelock, 204-19. London: Macmillan, 1973; part reprinted in *Paradise Lost*, edited by Scott Elledge, 442-59. New York: W. W. Norton and Co., 1975.

The anti-Miltonists, unlike many who admire his poetry, take seriously his use of words, though they condemn *Paradise Lost*'s style for emphasizing sound over sense and being monotonous, ritualistic, and incapable of producing concrete results or subtlety. Sometimes the anti-Miltonists (such as Leavis [see entry 31] and Eliot [see entry 28]) do not read the epic carefully, certainly not with the attention given to it by eighteenth-century editors (such as Bentley and the Richardsons), who remain in many ways Milton's best critics. While his verse occasionally shows signs of imprecision, insensitivity, and overemphasis, he usually controls syntax carefully, its complexity and Latinate constructions being essential to the subject matter. But the style of *Paradise Lost* is not consistently grand; it can be energetically direct and simple. Successful when they grow out of a tradition of etymology or epic practice, Milton's Shakespearean metaphors are blurred, mixed, and not tightly connected to their context. Word-play in *Paradise Lost* is controlled by the character who uses it or the decorum of the religious epic, particularly when etymologies reveal the true nature of things.

37   Ricks, Christopher. "Sound and Sense in *Paradise Lost*." *Essays by Divers Hands: Being the Transactions of the Royal Society of Literature* n.s. 39 (1977): 92-111. Reprinted in *The Force of Poetry*, 60-79. Oxford: Clarendon Press, 1984.

While *Paradise Lost* conveys mediated rather than immediate experience, it is no less great because it works from the outside. Milton often writes of things that can be felt only in the imagination, using sound, rhythm, and even rhyme to create superb poetry.

38   Sherry, Beverley. "Speech in *Paradise Lost*." *Milton Studies* 8 (1975): 247-66.

Renaissance writers argue that eloquence originates with Adam, is corrupted with the fall and then repaired, and has a regenerative power for fallen humans. Like other humanists, Milton agrees with these views and identifies eloquence (truth) with virtue. In *Paradise Lost*, God gives eloquence to Adam and Eve; after the fall, they lose the ability to pray eloquently in divine poetry, and they express themselves "in the restless rhythms of infernal speech" (253). Their

diction and tone change, becoming Satanic. While God is absolute eloquence, as the father of lies Satan is reduced to a speechless hissing.
Before the fall, Adam and Eve's complementary speeches mirror those
of the Father and Son, as signs of love and union. This mode is replaced by the monologue, a fallen form of utterance in *Paradise Lost*,
but Adam and Eve reestablish communication in Book 10's utilitarian
speeches. Having recovered some of the initial eloquence, Milton the
poet has a conversation with God, and the epic is the record of that
relationship.

39   Smith, Hallett. "No Middle Flight." *Huntington Library Quar-
        terly* 15 (1952): 159-72.
        Paradise Lost is deeply rooted in the hexameral tradition,
though Milton handles his subject as if it were new, something unat-
tempted yet in prose or rhyme. A similar paradox appears in the
poem's style, which has a certain grace even in the conclusion of stiff,
Latin constructions. Using both abstract and clear details, Milton's
baroque style conveys no visual effect. Since Milton assumes that his
weakness requires the muse's aid, he achieves the confidence to write
an adventurous poem that pursues no middle flight. He finds an answerable style for *Paradise Lost* because he believes its argument and
because this area of belief encompasses serious doctrine and poetic
fiction.

40   Sprott, S. Ernest. *Milton's Art of Prosody*. Oxford: Basil
        Blackwell, 1953. xi + 147 pp.
        In *Paradise Lost*, Milton's punctuation and phonetic spelling
are keys to understanding his prosody, which is based on lines of five
feet in iambic rhythm. Although most extrametrical supernumerary
syllables fall into place with elision, some few remain as a form of
license that Milton gives his verse. He creates variety by using inverted
feet, usually at the beginning of a line; loss of speech accent, typically
in the second foot; and caesuras in many different locations within
lines. See entry 22.

41   Steadman, John M. "*Ethos* and *Dianoia*: Character and Rheto-
        ric in *Paradise Lost*." In *Language and Style in Milton: A
        Symposium in Honor of the Tercentenary of "Paradise Lost,"*
        edited by Ronald David Emma and John T. Shawcross, 193-
        232. New York: Frederick Ungar, 1967. Reprinted in *Milton*

and the Paradoxes of Renaissance Heroism, 136-70. Baton Rouge: Louisiana State University Press, 1987.

Subservient to but interdependent with poetics, rhetoric in *Paradise Lost* makes a distinction between thought, or what a character says (*dianoia*), and character itself (*ethos*). Speeches in Milton's epic are thus not straightforward indexes of characters but of thought, for rhetorical techniques and moral purpose are not the same. The heroic poet and orator have different means (though both rely on the three main types of oration), but their ends—serving higher disciplines and pursuing humanity's beatitude—are identical. In *Paradise Lost* and *Paradise Regained*, deliberative oratory, which uses dialogue or debate to urge one to do or not to do something, plays an important role because of the poems' emphasis on the spiritual warfare of temptation. Because it pleads God's case, *Paradise Lost* emphasizes judicial oratory more than other heroic poems do. Satanic speech is usually based on lies, false testimony, or sophistical fallacies, and various characters rebut it with a standard method of debate and disputation. Aiming at truth, the ideal rhetoric is sincere and divinely inspired; unlike demonic speech, Christian rhetoric serves as ethical proof by reflecting the speaker's moral character. By emphasizing the antithesis between divine merit and human demerit, Milton radically changes the heroic poem's traditional nature.

42   Waters, Lindsay. "Milton, Tasso, and the Renaissance Grand Style: Syntax and Its Effect on the Reader." *Stanford Italian Review* 2 (1981): 81-92.

Like Tasso, Milton uses the Renaissance obscure style, which is characterized by complex syntax that suggests deeper meanings, overwhelms with confusion, and draws readers in by encouraging their struggle with the text. Both authors create confusion with the "inelegance of their asymmetrical profusions of syntactic units" (83). According to sixteenth-century Italian poets and critics, the best poetry, unlike rhetoric, should not merely move or persuade; it must use obscurity to overwhelm, enrapture, and yield new meanings. Tasso says the reader is expected to work at constructing the sense of the verses and at figuring out how they are connected. By using unusual syntax, Milton's grand style follows this advice, producing obscurity and an emotional effect on the reader.

For other studies of *Paradise Lost*'s prosody and style, see entries 4, 63, 74, 106, 216, 220, 225, 228, 282, 311, 371, 440, and 425.

6. THE BIBLICAL AND CLASSICAL EPIC TRADITIONS

43   Blessington, Francis C. *"Paradise Lost" and the Classical Epic*. Boston, MA: Routledge and Kegan Paul, 1979. xiii + 126 pp.

A parody of Greek and Roman epic heroes, Satan in *Paradise Lost* fails even by Homer's and Virgil's criteria. Milton's presentation of Satan alludes primarily to the *Aeneid* in the opening books, the *Iliad* during the war in heaven, and the *Odyssey* when he is on earth. The portrayal of God, the Son, and the messenger angels fuses the classical and Christian worlds, as Milton seeks common ground between them. While Satan never measures up to the pagan warriors' heroic, virtuous standards, the actions of the Father and his followers parallel, surpass, and Christianize those values. Beginning in a state of innocence, Adam and Eve can choose which values to follow. That they fail by falling into Satan's corrupt classicism makes the poem a tragedy, though Michael helps them regain some of their former purity. Each of *Paradise Lost*'s six parts adapts and revaluates one traditional epic convention while subsuming several others. The narrator's voice, Milton's greatest break with this tradition, largely synthesizes classical and Christian interests as he fulfills and extends the pagan world by returning it to its true source.

44   Boehrer, Bruce Thomas. "*Paradise Lost* and the General Epistle of James: Milton, Augustine, Lacan." *Exemplaria* 4 (1992): 295-316.

By removing lust from the infernal triad described in James—lust, sin, death—*Paradise Lost* formulates a version of desire that is related to Augustinian concepts. Although Milton follows Augustine in associating eros with sin, he distinguishes good and bad desire by rendering hell's populace erotic but impotent and by fighting the notion of Edenic sex without desire. Desire for Milton is ultimately the Lacanian Logos. Augustine's emphasis on will dominating desire means that neither Satan, who is consumed by desire, nor unfallen Adam, who is governed by will, can experience any sexual pleasure. Milton agrees that reason and choice form the basis of a legitimate union, yet he departs from Augustine by including a kind of desire in Eden—not lust, but a burning that seeks to remedy loneliness. Lacanian desire, best exemplified by Satan, produces a split between speaker and what is spoken, a process that informs not only language but genital eroticism in Eden. Where Augustine seeks to silence desire through repose in God, Milton cherishes it by describing a God who exists within uncertainty.

45   Collett, Jonathan H. "Milton's Use of Classical Mythology in *Paradise Lost.*" *PMLA* 85 (1970): 88-96.
        Milton attacks classical myths throughout his poems even as they contribute to his imagery, key themes, and genres. Over the years, he finds a truth and value in the myths, using them proleptically in *Paradise Lost* to anticipate major events. The myths associated with Satan present the pagan deities as fallen angels in a new guise. In descriptions of Eden and the first couple, Milton finds the myths effective and legitimate as types of the scriptural revelation Adam will receive. From the fall in Book 9 to the beginning of Book 11, classical myths virtually disappear in *Paradise Lost* because prolepsis is no longer needed and comparisons with the richly decorative fables are impossible.

46   Dobbins, Austin C. *Milton and the Book of Revelation: The Heavenly Cycle.* Studies in the Humanities, no. 7, Literature. University: University of Alabama Press, 1975. vi + 170 pp.
        By portraying the Son's exaltation as occurring before time and shifting the place where he assumes a mediatorial role from earth to heaven, Milton presents apparently questionable theology. But as *Christian Doctrine* indicates, God proclaims the Son's literal begetting as king of heaven in eternity—an act that provokes Lucifer's pride—and the Son metaphorically accomplishes his mediatorial office in time. *Paradise Lost*'s war in heaven is based primarily on a literal interpretation of Revelation 6.1-8 and 12.7-9, the portrait of Sin and Death on Revelation 6.8. Milton rejects the millennial position that anticipates Christ's imminent reign on earth; instead, Christ will complete his victory at the Last Judgment. While the desire (lust) to imitate God is not wrong, Lucifer perverts this by desiring to be his equal, an action Eve

imitates by aspiring to be Adam's equal. Milton brings the heavenly cycle to a second triumphant climax with Satan's capture and flight.

47   DuRocher, Richard J. *Milton and Ovid*. Ithaca, NY: Cornell University Press, 1985. 241 pp.

Entering into a dialogue with Ovid, Milton exposes *Paradise Lost* to the potential contamination and fragmentation of the *Metamorphoses*. Allusions to various Ovidian characters epitomize stages in Eve's development as a series of changes reveals her potentialities and weaknesses. In her earliest moments, she appears as a corrected Narcissus who escapes self-enclosure and a perfected Echo who initiates and responds to discourse. During the temptation, Eve shares Medea's fascination with a tempter, desire for glory, and reliance on experience. Adam and Eve in the final books transform the figures of Deucalion and Pyrrha from tragic lovers into pious supplicants. Milton upholds and undermines Satan's heroism by using Ovidian rhetoric and stylistic devices and by depicting the devil as an analogue of seemingly heroic but ultimately debased characters from the *Metamorphoses*. Satan continuously displays the attributes of a rhetor, beast, and hero, and *Paradise Lost* shows a pattern of counterheroism in which these roles appear in varying proportions. By revaluating Ovid's metamorphic epic, which itself revalues Homer's and Virgil's epics, Milton emphasizes his own changes in generic expectation (including the role of the narrator) and allows the reader to choose between Ovid's commitment to unending change and his own belief in divinely sanctioned teleological change. In creating a cohesive epic argument, Milton is more successful at interweaving Ovidian scenes than Virgilian or Spenserian ones.

48   Evans, J. M. *"Paradise Lost" and the Genesis Tradition*. Oxford: Clarendon Press, 1968. xiv + 314 pp.

Indifferent to the fall's doctrinal implications, Jewish interpretations disagree about such matters as the serpent's identity, the role of sex in the fall, and whether Adam's sin causes human mortality. Starting with Paul, Christian commentators argue for the interdependence of Adam's sin and Christ's sacrifice, and they view the fall as initiating hereditary sinfulness and its punishment of death. The fall is also central to the literary tradition, as pagan poetry is interpreted in Christian terms and vice versa. Eventually, the Edenic myth is used in opposition to dualism and as an alternative to classical literature. Book 9 of *Paradise Lost* is thus the culmination of extensive exegetical and literary traditions, with Milton blending allegorical, literal, and typological readings of the fall with biblical commentaries, epics, and plays on the same subject. However indebted his treatment of the fall is to earlier works, it is distinguished by its "profound originality" (221), particularly in portraying Satan's motives, the heavenly council, and an overabundant Eden.

49   Fiore, Peter A. *Milton and Augustine: Patterns of Augustinian Thought in "Paradise Lost."* University Park: Pennsylvania State University Press, 1981. x + 118 pp.

Augustine, who exerts a major influence throughout Milton's life, shapes *Paradise Lost*'s presentation of angels, created nature's metaphysical goodness, evil's lack of a nature, and the paradox in which evil is turned to good. According to Augustine and Milton's epic, the rebel angels oppose the Incarnation not because their natures are bad but because they prefer their own natures over a higher, supernatural perfection. Their perverted wills cause them to rebel against a hierarchical creation by asserting and thus rejecting the self. In their preternatural state, Milton's Adam and Eve follow the Augustinian tradition by being endowed with immortality, impassibility, superior knowledge, and integrity. While Milton agrees with Augustine that innocent Adam and Eve subordinate the senses and passion to reason, he disagrees about prelapsarian sexual relations. The single prohibition is "easy" and easily observed, so Adam's iniquity is all the greater since his sin breaks not one precept but the whole law. Yet humans are not basically corrupted after the fall, for they have remnants of their original excellence or divine image. In *Paradise Lost*, the Redemption, made up of the Son's Incarnation and mediation, is Augustinian—the final step in the plan of salvation and a pivotal concept that unifies Christian doctrine's many branches.

50   Gallagher, Philip J. "*Paradise Lost* and the Greek Theogony." *English Literary Renaissance* 9 (1979): 121-48.

Because Milton's story antedates all others, he can criticize them in advance and expose their errors by presenting the authentic narrative that classical literature will travesty. Satan inspires Hesiod's titanomachia, a distortion of the war in heaven, to promote devil worship, disguise usurpation as a myth of divine succession, and attempt to turn his defeat into something less than a complete rout, thus impugning God's omnipotence. What Hesiod sees as a genuine power struggle, a strife of glory in which Zeus requires allies, is in fact a pro forma war in which God needs no aid. In another attempt to qualify divine omnipotence, Satan inspires Hesiod's perception that Zeus's energies are insufficient to conclude the war, but Milton's God states that only the Son can end the war in heaven. By offering different interpretations of Hesiod's *Theogony*, Milton reveals its inconsistencies and reconstructs primordial truth from scattered fragments found in various Greek myths.

51   Hägin, Peter. "The Hero of *Paradise Lost.*" In *The Epic Hero and the Decline of Heroic Poetry: A Study of the Neoclassical English Epic with Special Reference to Milton's "Paradise Lost,"* 146-69. Bern: Francke Verlag, 1964.

   Rather than accepting the Renaissance definition of epic, which contains all the elements of what would be called neoclassicism, Milton in *Paradise Lost* focuses on an unheroic theme and unadorned, prosaic humans. Because he knows that the genre of the heroic poem is endangered, he relies on that literary tradition to show its devaluation. Adam and Eve, representing humankind, destroy the conventional expectation of a hero, for they undergo an internal struggle and do not have epic stature. *Paradise Lost*'s climax is Adam and Eve's expulsion from paradise, with their lives a failure and redemption only a promise. Since their drama occurs in the soul and the stage they appear on (the traditional epic machinery) is monumental, Adam and Eve are the poem's unheroic heroes. The narration of the war in heaven teaches them about the possibility of a fall and signals the appalling end of heroic warfare. Satan enables the first couple to appear at all, since their problem can be paraphrased by his, though the parallel ends with Satan's conscious revenge against God through Eve. Even before the fall, Adam and Eve have the consciousness of an ordinary person with a lifetime of experience—this everyman is *Paradise Lost*'s true hero.

52   Harding, Davis P. *The Club of Hercules: Studies in the Classical Background of "Paradise Lost."* Illinois Studies in Language and Literature, vol. 50. Urbana: University of Illinois Press, 1962. x + 137 pp.

   According to Renaissance theory, one writer imitates another to create original effects from the borrowed material, a pattern of literary conduct Milton chooses by turning to Homer and particularly Virgil when writing *Paradise Lost*. In the opening invocation, he asserts his epic's superiority and debt to its classical predecessors. Satan embodies the old heroism of Achilles, Turnus, and Odysseus, the system of values whose deficiencies are implicitly criticized in the pattern of Christ's life. To make the transition from Adam and Eve's innocence to the state of sin, Milton presents the illusion of innocence while allusions place shadows of doubts in the reader's mind. He uses three techniques—direct quotation, metaphor or simile, and verbal echo—to make the classical context evident throughout *Paradise Lost*. As the epic's prefatory note indicates, the choice of blank verse is radical and an enormous gamble, but Milton makes this verse form lofty and forces English to do the work of Latin.

53   James, Heather. "Milton's Eve, the Romance Genre, and Ovid." *Comparative Literature* 45 (1993): 121-45.

Eve's identification with the romance genre and Ovidian poetics—particularly with their themes of wandering—makes her a self-reflexive copy of Adam's imagination. In her feminine luxury, which resembles that of the garden, Eve is a text to be interpreted. Her differences from Adam provide the basis for a sound Miltonic marriage, but her ambiguous physical description makes her a commentary on sex and sexual politics that readers must decipher. Milton avoids the hazards associated with romance and Ovidian eroticism (such as excessive wandering and violence) by linking the hierarchies of gender and genre through the hierarchy of marriage and by dramatizing romance's inherent moment of suspended decision, which can end in transcendence or error. Eve's narcissistic tendencies at the pool are fulfilled—and divinely sanctioned—in Adam, her original. However, Adam disrupts their union by projecting his own imagination onto Eve, thereby inverting the order of subjection, and by confusing Eve with God. The Pygmalion and Orpheus myths model Adam's re-creations of Eve before and after the fall, respectively.

54   Kirkconnell, Watson. *The Celestial Cycle: The Theme of "Paradise Lost" in World Literature with Translations of the Major Analogues*. Toronto: University of Toronto Press, 1952. xxvii + 701 pp. Reprinted New York: Gordian Press, 1967.

Covering the millennium before Milton's age, Kirkconnell presents all or part of twenty-four analogues of *Paradise Lost*, including those by Avitus, Du Bartas, Cowley, and Vondel. He also includes a descriptive catalogue of 329 analogues.

55   Knoespel, Kenneth J. "The Limits of Allegory: Textual Ex-
        pansion of Narcissus in *Paradise Lost.*" *Milton Studies* 22
        (1986): 79-99.
        When Milton presents Eve's creation and the portraits of Satan
and Adam, he turns to Ovid for elements that psychologically animate
characters. The Ovidian tale of Narcissus stresses the role of understanding in perception; Milton's adaptation shows that understanding
and correction come not from a reliance on individual perception but
from guidance. In Eve's scene at the pool, Milton imitates Ovid's setting and Latin, but while Narcissus recognizes his own image and cannot hear the narrator's warning, Eve has no self-recognition and obeys
the warning voice by leaving her deceptive image. When she soon returns to it, however, her dangerous behavior implies self-reliance and
a movement away from reason and toward an image associated with
death and distortion. Adam misrepresents what occurs during Eve's
creation by interpreting her desire for a watery image as modesty. He
is attracted to Eve as a corporeal reflection of himself rather than of
God's image in him. Like Eve at the pool, Adam allows emotion to im-
pede rational choice; like Narcissus, he receives additional information
and guidance (from Raphael) but cannot comprehend them. Milton uses
the Narcissus myth to show not only sensual deception but also the act
of interpretation.

56   Kurth, Burton O. *Milton and Christian Heroism: Biblical Epic
        Themes and Forms in Seventeenth-Century England.* Berkeley:
        University of California Press, 1959. viii + 152 pp. Reprinted
        Hamden, CT: Archon Books, 1966.
        Transcending the tragic hero's suffering and the classical he-
ro's passions, the individual Christian's external and internal heroism
of faith and endurance, as dramatized in *Paradise Lost*, forms part of
the providential plan that transforms evil to good. Sacred narrative
poetry under the Stuarts turns to Homeric and Virgilian heroic forms
because authors doubt the propriety of writing a biblical epic. Following the examples of Du Bartas and Spenser, minor poets search for
ways to present a truly Christian protagonist, emphasizing the character's temptation, trial, and suffering. Only *Paradise Lost* and *Paradise
Regained* succeed in showing the full cosmic drama, drawing on the
hexameral and Old and New Testament literary traditions, while focusing on the first temptation and fall (the archetypal pattern of humanity's
struggle with evil) and on Christ's temptation. *Paradise Lost* makes
explicit the context of cosmic good versus cosmic evil in which Chris-

tian heroism is most meaningful. If Christ portrays the true heroism and Satan the false, Adam and Eve, though not essentially heroic, begin to seek salvation by repenting, thus making heroic action possible for future generations as they struggle with Satan.

57   Labriola, Albert C. "The Titans and the Giants: *Paradise Lost* and the Tradition of the Renaissance Ovid." *Milton Quarterly* 12 (1978): 9-16.

Milton's knowledge of the many commentaries on Ovid's *Metamorphoses*, which Sandys's 1632 edition synthesizes, influences the composition of *Paradise Lost*. From this interpretive tradition, Milton derives details of the Typhon myth, allegorical meanings for them, and an allegorical technique "that correlates classical mythology with a Christian frame of reference" (10). Typhon, according to Ovid, leads the Titans in a revolt against Jove, who slaughters them; for revenge, Earth, the Titans' mother, gives birth to a race of Giants. Sandys connects the Titans and fallen angels, the Giants and the sons of Seth. In Book 11 of *Paradise Lost*, Michael brings together all of these analogies in a lesson about vainglory and ambition that focuses on Satan, Nimrod, and fallen humanity. Milton also adapts the myth of the Titans and its commentaries when he describes hell, warfare, and the demons' anger and punishment. The epic presents the relationship between fallen angels and fallen humans as an adaptation of the relationship between the Titans and the Giants.

58   Low, Anthony. "Milton and the Georgic Ideal: *Paradise Lost*." In *The Georgic Revolution*, 310-22. Princeton, NJ: Princeton University Press, 1985.

His life a testimony to the Virgilian georgic virtues of labor rather than military prowess, Milton creates in *Paradise Lost* a broad movement from pastoral to georgic. Adam and Eve enjoy pastoral otium before the fall, but they enter the larger world's bleak landscape at the end; heavenly life is characterized by pastoral delights until the war, when the rebels parody georgic activity by ripping up the soil, which the Son later restores in a miraculous georgic moment. As he builds his empire, even Satan is a laborer, an aspect of his personality that Milton uses to warn against the false pursuit of imperial georgic. In pastoral Eden, georgic elements illustrate humanity's dignity, the satisfactions of prelapsarian life, and the lack of distance between Eden and what fallen humanity may still find through grace. Labor in the fallen world Adam and Eve enter is both an unpleasant, unavoidable curse and something that can be turned to good.

59   McColley, Grant. *"Paradise Lost": An Account of Its Growth and Major Origins, with a Discussion of Milton's Use of Sources and Literary Patterns.* Chicago, IL: Packard and Co., 1940. ix + 362 pp. 4 illustrations. Reprinted New York: Russell and Russell, 1963.

Though Milton draws on religious writing in general, classical works, philosophy, and so forth, *Paradise Lost*'s most important single source is the genre of hexameral literature, followed in terms of general scope and major divisions (Satan's rebellion and the war in heaven; creation; temptation and fall; and paraphrases of biblical history). When Raphael discusses astronomy with Adam in a section derived from Ross's and Wilkins's works, the angel uses dialectic to demolish many cosmological speculations. Such sources as the Bible, Shakespeare, Spenser, and Du Bartas shape major and minor structural patterns in *Paradise Lost*. As the Trinity manuscript and Milton's reflections on the craft of poetry indicate, the true poet must read extensively, be divinely inspired, and write to praise God or the nation. Milton probably started writing *Paradise Lost* in 1652 and finished in 1663, but he did not compose the books in the order in which they were published.

60   Martz, Louis L. *"Paradise Lost*: Figurations of Ovid." In *Poet of Exile: A Study of Milton's Poetry*, 203-44. New Haven, CT: Yale University Press, 1980. Reprinted 1986.

Milton follows Ovid's example of structuring a poem in sections or panels whose characters, actions, details, and styles are compared to or contrasted with those in surrounding sections. Ovid's presence is especially pronounced in Milton's Eden, a realm where change is imminent and the threat of destructive power lurks everywhere.

61   Patrides, C. A. *Milton and the Christian Tradition.* Oxford: Clarendon Press, 1966. xvi + 302 pp. Part reprinted in *On Milton's Poetry*, edited by Arnold Stein, 111-33. Greenwich, CT: Fawcett Publications, 1970.

Christian Doctrine views the Son as subordinate to the Father, but *Paradise Lost* presents the persons of the Trinity in orthodox terms, as united and equal. Denying the doctrine of creation *ex nihilo*, the epic advances the idea that all creation is based on God's preexistent idea and occurs primarily to disseminate divine goodness. Created nature is orderly, hierarchical, and entirely subordinate to the providential plan. The concept of original sin, though lacking biblical support, becomes orthodox doctrine to which Milton turns when Adam and Eve fall by eating the fruit, an act indifferent in itself but significant as a test of obedience that affects the microcosm and the macrocosm. With its basis in satisfaction to divine justice, the Protestant theory of atonement makes it difficult to contemplate love as the absolute lord of life and death, a problem *Paradise Lost* does not solve by implicitly opposing the Son's mercy and the Father's justice. The epic achieves a balance of justification by faith and works, yet Milton cannot convince readers that free will and divine foreknowledge exist simultaneously. While history in the Greco-Roman view is a series of cycles, the Judeo-Christian perspective describes it as linear, unfolding in a sacred framework under God's vigilant eye. For Milton, history is a Christo-centric record of God's constant intervention in the world's affairs, ending in the great conflagration.

62   Pavlock, Barbara. "Milton's Criticism of Classical Epic in *Paradise Lost* 9." In *Eros, Imitation, and the Epic Tradition*, 187-218. Ithaca, NY: Cornell University Press, 1990. Reprinted in *Vergil*, edited by Craig Kallendorf, 291-314. New York: Garland, 1993.

By portraying Eve in the paradigm of the abandoned female and Satan as the "hero" who lures her with erotic language and leaves her to a dreadful fate, Milton implies a critical judgment of the classical epic tradition. Marriage in *Paradise Lost* attains the status of a new heroic value, perhaps an ideal to influence Milton's society concerning complementary relationships between men and women. In the separation scene, Eve presents the case for Christian liberty; Adam, for responsibility in the context of freedom. With its context of marital union, Milton's simile describing Eve's departure (9.386-92) differentiates his heroine from women presented in similes by Tasso, Virgil, Apollonius, and Homer. The simile describing the garden through which Satan prowls (9.439-41) links him to Odysseus and his manipulation of Nausikaa for self-aggrandizement. By connecting love and pious behavior, Milton undermines his predecessors' ethical structures. Adam, a complex analogue of Aeneas, fails in Christian piety and does not respond to the fallen Eve's dilemma by attempting mediation with God. When Adam and Eve violate their piety to God, they pervert their mutual love.

63   Porter, William M. *Reading the Classics and "Paradise Lost."* Lincoln: University of Nebraska Press, 1993. xii + 222 pp.

Milton's allusions to classical texts operate centrifugally, leading away from his epic and toward ancient works; readers must compare each allusion's significance in its two contexts, Miltonic and classical. Just as Milton issues challenges to the classics in *Paradise Lost*, so they complete the hermeneutic dialogue by turning his critiques back on themselves. He sees Hesiod as a classical archetype of the divinely inspired poet and a writer who addresses the matters that would later interest Moses. Besides being filtered through Virgil, Milton's allusions to Homer are included more for their prestige than their context. Books 1-2 of Milton's epic correspond to the infernal part of Aeneas's descent, Books 11-12 to the Elysian part. Both Adam and Eve are linked to Dido, and *Paradise Lost* connects the Son and Augustus as one way of engaging the *Aeneid*'s political dimension. The "Latinity" of Milton's epic style, particularly the diction, is an important part of his "intertextual or interlingual strategy" (134).

64   Quint, David. "The Boat of Romance and Renaissance Epic." In *Romance: Generic Transformation from Chrétien de Troyes to Cervantes*, edited by Kevin Brownlee and Marina Scordilis Brownlee, 178-202. Hanover, NH: University Press of New England for Dartmouth College, 1985. Translated as "La Barca dell'Avventura nell'Epica Rinascimentale," *Intersezioni* 5 (1985): 467-88. Revised version in *Epic and Empire: Politics and Generic Form from Virgil to Milton*, 248-67. Princeton, NJ: Princeton University Press, 1993.

Celebrating a triumphant, imperial papacy's absolute power, Tasso in *Jerusalem Delivered* incorporates romance, a genre of potential aimlessness and dependence on random chance, into the plot of conquest and manifest political destiny. To distinguish the epic enterprise from its romance double, Tasso also alludes to Boiardo when he juxtaposes two versions of the boat of adventure. Milton satirically collapses the genre into Satan's bad romance in *Paradise Lost*, while the larger story of Adam and Eve reclaims and revalorizes romance's open-endedness and contingency. When Milton describes Satan's journey through chaos in Book 2, his main subtext is Vasco da Gama's journey around the Cape of Good Hope in Camoëns's *Lusiads*. By suggesting that such imperialistic voyages are the devil's work, Milton continues his poem's general rejection of imperialism and the Virgilian epic of empire. Transformed from epic voyager to romance adventurer, Satan takes advantage of and depends on the occasion that chance brings. The epic deed is thus deflated into an adventure with merely momentary significance, for Milton devalues the enterprise of discovery as a literary subject matter.

65   Radzinowicz, Mary Ann. "'Smit with the Love of Sacred Song': Psalm Genres" and "'Light . . . from the Fountain of Light': Psalm Themes." In *Milton's Epics and the Book of Psalms*, 135-69 and 170-99. Princeton, NJ: Princeton University Press, 1989.

        Besides contributing psychological fluidity and focusing intense expressive utterance, psalm genres help Milton shape *Paradise Lost* into a mode of worship. His invocations adapt the conventions of the prophetic psalm genre, the heavenly choir in Book 3 and other hymns are governed by the hymnal psalm, and the poet's role as teacher and Abdiel's conduct as loyal angel draw on the wisdom song. Tragic movements and statements about "all our woe" imitate the Psalms of lamentation, which often develop into moments of thanksgiving.

        Milton sees the Book of Psalms as containing revealed truths and an account of the process by which they are acknowledged. In *Paradise Lost*, he uses psalm themes to produce "the encyclopedism of copia" (170) and give a comprehensive representation of process or causality. From one cluster of Psalms, Milton creates a drama of death's unfolding meaning, including his unorthodox mortalist view; another cluster presents the orthodox and materialistic theories of creation.

66   Revard, Stella P[urce]. "The Heroic Context of Book IX of *Paradise Lost*." *JEGP: Journal of English and Germanic Philology* 87 (1988): 329-41.

        In the classical epic tradition, the two principal male adversaries, having been kept apart for the whole poem, finally meet in battle. Milton dismisses such a heroic encounter in the invocation to Book 9, yet that book does not contain the patience and heroic martyrdom he promises. By encountering Eve, Satan shuns traditional single combat; instead, he uses unmilitary strategies of fraud and flattery, cowardice and indirection. He will, however, have to face and be conquered by the second Adam. With his offer to die for humanity, Christ presents the pattern for heroic martyrdom, parodied by Adam's evasion of God's condition, disobedience, and choice to die with Eve rather than for her. If the epic duel is left unfulfilled and the roles of battle hero and heroic martyr are contrasted in Book 9, Book 12 merges the two as the Son achieves revenge by dying on the cross and teaching Adam about true heroism. Half divine, strong, and capable of changing the course of history, the Son in *Paradise Lost* resembles Achilles and Aeneas, and he unites the classical and Christian hero.

67   Rosenblatt, Jason P. *Torah and Law in "Paradise Lost."*
      Princeton, NJ: Princeton University Press, 1994. xi + 274 pp.
      In Books 5-8 of *Paradise Lost*, Milton's positive portrayal of Edenic Mosaic law, which is benign and easy to keep, owes a great deal to his prose tracts from 1643-45. With the fall comes the need for a savior, and *Christian Doctrine* is the matrix for the typology, Pauline perspective, and negative conception of the law in the epic's final books. The invocations to Books 1 and 3 are illuminated by an extensive Platonic and Hebraic historical and allegorical tradition that portrays Moses as a poet-prophet with unmediated human accomplishments. Starting with the invocation to Book 9, however, Moses bridges the gap between perfection and sin because he is united with Adam and the narrator as sinners excluded from sacred ground and in need of divine intervention. Adam and Eve do not preserve the law's sanctity from "contamination by a demonic parody of the gospel and by the premature introduction of an ethos that is in part genuinely Pauline" (167). Adam's soliloquy in Book 10.720-844 dramatizes Milton's turning away from Torah after the fall to meditate on the Pauline theme that faith and law are contradictory. The Epistle to the Hebrews is the main source of Books 11-12, in which Michael expounds the typology of Moses and demonstrates the Mosaic law's inferiority to justification by faith.

68   Rumrich, John Peter. "Metamorphosis in *Paradise Lost*." *Viator: Medieval and Renaissance Studies* 20 (1989): 311-25.

Unlike his contemporaries, Milton revises rather than abandons Ovid, particularly in his formulation of the fall as a metamorphosis. Similar to Aristotle and Anaxagoras, Milton believes in the necessity of change in salvation, whereby humans' spiritual and material being is improved when harmonized with the will of God. While Adam and Eve maintain a positive fluidity through wholesome nourishment, the fallen angels, because of their voluntary alienation from God, feed on and are hardened by the hell without and within. The motivation behind metamorphosis in *Paradise Lost* is love, whether the instantly achieved angelic form or the more involved human process. Although Adam and Eve's marriage has great metamorphic potential, the opposing forces of required obedience and unbidden love threaten to draw Eve back into destructive narcissism. The fall, caused by the departure from God's will, brings metamorphic regression. The only certainties in Milton's universe are God's goodness and the endurance of his glory; whoever endures and trusts in these can be part of the change that turns defeat into victory.

69   Ryken, Leland. "*Paradise Lost* and Its Biblical Epic Models." In *Milton and Scriptural Tradition: The Bible into Poetry*, edited by James H. Sims and Leland Ryken, 43-81. Columbia: University of Missouri Press, 1984.

Milton uses biblical epic models in *Paradise Lost* to replace the epic tradition's heroic values with pastoral and domestic ones, its theme of human greatness with an emphasis on divine greatness and human smallness, and its physical motifs with spiritual ones. The Son's role as epic hero, and Adam and Eve's as failures, illustrates Milton's substitution of human values and action with the divine and his separation of the two realms. Following the model of Genesis, *Paradise Lost* presents Adam and Eve with domestic values elevated to the status of an epic norm. Based on Revelation, a shift of motifs from the earthly or physical to the heavenly or spiritual plane appears in the war in heaven and the kind of heroism, dominion, and empire that Milton advocates. *Paradise Lost* consistently uses an anti-epic strategy of subverting the classical heroic tradition by following biblical epic models.

70   Shumaker, Wayne. "*Paradise Lost* and the Italian Epic Tradition." In *Th'Upright Heart and Pure: Essays on John Milton*

Commemorating the Tercentenary of the Publication of "Paradise Lost," edited by Amadeus P. Fiore, O.F.M., 87-100. Pittsburgh, PA: Duquesne University Press, 1967.

When Milton rejects an Arthurian subject for his major poem, he also rejects chivalric themes and the Italian epic tradition, the only epic form that had demonstrated popular and critical appeal in Europe. He thus chooses a simple, focused plot, with fewer actions and fewer, more carefully delineated characters. Unlike writers of Italian romance epics, Milton has little interest in magic: "the universe of *Paradise Lost* is infinitely clearer, saner, and simpler than the necromantic one of his Italian predecessors" (97). If the Italian epics' main values are honor, valor, and romantic love, Milton's poem advocates the higher ideals of patience and heroic martyrdom. Boiardo, Ariosto, and Tasso use ottava rima, but Milton's choice of blank verse is boldly original.

71   Sims, James H. *The Bible in Milton's Epics*. Gainesville: University of Florida Press, 1962. vii + 283 pp.

In *Paradise Lost* and *Paradise Regained*, Milton uses biblical allusions to create a sense of reality, truth, and authority. Even the episodes and characters he invents are based on or expansions of Scripture. With his thorough training in biblical languages, he sometimes transliterates Greek or Hebrew into English and presents a translation, provides variant translations of certain texts, and follows the Vulgate's words or phrasing. Biblical allusions heighten the dramatic effects when Milton foreshadows events and establishes setting, time, and character, often by associating them with a scriptural context. By reiterating biblical phrases, he unifies each epic's theme while connecting *Paradise Lost* to *Paradise Regained*.

Sims includes an "Index of Biblical References" contained in each line of Milton's epics.

72   Steadman, John M. *Milton and the Renaissance Hero*. Oxford: Clarendon Press, 1967. xx + 209 pp.

Radically spiritualizing the epic's conventional argument and revising the formulas that define a hero, Milton consigns the traditional heroism of strength and courage (*fortezza*) in its vicious mode to the devils and the heroism of fortitude associated with wisdom (*sapientia*) to Christ. Satan's portrait in *Paradise Lost* discredits his heroic pretensions and the *fortezza* formula itself because might without piety is a falsely heroic attribute. Such characters as Abdiel and Christ reveal strength in apparent weakness. Milton reduces the *sapientia* formula to an opposition between God's wisdom and the world's. To pursue the public's welfare, a character must join these formulas to the idea of the *dux* or good leader who is always a loyal subject of God, a role Christ fills, Satan inverts, and Adam abrogates. Like all of these qualities, love can be a brutish passion or heroic virtue; Adam and Eve illustrate both the idol and the true image of love. Satan displays false magnanimity and vainglory, which seeks the peers' approval rather than God's. In *Paradise Lost*, true glory comes from shame, and virtue from obedience. Milton's epics emphasize moral virtues instead of the actual heroic deed.

73   Steadman, John M. *Milton's Biblical and Classical Imagery*. Pittsburgh, PA: Duquesne University Press, 1984. xii + 258 pp.

Milton uses the classical tradition as a figurative commentary on or antithesis of the biblical one. In *Paradise Lost*, Satan's actions, beginning with a martial context and culminating in a moral battle, link the classical epic tradition and the biblical epic of Job. Milton's plot differs from Renaissance norms by focusing on the antagonist's temporary victory and the epic hero's defeat, while presenting the heroic archetype (the Son) primarily through retrospective and proleptic episodes. A paradoxical compromise between truth and myth, the metaphor of a Christian muse is a variant on a classical literary convention as well as a symbol for revelation, the poet's musings on sacred themes, or—as *Paradise Lost* implies—the Holy Spirit. When Milton invokes the meaning of Urania and not the name, he is following an etymological approach and interpreting her name literally as "Heavenly," for she is closely related to God's internal efficiency, decrees, and foreknowledge. The epic's opening invocation calls to two powers: first to a personification of celestial song and then to God. Milton's description of a fire in hell that sheds no light follows traditional uses of this image, appears as *Paradise Lost*'s first example of the Christian marvelous, and shows the penal nature of hell, a region that affects vision and the knowledge one can gain from it.

74   Steadman, John M. *The Wall of Paradise: Essays on Milton's Poetics*. Baton Rouge: Louisiana State University Press, 1985. vii + 156 pp.

Based on the synthetic tradition of sixteenth-century Italian criticism, Milton's conception of the poet's office indicates that eloquence is an instrument of civil and moral education and that the arts serve the ends of religion. When Milton selects the tragic matter of Adam's failure for *Paradise Lost*, he rejects the traditional Renaissance view of a heroic poem's proper subject, though Aristotle and classical poets sanction such a choice. His most significant departure from the classical and Renaissance tradition is the rejection of a martial theme in favor of spiritual combat. In choosing a subject for his epic, Milton realizes that the theme must receive the ideal form of an epic plot and delineate an ideal pattern of heroic virtue; he achieves a compromise between the ethical requirement for a universal *moralitas* (the testing of virtue in spiritual combat) and the emphasis on an extraordinarily virtuous and eminent hero (Adam). In Italian literature, which sets the precedent for English writers, blank verse becomes conventional through practice rather than theory. Neoclassical critics disapprove of allegory in a heroic poem, but the Aristotelian tradition and Italian commentaries affirm the poet's license to describe impossibilities for the sake of their allegorical content.

75   Treip, Mindele Anne. "Debts to Renaissance Allegory in *Paradise Lost*," "Allegorical Poetics in *Paradise Lost*," "Allegory and 'Idea' in *Paradise Lost*," and "'Real or Allegoric': Representation in *Paradise Lost*." In *Allegorical Poetics and the Epic: The Renaissance Tradition to "Paradise Lost,"* 126-37, 138-49, 150-67, and 169-256. Lexington: University Press of Kentucky, 1994.

At least one-fifth to one-quarter of *Paradise Lost* is rendered allegorically or contains devices recognizable from the tradition of allegorical methodology. The tradition of interpreting Scripture allegorically shows Milton the need to sustain the truth of his epic's literal level. He also aligns his poem with historical and contemporary models that emphasize the moral level and use both intermittent and sustained allegory.

Tasso's work is the main source for the theme and model that allow Milton to correlate a historical narrative, biblical narrative history, and allegorical fiction that displays a moral concept.

Milton joins the allegorical epic's humanist tradition, which assumes that the poet resembles a divine theologian and that all poetry expresses some prior Idea (or oblique intention) about the moral life, such as justifying God's ways and the existence of evil.

Although critics have applied a kind of poetic fundamentalism to *Paradise Lost* for three centuries, literal expression and figurative expression are not mutually exclusive. *Christian Doctrine* formulates hermeneutic principles of attending to context and balancing strictness in some respects with figurative latitude in others, principles that are crucial to *Paradise Lost*'s aesthetic. Speaking to Adam, Raphael infers a mode of narrative allegory for his account and implicitly a poetics of allegory for Milton's epic. Everything in *Paradise Lost* that is fictive and the poet's invention is in some way allegorical, a fact that makes its historical component no less real.

76   Webber, Joan Malory. "*Paradise Lost*." In *Milton and His Epic Tradition*, 103-63. Seattle: University of Washington Press, 1979.

In the epic tradition, the hero completes his quest and his society is accepted, but "neither the culture nor its preservation is as important as self-conflict and self-knowledge" (103), including the hero's acceptance and transcendence of mortality. From 1640 to 1660, Milton tries to realize a new society worthy of his epic praise. *Paradise Lost* and *Paradise Regained* continue his battle against those external things that cause the revolution, such as tradition and the people's love of their own slavery, as he celebrates and subverts his culture's ideals. The epic begins in a cave of the human condition (hell) to remind readers that they are fallen and their sources of trust or authority are few. Satan in *Paradise Lost* is a fragmenting force, an impeder of life, like King Charles I; God is not a character but a creative force of life or a direction. By singing of creation, the poet reveals God's discovery of himself and thus of otherness and death. If Milton's Satan is a critique of classical heroes, his God is a critique of classical deities. As they journey into consciousness in *Paradise Lost*, God, the Son, Adam, and Eve are all isolated figures. Milton constructs his poem on dualities, oppositions, dividedness, and androgyny.

Other studies that explore *Paradise Lost* and the biblical and classical epic traditions are identified in entries 105, 130, 154, 169, 205, 246, 263, 278, 312, 327-28, 368, 371-72, 382, and 436.

7. REPUTATION AND INFLUENCE

77   Baker, C. H. Collins. "Some Illustrators of Milton's *Paradise Lost* (1688-1850)." *Library*, 5th series, 3 (1948): 1-21, 101-19. 10 illustrations.

On the fringes of gothic-baroque art, *Paradise Lost*'s first illustrations use engraving processes well-suited to the imperial gesture or heroic figures in close design. Turner's landscapes later show artists who have the resources of mezzotint how to create the high imagery Milton conceives. Baker provides a catalogue of the artists and subjects of *Paradise Lost*'s early illustrations.

78   Barker, Arthur [E.]. "'. . . And on His Crest Sat Horror': Eighteenth-Century Interpretations of Milton's Sublimity and His Satan." *University of Toronto Quarterly* 11 (1942): 421-36.

Late seventeenth- and early eighteenth-century commentators consider *Paradise Lost* sublime yet unpolished and not truly epic in subject. Milton's sublimity is first conceived as a theory of religious elevation and later of delightful sensationalism. Near the end of the eighteenth century, writers begin to emphasize Satan's sublimity, sympathize with him, and humanize him.

79   Boss, Valentin. *Milton and the Rise of Russian Satanism*. Toronto: University of Toronto Press, 1991. xxvi + 276 pp.

Milton's Satan has a varied career in Russian literature. Initially ignored, perhaps because he is closely linked to the Antichrist and Peter the Great, he soon appears in all of his biblical intensity and then as a gentleman and nontheological figure of evil. Russian imitations and translations of *Paradise Lost* reveal a sympathetic view of Satan in the eighteenth century. In the late part of that century, the French Revolution turns him into a political figure, with portrayals of him as a freethinking revolutionary and a Prometheus figure becoming touchstones of political and religious orthodoxy. Russian Romantics see Satan as a secularized heroic figure. Later developing into the ideologue of a new conception of evil, Milton's character assumes a post-revolutionary role that both fascinates and repels readers. After 1917, the radical intelligentsia transforms Satan into almost a purely political creature; following the Bolshevik Revolution, he takes his place as a prince of light in the battle against imperialism. "With *glasnost'* and *perestroika* this prestigious phase in Satan's career as an intellectual pillar of the Marxist-Leninist establishment has come to an end" (163).

Boss includes three indexes: "Milton's Interest in Russia"; "An English Oration Concerning Milton's Satan from Lermontov's School"; and "A Chronological Distribution Table [of Russian Manuscripts and Printed Book Translations of Milton's Writings before World War I]."

80   Eliot, T. S. *Milton*. Oxford: Oxford University Press, 1947. 19 pp. Reprinted as "Milton II" in *On Poetry and Poets*, 165-83. London: Faber and Faber, 1957; reprinted in *The Modern Critical Spectrum*, edited by Gerald Jay Goldberg and Nancy Marmer Goldberg, 175-86. Englewood Cliffs, NJ: Prentice-Hall, 1962; reprinted in *Milton: "Paradise Lost," a Casebook*, edited by A. E. Dyson and Julian Lovelock, 77-84. London: Macmillan, 1973. Frequently reprinted.

Readers of Milton should always be alert to their potential prejudice against his religious views, politics, or character. One cannot say that his verse exerts only a harmful influence on other poets (see entry 28), for the imitators are responsible for their own work and, in the case of future poets, perhaps readers can hold no opinion about what good or bad influences mean. The seventeenth-century dissociation of sensibility is the result of many complex causes, not just Milton. Writing a style that is a sequence of original acts of lawlessness, Milton creates a personal style far removed from prose and ordinary speech. A lack of interest in and understanding of individual humans leads him to choose the subject of Adam and Eve, and a weak visual imagination leads him to create richer sounds and better images of light, darkness, and vast size.

81   Newlyn, Lucy. *"Paradise Lost" and the Romantic Reader*. Oxford: Clarendon Press, 1993. xii + 295 pp.

Deified by eighteenth- and early nineteenth-century readers and seen preeminently as the author of *Paradise Lost*, Milton acts as a moral guide and political hero. Romantic responses to Milton contain a noteworthy inconsistency: as critics, the Romantics caricature him as authoritarian; as practicing writers, they admire and imitate "the indeterminacies of his style and meaning" (69). Rather than having to choose between *Paradise Lost*'s didacticism and the subtext that subverts it, a Romantic reading finds a kind of truth in the plurality of perspectives and suspension of choice that the epic narrator denies. Instead of believing that *Paradise Lost* relates a coherent republican allegory, Romantic writers see a divided treatment of the relationship between earthly politics and religious truth. In response to Milton's apparent misogyny and Eve's subjection, a male line of feminist writing leads from Milton through Pope and to the major Romantic poets (see entry 88). The Romantics use Eve to represent both a craving for liberty, which can be achieved only through transgression, and the difficulty of reconciling imagination with the constraints of the real. By imitating, echoing, or reworking *Paradise Lost*, Romantic writers seek to gain poetic credibility and claim quasi-scriptural authority. Using a revisionary procedure, Blake in *Milton* undermines the voice of Milton's narrator, acknowledges that parallels between opposites proliferate in *Paradise Lost*, and intends to correct all that is wrong-headed about Milton's epic.

82   Paulson, Ronald. "The Miltonic Scripture." In *Book and Painting: Shakespeare, Milton and the Bible. Literary Texts and the Emergence of English Painting*, 99-151. Knoxville: University of Tennessee Press, 1982. 46 illustrations.

If Shakespeare skeptically questions all organizing structures, Milton's "illustration" of Genesis in *Paradise Lost* organizes experience around simple paradigms, such as the duality of light and dark or height and depth. His similes show a settled georgic order in the world and remove humans from that order, leaving them in a dark area without the divine effect needed to interpret signs. Though Milton and the Old Testament fulfill the eighteenth-century need for order, at the end of the century Blake rewrites Milton and sets New Testament fiction against Old, while other artists turn Shakespeare into a Miltonic poet or recognize that his plays offer models for undermining forms. Carrying negative capability into a contrary egotistical sublime, Blake and other artists have a Miltonic point of view. The landscapes in Turner's illustrations of Shakespeare Miltonize the dramatic text and aestheticize Milton's moral contrast of light and dark by turning it into a Shakespearean fable about the artist controlling nature.

83   Pointon, Marcia R. *Milton and English Art*. Manchester: Manchester University Press, 1970. xliii + 276 pp. 218 illustrations.

Early illustrators of *Paradise Lost* try to enlighten or explain the poem in work reminiscent of medieval and sixteenth-century manuscript and Bible illumination. In the mid-eighteenth century, artists associated with Hogarth advocate modern rococo and baroque styles, which are followed by a period of intensified illustration of Milton using either a neoclassical or melodramatic, sublime style. Blake, having assimilated the Milton illustrations of the 1790s, does more than other artists to incorporate his interpretations of *Paradise Lost* into the pictorial symbolism of his designs. In the nineteenth century, the neoclassical style of illustration matures, the sublime style gaining new dimensions in Martin's work.

84   Schulman, Lydia Dittler. *"Paradise Lost" and the Rise of the American Republic*. Boston, MA: Northeastern University Press, 1992. xiii + 273 pp.

Attracted to Milton's defense of republican liberty, which requires a virtuous, educated citizenry, eighteenth-century Americans give *Paradise Lost* a central place in the popular consciousness. The fall is seen as a religious and political story conducive to reflection on the paradoxes of the early commercial republic because Milton shows both human fallibility and free, rational choice. Acting as a perversion of the orator-statesman who awakens right reason, his Satan is a manipulative tyrant and a slave to "the single-minded pursuit of self-interest" (58). Though the government of heaven is formally an absolute monarchy, it also resembles the free republican commonwealth praised in Milton's pamphlets. Early Americans receive a legacy of Puritanism and Commonwealth thought, including Milton's, that includes ideas about millenialism, inalienable rights, the legitimacy of certain kinds of revolution, the importance of education, and the superiority of mixed and balanced government. The imagery of *Paradise Lost* permeates American culture, as the poem "reached increasingly wider American audiences in the first decades of the Republic" (181). See entry 87.

85   Shawcross, John T., ed. *Milton: The Critical Heritage*. London: Routledge and Kegan Paul, 1970. xi + 276 pp.
      Covering the years 1628-1731, Shawcross includes statements by Milton and others about his writings. A large section is devoted to early eighteenth-century comments on *Paradise Lost*. See entry 86.

86   Shawcross, John T., ed. *Milton, 1732-1801: The Critical Heritage*. London: Routledge and Kegan Paul, 1972. xi + 439 pp.
      The companion to Shawcross's volume of commentary on Milton from 1628-1731 (see entry 85), this book contains statements reflecting *Paradise Lost*'s reception and reputation in the eighteenth century.

87   Stavely, Keith W. F. "Prophetic Strain: The Representation of Puritan Culture in *Paradise Lost*." In *Puritan Legacies: "Paradise Lost" and the New England Tradition, 1630-1890*, 19-97. Ithaca, NY: Cornell University Press, 1987.
      The broad sense of vitalism and immanence implied by antinomianism appears in *Paradise Lost*'s dignified creation, permeated by God's light. Not a spokesman for only a reforming middle class, Milton integrates antinomianism and Arminianism by creating a universe in which every creature is challenged to participate and make choices. The ambivalence of sexual politics in prelapsarian Eden—Adam and Eve are both equal and unequal—represents Puritan domestic doctrine and the relationship of the Puritan church and state. After a number of events leave Adam and Eve uncertain about the boundary between subordination and autonomy in their relationship, each concentrates on consolidating a position rather than listening to the other person. The separation scene shows that the growing uncertainty becomes an irritant and a reason for confrontation. Satan thus does not need to initiate strife; he works with the conflict that develops in Adam and Eve's contradictory, ambiguous relationship. In his portrait of Satan, Milton may be representing the ambiguity in Protestant and Puritan activism—that is, the grandeur of the emergent capitalist revolution as well as the license it gives to self-interest and ambition. See entry 84.

88   Wittreich, Joseph. *Feminist Milton*. Ithaca, NY: Cornell University Press, 1987. xxiii + 173 pp.

From about 1700 to 1830, female readers of *Paradise Lost* view Milton as an ally in their effort to transform the received ideology concerning the sexes because his three major poems critique and explode the biblically sanctioned and culturally reinforced traditions of patriarchy and misogyny. His representation of woman is ambiguous, its conflicting signals harboring an elaborate system of subversion. In the eighteenth century, his epic is first and foremost the property of the popular culture, whose interpretations differ from the elitist movement's views, which become canonized as the age's orthodoxies. The popular culture and female readers find in Milton a sponsor of women's liberation and an interrogator of patriarchal religion and masculinist society. His realistic portrait of women contains an idealism that allows for and honors sexual difference, potential for self-improvement, and certain attributes worthy of general emulation and admiration. Using deconstructive strategies not as ends in themselves, Milton's early readers see them as tactics of subversion rife with ideological significance. Satan generates patriarchal attitudes before the fall, at which point man assumes that role and too successfully instills them in woman. Milton is of Eve's party and he knows it very well.

For other studies that examine *Paradise Lost*'s reputation and influence, see entries 17, 144, and 171.

8. CRITICS ON CRITICISM OF
PARADISE LOST

89   Adams, Robert Martin. "The Devil and Doctor Jung." In
      Ikon: John Milton and the Modern Critics, 35-59. Ithaca, NY:
      Cornell University Press, 1955. Reprinted 1966.
      Jungian or archetypal criticism too often locates aesthetic value
in farfetched parallels between works. Rather than being *Paradise
Lost*'s tragic hero or a Prometheus figure, Satan is a secondary character who does not develop consistently in one direction and whose energy cannot be explained by calling him archetypal. If Milton wants the
reader to see a Prometheus figure in the epic, that character is Adam.

90   Alpers, Paul J. "The Milton Controversy." In *Twentieth-
      Century Literature in Retrospect*, edited by Reuben A. Brow-
      er, 269-98. Cambridge, MA: Harvard University Press, 1971.
      Despite attacks on Milton's preeminence by Leavis (see entries
30-31), Eliot (see entry 28), and Waldock (see entry 221), their
opponents remain silent until the publication of Ricks's *Milton's Grand
Style* (see entry 36)—and even that book, while it ably defends Milton's
personality, does not provide a comprehensive response to earlier criticisms of his verse. *Paradise Lost* sometimes emphasizes words over
things, as Leavis argues, yet it does so not because of artistic incompe-
tence but to illustrate the problem of what human art can apprehend.
Milton's syntax is shaped by the auditory imagination rather than patterns of speech or thought, as Eliot insists, and not because of poetic
impoverishment but to produce an intense engagement. Leavis bases his
rejection of Milton on a revaluation of nineteenth-century critical attitudes that praise the poet's character rather than his intelligence. Viewing truth objectively and perhaps dogmatically, Milton finds human nature fixed and general, a perspective that in some ways liberates his
poetry. Waldock sees a contradiction between *Paradise Lost*'s categori-
cal moral interpretations and its dramatic life; if readers are participants

in the poem's words, however, they realize the moralizing is accurate and appropriate. Rather than rendering the dramatic development of a mind, Milton's poetry successfully contemplates truths, attitudes, and traditions.

91   Bergonzi, Bernard. "Criticism and the Milton Controversy." In *The Living Milton*, edited by Frank Kermode, 162-80. London: Routledge and Kegan Paul, 1960.

The modern view of Milton—general admiration mixed with some reservations—starts with his earliest critics, though they never doubt his greatness. Such critics as Leavis (see entries 30-31), Eliot (see entry 28), and Waldock (see entry 221), however, aim to reduce his stature as a classic. Using the stance of a critic, Eliot still speaks as a practicing poet who rejects what he cannot use, including Milton. Anti-Miltonists point out that a true controversy does not exist because the upholders of the poet's reputation refuse to join the debate. No one has responded to the anti-Miltonists for one simple reason: their criticisms are unanswerable and irrefutable within the terms of reference in which they are stated. But they are wrong, as one can argue only by examining the appropriateness of the formulas that state the case. Leavis demands organic poetry that is like speech (subtle, expressive, and sensitive), a criterion that omits too much, particularly ritualistic art. Waldock requires a monistic narrative and moral naturalism that are more relevant to a novel than a Christian epic.

92   Corthell, Ronald J. "Milton and the Possibilities of Theory." In *Reconsidering the Renaissance: Papers from the Twenty-First Annual Conference*, edited by Mario A. Di Cesare, 489-99. Binghamton, NY: Medieval and Renaissance Texts and Studies, 1992.

Because of their reliance on thematics of binary oppositions, various critics' subversive readings of Milton may not be desirable or even possible. Theory cannot help people understand Milton, but it can make them think about the complex issues that arise when reading his poetry.

93   Fish, Stanley. "Transmuting the Lump: *Paradise Lost*, 1942-1982." In *Literature and History: Theoretical Problems and Russian Case Studies*, edited by Gary Saul Morson, 33-56. Stanford, CA: Stanford University Press, 1986.

As both products and objects of the critic's activity, literary works are constituted by questions that are meaningful only in relation to "prevailing institutional conditions" (36). Professional readers and writers, relying on what has previously been stated, create an ideological and political situation that determines what assertions make convincing sense. Reconfirming an old orthodoxy while challenging a new one, Lewis in 1942 (see entry 167) regards Books 11-12 of *Paradise Lost* as barely part of the poem, but by 1982 critics see them as its very center. A structural criterion that affirms literature's value as literature leads one to condemn Books 11-12 as inartistic because doctrinal matters dominate the poetry or drama. To counter this view, critics spatialize *Paradise Lost* and later redefine the poetic to include theology, noting that theological material makes doctrinal matters available for dramatization. The rehabilitation of these books is well under way by 1959.

94   Keener, Frederick M. "Parallelism and the Poets' Secret: Eighteenth-Century Commentary on *Paradise Lost*." *Essays in Criticism* 37 (1987): 281-302.
    Paradise Lost is constructed with many parallel elements, such as the various trinities, that form and qualify its meaning, yet eighteenth-century readers are only minimally aware of them and pursue their implications very little. Eighteenth-century annotations are concerned, however, with parallels between *Paradise Lost* and other literary works, particularly classical ones. Parallels and repetitions remain the poet's secret for three centuries, but methods of reading have changed more than most scholars realize.

95   Oras, Ants. *Milton's Editors and Commentators from Patrick Hume to Henry John Todd (1695-1801): A Study in Critical Views and Methods*. London: Oxford University Press, 1931. 381 pp. Reprinted New York: Haskell House, 1964.
    Paradise Lost's eighteenth-century annotators range from the undisciplined Hume to the narrow-minded Bentley, from the scholarly Pearce to the enthusiastic Richardsons and Peck. Bishop Newton's variorum edition (1749) marks the first attempt to collect the valuable annotations of Milton's writing, and Todd's edition (1801) includes a great deal of the work done during the entire eighteenth century. Much of this commentary is characterized by its interest in etymology as well as biblical and classical sources.

96   Redman, Harry, Jr. *Major French Milton Critics of the Nine-
         teenth Century*. Pittsburgh, PA: Duquesne University Press,
         1994. xiii + 390 pp.
         Until almost the end of the nineteenth century, French readers
view Milton only as a prose polemicist. His poems become more wide-
ly known after the French Revolution, and in the nineteenth century
"most French Milton critics were enthusiastic about their author, what-
ever reservations they may have had about his political commitments
and activities" (6-7). French Romantics come close to seeing Satan as
the hero of *Paradise Lost*, but they do not make this claim explicitly.
Some authors, including Pichot, Vigny, Hugo, and Villiers, write fictional works about Milton, and other prominent French authors allude
to him in their writing. Redman discusses the criticism of fifteen
French Milton critics of the nineteenth century. Though these writers
have diverse reactions to *Paradise Lost*, many comment on Milton's
powerful imagination, deep disillusionment, and sublime poetic style.

9. GENERAL CRITICISM OF
PARADISE LOST

97   Allen, Don Cameron. "Description as Cosmos: The Visual
      Image in *Paradise Lost*" and "The Descent to Light: Basic
      Metaphor in *Paradise Lost*." In *The Harmonious Vision: Stud-
      ies in Milton's Poetry*, 95-109 and 122-42. Revised edition
      Baltimore, MD: Johns Hopkins Press, 1970.

      Visual imagery, which depends on words suggesting color,
motion, and shape, plays an important role in *Paradise Lost*, despite
what some critics claim. In Book 3 and elsewhere, Milton thinks of
light as a graduated divine impulsion: readers cannot see essential light,
but when it descends into materiality light,becomes shadowy. What one
perceives as colors are simply broken beams of the eternal ray. The use
of colors thus confesses one's imperfection, so Milton's description of
heaven is appropriately bathed in an essential light that is almost without color. Deprived of light, the demons are removed from God. Earth
in *Paradise Lost* is a world of half lights until the fall brings darkness
as readers know it.

      Milton believes in the literal interpretation of the Bible but he
also finds allegory and a dynamic typology that changes as history unfolds, two techniques that are relevant to *Paradise Lost*, which might
be called an allegory about allegory. Like other elements from pagan
culture that Milton enlists to support Christian myths, Orpheus appears
as a type of Christ and one of Milton's own predecessors as poet-
theologian, while Hercules is another savior and Christ figure. In
Paradise Lost, as in the Christian scheme and the lives of Orpheus and
Hercules, one humbly descends into the dark to ascend triumphantly to
the light, a movement the demons pervert. Although Satan is associated
with the darkness of damnation, Christian tradition also portrays the
dark God in the divine night. Light itself must descend in *Paradise Lost*
so humans may see.

51

98   Armstrong, Wilma G. "Punishment, Surveillance, and Discipline in *Paradise Lost.*" *Studies in English Literature, 1500-1900* 32 (1992): 91-109.

Like Foucault, Milton focuses on areas of control and authority in society, particularly the internalizing of control. Most of the forms of punishment that Foucault traces through history—from Greek and Roman exile to modern imprisonment and surveillance—are applied to Satan and his followers. The torment in hell is a social ritual that reenacts their crime and inscribes it on their bodies. Adam and Eve receive the same varied forms of punishment, and even paradise is defaced and deformed. Through the Son, Adam and Eve may experience the Germanic form of punishment, which involves atonement, compensation, and fines. Using imprisonment to reform the offender, surveillance by an omnipotent, omniscient God and his angels is pervasive in Milton's poetic universe. Yet the frequent failures in surveillance testify to the imperfect system that God commands as well as the internalized locus of responsibility to God in the epic. Milton sees self-surveillance or discipline as positive and productive; indeed, it leads to true liberty because it focuses the individual's attention on God. See entry 162.

99   Babb, Lawrence. *The Moral Cosmos of "Paradise Lost."* East Lansing: Michigan State University Press, 1970. x + 166 pp.

Literal knowledge comes from study and accommodated knowledge of suprahuman matters comes from revelation, both leading to a virtuous life, while forbidden knowledge involves what God chooses not to reveal. For prelapsarian Adam and Eve, the world is wholly good and evil exists only potentially, so the forbidden fruit provides unnecessary knowledge of what they already understand. Because the study of nature leads to knowledge of God, *Paradise Lost*'s humanistic-Christian cosmos uses scientific material, especially astronomy, for pious ends. Though Milton eventually becomes aware of the heliocentric theory's reasonableness, his epic tries to reconcile the obviously incompatible Ptolemaic astronomy and Hebrew cosmology. Materialism, which distinguishes creatures of flesh from those of spirit only by degree, unifies the creation. The spatial relationships in and between the epic's various settings—heaven, earth, chaos, hell—are highly original.

100   Barker, Arthur E. "*Paradise Lost*: The Relevance of Regeneration." In *"Paradise Lost": A Tercentenary Tribute*, edited by

Balachandra Rajan, 48-78. Toronto: University of Toronto Press, 1969.

By showing the continuous development of human powers in relation to God's purposes, *Paradise Lost* expresses the "transcendentalizing process" of descending into the darkness of sin and then ascending into holy light (52). Milton never encourages escapism from the world or withdrawal into spirituality; he makes readers face the despair in the human condition and then asserts the dignity of regenerated human nature. In the opening books in hell, they see the archetype of fallen human endeavor and experience because the epic focuses on the developing human situation. Satan enacts a parody of the Son's mediatorial role and of regeneration. When Adam and Eve fall, readers recognize the perversities that will follow, but they also sense their loss of opportunity for self-development, a process the first sin parodies. Books 11-12 complete the pattern of history and prepare Adam and Eve to face the fallen world.

101   Barker, Arthur [E.]. "Structural Pattern in *Paradise Lost*." *Philological Quarterly* 28 (1949): 17-30. Reprinted in *Milton: Modern Essays in Criticism*, edited by Arthur E. Barker, 142-55. London: Oxford University Press, 1965.

In times of tension, Milton finds security in traditional forms. He modifies *Paradise Lost*'s structure from ten books to twelve—that is, away from a five-act epic structure—to shift the emphasis from Satan's tragic turning of God's work with the fall to the creation and Adam's conversation with Raphael. Not only does the twelve-book version alter the *Aeneid*'s large structural pattern, but it also places more weight on the Son's ultimate triumph, on mercy, love, and restoration. The ten-book structure can be divided into two blocks of five books each; the twelve-book structure can be divided into thirds (focusing on Satan, the Son, and humanity), quarters, and halves (which balance evil frustrated and creation). Milton changes *Paradise Lost*'s structure to reduce Satan's power over the poem.

102   Belsey, Catherine. *John Milton: Language, Gender, Power*. Oxford: Basil Blackwell, 1988. xi + 114 pp.

Paradise Lost, like most of Milton's poetry, presents a turning point in the relationship between heaven and earth, the fall, as well as a second turning point, the Redemption. Because God, the core of the poem, is and is beyond difference, he cannot be defined, and thus the signifier's materiality and truth's textuality emerge. Not a feminist text,

Paradise Lost nonetheless depends on the failure of Eve's submission, on her independence and assertiveness, as she initiates the emergence into difference. Though the epic cannot acknowledge the precarious meaning of sexual difference, it uncovers precisely this point and the related idea that patriarchy is caused by a fear of female sexuality, which even in the prelapsarian world is a force man must subdue. After the fall, God reinstates the same patriarchal order that produced it. Only in Raphael's narrative about angels whose difference is internalized do readers see the possibility of a world beyond essences and the release of sexual being from power. *Paradise Lost* struggles with the relationship of God (the transcendental signified) and the Son (the signifier or Word) as differentiated beings. To fulfill his desire, God will eliminate difference by repossessing his creation to form a divine unity, but the price for this is the final and absolute fixing of difference.

103   Bercovitch, Sacvan. "Three Perspectives on Reality in *Paradise Lost*." *University of Windsor Review* 1 (1965): 239-56.
        The perspective of each level of action in *Paradise Lost*—angelic, demonic, human—contrasts with that of the others. To dramatize the Son's mercy, Milton restricts God to the viewpoint of justice; together, the Father's and Son's complementary perspectives present reality in its fullest meaning, just as Raphael's and Michael's narrations together combine love and justice to reveal the total view of universal order. Vacillating between a perspective based on despair and one based on pride, Satan uses illusion and self-delusion to rebel against God or reality itself. Adam and Eve embody the divine perspective of justice and love before the fall, the demonic perspective after they sin, and finally a postlapsarian synthesis of these views. See entry 175.

104   Blamires, Harry. *Milton's Creation: A Guide through "Paradise Lost."* London: Methuen, 1971. x + 308 pp.
        Blamires provides a book-by-book introductory reading of *Paradise Lost* that focuses on every significant passage and episode.

105   Blessington, Francis C. *"Paradise Lost": Ideal and Tragic Epic.* Boston, MA: Twayne Publishers, 1988. xiv + 144 pp.
        Milton conceives *Paradise Lost* as a national document that belongs to the tradition of classical and Renaissance Italian epics. Satan

acts as the pure will to power with no morality, a character of strength, rhetorical skill, and noble suffering whose anger and despair eventually dominate his personality. His story is about "cosmic frustration" (29). Because God values freedom more than control, he allows evil to exist and creatures to prove their obedience. The Son, with powers granted by the Father, acts as warrior, judge, co-creator, and mercy giver; his is a force of re-creating and converting evil to good. Shaping their natures by obedience, labor, and communication, Adam and Eve can rise to a more spiritual state. Eve, though inferior to Adam, is in one sense the poem's true human hero, for she saves him. If the epic's major crisis is the marital dispute, its conflict—and the test of human free will—occurs when Adam and Eve desire that which they know is wrong. In the closing books, Michael teaches Adam about the fallen world produced by his actions, including the facts of death, suffering, and triumph.

106   Bradford, Richard. "Milton's Graphic Poetics." In *Remembering Milton: Essays on the Texts and Traditions*, edited by Mary Nyquist and Margaret W. Ferguson, 179-96. New York: Methuen, 1987.

In the century after *Paradise Lost*'s publication, detractors accuse its blank verse of having "interlineal syntactic promiscuity" (179), while others attempt to recognize the style's own internal logic. Modern critics, continuing the tradition, generate meanings from the epic's shifting surface and then neutralize them by referring to a stable point, an assumption about the poem's meaning and stylistic intention. The spoken poem is too often privileged by treating the typographical object as a mediating practical necessity. By presuming to master and reconcile the text's destabilized signifiers and the context's assumed signifying intentions, many analyzers of Milton's verse fragment the referential and rhetorical categories. *Paradise Lost*'s overall textual identity is distinct from its particular internal dramatic contexts (or voices); only a reader can arbitrate between them and act as the arbiter of meaning.

107   Broadbent, J. B. *Some Graver Subject: An Essay on "Paradise Lost."* London: Chatto and Windus, 1960. viii + 304 pp. 4 illustrations. Part reprinted in *Milton's Epic Poetry: Essays on "Paradise Lost" and "Paradise Regained,"* edited by C. A.

Patrides, 132-56. Harmondsworth: Penguin Books, 1967; part reprinted in *Paradise Lost*, edited by Scott Elledge, 460-68. New York: W. W. Norton and Co., 1975.

While the earlier seventeenth-century reading public in England feels a need for a nationalistic Christian epic, by the 1650s Milton's countrymen no longer want such a poem. *Paradise Lost*'s neoclassical elements make it a contemporary work, while its subject is anachronistic. Just as the opening invocation subverts all pagan literature that had been thought sublime, the portrait of hell and Satan reveals human powers corrupted by pride. Though the narrator's comments frequently undercut the demons, Satan's personality is based on the prototypical epic hero. God is a legalistic character who presents ineffectual arguments in antiquated, bare speeches, but the Son uses more flexible and sensitive rhetoric. If Milton's heaven inconsistently mixes the apocalyptic and the emblematic, his description of paradise brings together the idea and symbolic expression of innocence. *Paradise Lost* lacks unity because such incidental episodes as the creation and Raphael's lectures are not integrated into its central theme, which does not itself have epic stature.

108   Brockbank, Philip. "'Within the Visible Diurnal Spheare': The Moving World of *Paradise Lost*." In *Approaches to "Paradise Lost,"* edited by C. A. Patrides, 199-221. London: Edward Arnold, 1968.

In *Paradise Lost*, Milton give aesthetic and moral validity to the astronomical order, inviting readers to marvel at the creation's bounty, rhythm, and miraculous solicitude for human life. The fall of Lucifer, for example, despite its long tradition of moral and theological commentary, receives attention as an event in space and is associated with other flights through the void in the epic. The diurnal harmonies of the cosmos—particularly in Adam and Eve's realm and relationship—are accompanied by points of instability that Satan exploits, indicating that order and felicity can breed chaos and misery. With the fall, the instability is aggravated, for moral offenses bring mutations in the created order, but the diurnal rhythm survives in changed form as a consolation. The postlapsarian world's asymmetries offer new possibilities and opportunities.

109   Buhler, Stephen M. "Kingly States: The Politics in *Paradise Lost*." *Milton Studies* 28 (1992): 49-68.

The Son's rule by merit is consistent with the view expressed in Milton's prose: meritocracy is the form of government most in accord with natural law and divine precept. While the Son demonstrates his merit by loving service to fallen humanity, various characters respond to his kingship with different forms of dominion. For the Son and all true rulers, however, governing and serving are the same, a lesson that even the loyal angels do not fully grasp. In *Paradise Lost*, Satan displays the more familiar patterns of kingship, which use regal trappings, ornate pomp, and courtly servility. He misreads the nature of the Son's kingship and all true authority, seeing Christ as stealing power and appropriating much of the angelic order and degree. Comprehending his own threatened office in terms of title, prestige, and the homage offered by those ruled, Satan misunderstands the difference between service and servility. Milton's prose indicates that the Stuart court's behavior is patterned on the Satanic original.

110   Burden, Dennis H. *The Logical Epic: A Study of the Argument of "Paradise Lost."* Cambridge, MA: Harvard University Press, 1967. ix + 206 pp.
Milton insists that *Paradise Lost*'s subject—asserting providence and justifying God's ways—is rational, as are God and the Bible. His portrayal of Edenic life logically extends and clarifies the Genesis account by providing details about food, climate, light labor, love, and the serpent. Hell is also presented systematically, with its residents creating a Satanic (or pagan) literature and philosophy that promote fate and chance, which are countered by *Paradise Lost*'s poetry and theme of free will and responsibility. Milton expands Genesis by presenting the fall without indicting God's providence but instead exemplifying it, as the episode dramatizes a logical exercise on the conflicting ideas of choice and chance. Neither provocative nor tempting (unlike the fruit in hell), the fruit in Eden is a thing indifferent. Once Eve chooses to eat of it, her values and the poem move into a Satanic mode. As a source of solace, and only secondarily as a union of flesh, marriage in *Paradise Lost* is a rational institution. Not deceived, Adam cannot be persuaded to eat the fruit; he freely and somewhat hastily chooses to fall and then rationalizes the decision as a Satanic tragedy of necessity, which is now instituted as a literary genre.

111   Bush, Douglas. *"Paradise Lost" in Our Time: Some Comments.* Ithaca, NY: Cornell University Press, 1945. ix + 117

pp. Frequently reprinted; part reprinted in *Milton: Modern Essays in Criticism*, edited by Arthur E. Barker, 156-76. London: Oxford University Press, 1965; part reprinted in *Milton: A Collection of Critical Essays*, edited by Louis L. Martz, 109-20. Englewood Cliffs, NJ: Prentice-Hall, 1966; part reprinted in *Milton's Epic Poetry: Essays on "Paradise Lost" and "Paradise Regained,"* edited by C. A. Patrides, 33-54. Harmondsworth: Penguin Books, 1967.

Some modern critics attack Milton's religious beliefs, poetic art, and personality, but they speak in unexamined, unsupported generalizations. According to Milton, the poet-priest holds a high office, which he uses to sing of liberty, right reason, and eternal providence. In *Paradise Lost*, he justifies God's ways on the basis of humanity's rational freedom of moral choice and the love and grace God offers to make regeneration possible. Pride is the root of human sin; religious humility is humanity's great need. The poem reveals a large gap between its concrete epic material and abstract, spiritual theme. Starting with his first speech, Satan, hardly a glorious character, condemns himself by understanding neither true liberty nor slavery to passion and pride. Prelapsarian love between man and woman or man and God, on the other hand, illustrates the function of right reason. While Eve displays pride, Adam errs by subordinating reason to his senses and a creature of inferior intellect. A great practitioner of classical art, Milton in *Paradise Lost* uses simple and grand styles, generalized descriptions, numerous allusions, and a wide variety of movement and tone.

112   Carnes, Valerie. "Time and Language in Milton's *Paradise Lost*." *ELH* 37 (1970): 517-39.

In *Paradise Lost*, prelapsarian time is defined in terms of order and is thus analogous to eternity, while after the fall it is an expression of disorder. Every unfallen created thing is a theophany of eternity—imperfect now but perfect in the fulfillment of time. After the fall, when time becomes limited or finite, events past and present are not just anticipated but also retrospective. Each level in Milton's hierarchy—diabolic, human, angelic, and divine—has its own perception and experience of time, which are expressed in its own morally revealing language. Milton's God speaks an absolutely typological, compressed language that avoids figurative expression since he exists outside of time and space, rendering all things as one to him. Unfallen Adam and Eve also use literal language, but as an instinctive echo of God and because they lack any experience beyond Edenic life. The progressive decay of their language after the fall points to their progressive moral deterioration. In Books 11-12, time again becomes reordered as its former resemblance to eternity is restored and it acts as a potential instrument of redemption.

113   Carrithers, Gale H., Jr., and James D. Hardy, Jr. *Milton and the Hermeneutic Journey*. Baton Rouge: Louisiana State University Press, 1994. xii + 256 pp.
        Because of Milton's emphasis on grace, the central theme of love in *Paradise Lost* "ascends to the level of the meaning and purpose of life" (18). A divine pageant of creativity subsumes the fall in a poem filled with movement and dynamism, including Satan's endless deterioration and humanity's unfortunate fall. *Paradise Lost* is also an Augustinian journey, particularly in terms of the interior movements toward and away from the love owed to God. Impelled and required by love, the acts of knowing and naming provide significant definitions of humanity and appear as central manifestations of grace. The different natures of Adam's and Eve's dreams suggest that Milton sees a disparity in the characters' capacities, Eve's being the greater.

114   Carrithers, Gale H., Jr., and James D. Hardy, Jr. "Miltonic Dialogue and Metadialogue in *Paradise Lost*: An Exploratory Essay." In *Compendious Conversations: The Method of Dialogue in the Early Enlightenment*, edited by Kevin L. Cope, 54-64. Frankfurt am Main: Peter Lang, 1992.
        Milton's attempts to communicate, to justify God by transcending traditional epic dialogue, can be explained in terms of love. Miltonic dialogue consists of presence, a function of love, and persistence, a function of power, both illuminated by grace. Dialogically engaged with his text, the narrator creates a relationship with his audience and his muse that is more communion than communication. Urania acts as the necessary mediator who keeps Milton from falling into sin. In her playful song, she expresses the love necessary for effective dialogue. Miltonic dialogue remains forever dynamic and imperfect, while metadialogue stands as transcendent and divinely complete; only grace can give a glimpse of the latter through the former.

115   Cirillo, Albert R. "Noon-Midnight and the Temporal Structure of *Paradise Lost*." *ELH* 29 (1962): 372-95. Reprinted in

Milton's Epic Poetry: Essays on "Paradise Lost" and "Paradise Regained," edited by C. A. Patrides, 215-32. Harmondsworth: Penguin Books, 1967; reprinted in *Critical Essays on Milton from "ELH,"* 210-33. Baltimore, MD: Johns Hopkins Press, 1969.

Paradise Lost's structure is based on a double time scheme through which events expressed in temporal terms occur simultaneously in the eternal present that is the epic's key setting. Moving in a cycle, the Platonic great year is completed and renewed when all heavenly bodies are realigned, as they were at the creation, in an eternal noon. Many important events in *Paradise Lost*—including Satan's defection and defeat by Christ, Eve's dream, the descent of Raphael, Adam and Eve's fall, Satan's return to hell, and the Crucifixion—occur at noon or midnight, disparate and concordant polarities imaged in the great year's noon. Milton juxtaposes events in an eternal framework that justifies God's ways by showing how the Crucifixion, the noon of eternal life and the ultimate eclipse of Satan, resolves the noon-midnight ambiguity. Time contributes to the poem's structure by acting as a metaphor for the eternal.

116   Clark, Ira. "A Problem of Knowing Paradise in *Paradise Lost*." *Milton Studies* 27 (1991): 183-207.

The many narrators in *Paradise Lost* repeatedly declare "their problems of telling caused by problems of knowing" (183). As indicated by various techniques, including a focus on naming and the insufficiency of fallen language, readers are frequently reminded that they cannot know what they imagine about the obviously incomprehensible realms of hell and heaven. Listening to Raphael's narration, Adam and Eve must recognize their inability to know heaven (though they have fewer problems than fallen readers) so they can gain some notion of it. Confessing the impossibility of telling about paradise, the epic narrator reminds readers that their gap in knowing and language makes paradise incomprehensible. The presentation of the first couple requires both an innocent ignorance and a knowing that comes with guilt. They know and they do not know; they know and name what they cannot. Readers must keep in mind that they cannot know whether the implications and entailments they infer refer only to them and their fallen perception or present a state of paradise. Nor can they know whether Adam and Eve's "simultaneous lack-knowledge and knowledge in and of Paradise" (204) is a condition of language since Babel, before Babel, or before the fall.

117   Colie, Rosalie L. "Time and Eternity: Paradox and Structure in *Paradise Lost.*" *Journal of the Warburg and Courtauld Institutes* 23 (1960): 127-38. Reprinted in *Paradoxia Epidemica: The Renaissance Tradition of Paradox*, 169-89. Princeton, NJ: Princeton University Press, 1966; reprinted in *Milton: Modern Judgements*, edited by Alan Rudrum, 189-204. London: Macmillan, 1968.

Christian doctrine asks the believer to accept many paradoxes, including the existence of both divine foreknowledge and human free will and of eternity and time. God's omniscience and act of creation occur in the medium of his eternity as well as in time. Though such paradoxes are central to *Paradise Lost*, from the human point of view the narrative is necessarily governed by chronology yet, from the dominating perspective of eternity, it is all *in medias res*. As the epic proceeds, Milton shifts to the human point of view, as Adam enters history and begins to understand it from God's perspective. Because Adam is in each believer, as is Christ, historical times fuse. The poet resembles God by focusing on the act of creation and having an aspect of foreknowledge through revelation and the Bible. Though Milton cannot explain the various paradoxes, his efforts to reconcile them affect *Paradise Lost*'s structure because it makes readers experience them.

118   Cooley, Ronald W. "Reformed Eloquence: Inability, Questioning, and Correction in *Paradise Lost.*" *University of Toronto Quarterly* 62 (1992-93): 232-55.

Paradise Lost defines and practices a reformed eloquence that depends on classical and humanist conventions but is stripped of the duplicity that characterizes Satan's discourse. Full of presumption and pretense, Satan's speeches resemble the declarative rhetorical exercises in *Of Education*, and both are countered by a process of revelation, inquiry, and corrective dialogue. The facile rhetorical questions and affected aporia during the debate in hell are set against Adam's pursuit of knowledge in his dealings with Raphael and Michael. For prelapsarian Adam and Eve, Raphael presents questioning as the paradigm that leads to knowledge and God; after the fall, Michael offers the paradigm of correction. *Paradise Lost* puts these two models into practice in Book 2, where Satan and his followers cannot answer their own questions and where one demonic speaker corrects another by giving unsought answers to rhetorical questions. Even the narrator undergoes correction in Books 11-12, as he relinquishes his inspired status, hands over narrative authority to Michael, and joins Adam as a recipient of redemptive instruction.

119   Cope, Jackson I. *The Metaphoric Structure of "Paradise Lost."* Baltimore, MD: Johns Hopkins Press, 1962. ix + 182 pp.

By producing a spatialized form of logic that reduces reality to a visual object, Ramism influences Milton's use of metaphor in *Paradise Lost*, in which chaos parodies heaven's dimensionless quality. Space in the epic's cosmos is "the vehicle of imperfection and of pain" (57) and the antithesis of a circumscribed area. For Milton's God, time becomes space, because it is both the creature and the symbol of the fall. Restating the epic's argument by implication, space is a sign of humanity's imperfection yet also the instrument of their glory, for it will ultimately turn to spirit. Throughout *Paradise Lost*, microcosmic falls and resurgences express the main action and bring episodes into the focus of the fortunate fall's development. Paradox governs many images in the epic, as light carries the potentiality of darkness, sight of blindness, and fall of ascent. In the first two invocations, Milton shifts from poetic to prophetic inspiration, suggesting a movement from Old Testament songs to Christ, the light of the world. The dialogue in heaven is structured by schematic repetition, and it uses irony and paradox to express the fortunate fall.

120   Cox, Catherine I. "Dance and the Narration of Providence in *Paradise Lost." Milton Studies* 26 (1990): 159-92. 10 illustrations.

In his narrative about God's announcement of the Son, Raphael associates the revelation of the providential plan with the angelic dance that celebrates God's goodness. Revealing and imaging God's providential care and his mind's harmony, the dance is an act of reciprocity: the angels, having received the Son as the Father's greatest gift, return their love. But Satan, in the first conscious deception, is a dissembler in the divine dance. The dance of the stars emphasizes the idea of correspondence, yet dissonance grows with greater distance from God. When readers approach Eden, the dance's generative values become stronger, as all of nature and the first couple participate in a procreative dance. This innocence is contrasted with images of postlapsarian revels and lascivious dances based on demonic motions.

121   Crosman, Robert. *Reading "Paradise Lost."* Bloomington: In-
        diana University Press, 1980. xi + 262 pp.

Because reading is an interpretive act involving choices, how readers learn to understand *Paradise Lost* and thus to discover them-selves is part of the poem's meaning. Milton confuses and misleads readers into the very errors condemned by his paradoxical poem, just as he exposes them to evil so they can recognize it and make choices. Contributing to the confusion, the narrator simultaneously affirms and ignores the truth to teach readers to distrust him as well as their senses and *Paradise Lost* itself. The clash and resonance of different points of view—Satanic, divine, fallen, unfallen—establish a pattern of logic and vision that shows readers how to make the choice to love God. When the reader meets Adam and Eve, they have a double perspective: they move forward in complexity even as the reader moves backward to-ward their innocence; later the reader must see the fall as both comic and tragic. Raphael's stories, filled with absurdities and contradictions, contain no lessons for Adam but many for readers, though the angel, like the narrator, indicates that he cannot present anything resembling the truth without the receiving mind's active collaboration. If *Paradise Lost*'s first ten books teach how to read the poem by trial and error, the last two show how to interpret the Bible or human history, of which readers are a part. See entries 137 and 163.

122   Crump, Galbraith M., ed. *Approaches to Teaching Milton's
        "Paradise Lost."* New York: Modern Language Association
        of America, 1986. x + 201 pp. 9 illustrations.

Crump's volume is divided into two main sections: Materials (including Editions and Aids to Teaching) and Approaches (seventeen essays organized into sections on General Overviews, Specific Ap-proaches, and Teaching the Backgrounds and Contexts).

123   Curry, Walter Clyde. *Milton's Ontology, Cosmogony, and
        Physics.* Lexington: University of Kentucky Press, 1957. vii
        + 226 pp. Reprinted 1966.

In *Christian Doctrine* and *Paradise Lost*, Milton defines God in metaphysical terms as a being whose essence is infinite, inviolable, and incommunicable, and in operational terms as the efficient cause of effects, including all created things. The epic presents chaos and old night as parts of a divine, intelligible triad, as described in Neoplatonic theology's interpretations of Pythagorean and Orphic cosmogony. If Raphael's report on the creation initially lacks clarity, when material forms a sphere he explains the completion of an instantaneous creation; with the Spirit's introduction in the second step, Raphael, unlike Uriel, emphasizes the light that gives a vital warmth to the fluid mass. The Spirit communicates to prepared matter creative powers, such as "the energic forms of the Sun" (116), which await actuation. A generator of powers and lord of the physical universe, the sun changes crude or refined materials into useful forms. *Paradise Lost* identifies light with God's emanating power used by a hierarchy of causes in the creation. According to Milton's scale of nature, all things are created from one homogeneous matter differentiated by a plurality of forms into a multiplicity of appropriate matters. The human spirit's moral disposition determines the material body's purity.

124   Damrosch, Leopold, Jr. "Art and Truth in *Paradise Lost*." In *God's Plot and Man's Stories: Studies in the Fictional Imagination from Milton to Fielding*, 72-120. Chicago, IL: University of Chicago Press, 1985.

Paradise Lost's goal is "to show that man has no right to accuse the God who rightly accuses man" (73), an issue Milton wants readers to confront through a problematic myth mediated by ambiguous symbols. Because doctrine in his age requires imaginative re-creation, he mythicizes fiction and fictionalizes myth. While recognizing the danger of invention, he reinvents truth to be faithful to it in an epic that is a myth of the inner life. Milton's God, like the Son, remains too abstract and insufficiently anthropomorphic; he is rationally loquacious yet emotionally distant. As something both freely chosen by humans and inflicted on them, as a powerful force and nothingness, evil has a paradoxical role from which the concept of Satan is built. Satan, the symbolic form of the modern unhappy consciousness, feels alienated from external reality and thus tries to order his inner experience or subjective illusion. The knowledge Adam and Eve may not possess is destructive, for one must live the knowledge of good and evil, a step that entails death. Replacing causal explanation with psychological drama, Milton presents the fall as a series of stages.

125   Daniells, Roy. "*Paradise Lost*: Unity, Power, and Will," "*Paradise Lost*: Space and Time," "*Paradise Lost*: Personages

and Plot," "*Paradise Lost*: Paradox and Ambiguity," and "*Paradise Lost* and Roman Baroque." In *Milton, Mannerism and Baroque*, 64-86, 87-99, 100-16, 117-31, and 170-93. Toronto: University of Toronto Press, 1963.

Unity, power, and will are central to Milton's discussion of God in *Christian Doctrine* and the perspectives of Satan and God in *Paradise Lost*. While God's will is inexplicable and absolute, all acts of will in the epic are finally causeless and irrational. As forces that establish, preserve, or disrupt unity, power and will pervade the poem.

Like a baroque church, *Paradise Lost* is conceived as an architecturally and ideologically complete work that leads upward from hell to Eden at the center and then to the highest point. The bower, garden, and Eden are all located concentrically about a single axis stretching from God's will to humanity's.

The epic's characters have a baroque quality because they are embodiments of absolutes.

A baroque poem, *Paradise Lost* thrives on paradox, incongruity, and ambiguity, all provoked by the massive unity Milton seeks.

The works and careers of Milton, Bernini, and Borromini have a great deal in common.

126   Darbishire, Helen. *Milton's "Paradise Lost."* London: Oxford University Press, 1951. 51 pp. Reprinted Folcroft, PA: Folcroft Press, 1969.

While Milton's reputation has fluctuated in the past three centuries, such astringent commentators as Bentley and Johnson at least ask the right questions about *Paradise Lost* and alert readers to the boldness, violence, and tendency to paradox in its phrasing. Milton supervises the printing of his epic and uses a personal spelling system to ensure that lines are read correctly (see entries 2, 9, and 11-12). By having a sure sense of Adam's and Eve's physical reality, the poet brings these characters to life, Eve more fully than Adam. The temptation scene reveals a keen insight into the human heart, the kind of perception a dramatist has but that Milton supposedly lacks. After their fortunate fall, the couple can develop morally and spiritually.

127   Davies, Stevie. *Images of Kingship in "Paradise Lost": Milton's Politics and Christian Liberty*. Columbia: University of Missouri Press, 1983. i + 248 pp.

Milton expresses his contempt for Charles I and for Charles II's restoration—indeed, for all human monarchs—in images of kingship associated with such evil figures as Satan (the father of kings), Death, and Nimrod. If each of Satan's royal descendants specializes in one aspect of false kingship, he includes all as he towers over them. Milton defines the monarchical principle as an undoing of order by violent, tyrannical individuals who establish a cyclic pattern of corruption in human life. God rules as father and king, two roles earthly monarchs sacrilegiously unite, and in heaven the hereditary principle of rule is benign. A plagiarist, Satan offers only the perversion of God's monarchy. Before the fall, Adam and Eve are both kings, dispensing an earthly form of the divine justice, and a republic of two. With the fall, Adam is identified with King Solomon.

128   Davies, Stevie. "*Paradise Lost*: The Maladaptive Eye." In
         Milton, 95-152. New York: St. Martin's Press, 1991.
         The language of *Paradise Lost* reveals an epic centered on the experience of insecurity, which Milton knew first-hand. As a kind of dream-poem, the epic emphasizes the conflicts of inner consciousness, often mirrored by the external world's instability. Even paradise is defined by confusion. Taking his lead from such Renaissance scientific discoveries as the microscope and Galileo's telescope, Milton distorts the external world of his epic to assert the importance of perspective. He reveals his own struggles through the epic's vivid, chaotic language and the discordances that meet Satan's eyes and ears. The treatment of God most strongly reveals Milton's efforts and language's limits. However, the disproportions of language and maladaptions of Milton's eye lessen the reader's reliance on sensory input and thus point toward the nonsense that is possibly the only way to make sense of God. Despite Milton's attempts to justify God, a schism between divine justice and mercy is never resolved.

129   Demaray, John G. *Milton's Theatrical Epic: The Invention and
         Design of "Paradise Lost."* Cambridge, MA: Harvard University Press, 1980. xviii + 161 pp. 16 illustrations.
         For Milton, the artistic imitation of reality consists in using reason to comprehend immaterial substantial forms or essences and then using words to clothe them in sensuous imagery. When planning *Paradise Lost*, he seeks a structure that can contain diverse literary-theatrical modes and genres, such as the *sacre rappresentazioni*, court masques, triumphs, and *drammi per musica*. The Trinity manuscript shows Milton's evolving theatrical ideas, as his reading, friends, and experiences in Italy all contribute ideas about theatrical structures that

influence his epic's cosmic setting, angelic descents, soliloquies, and division into ten or twelve books. The first ten books reflect a transformed masque of opposites; the final two books, a transformed, visionary processional masque. As the realm of grand illusion and excess, *Paradise Lost*'s hell develops themes from *Comus*, outlines of sacred representations, and *In Quintum Novembris*. Elements of the antimasque appear in hell to form a sharp contrast with both the idealized masque of Hymen in Eden's opening episode and heaven's presentation of ceremonial masquelike triumphs. Books 11-12 use the themes, didacticism, and flat characters of the digressive intermezzi that conclude Renaissance *sacre rappresentazioni*.

130   Demaray, John G. "Milton's Universal Epic and the Cosmographical-Historical Revolution: Inward Vision and Eyewitness Discovery." In *Cosmos and Epic Representation: Dante, Spenser, Milton and the Transformation of Renaissance Heroic Poetry*, 176-209. Pittsburgh, PA: Duquesne University Press, 1991. 11 illustrations.

As a correlative to medieval historical typology, Milton in *A Brief History of Moscovia* and "Adam Unparadised" develops a new conception of how history and geography might be most reliably presented. He comes to believe that one produces accurate history and geography not by studying medieval chronicles and iconography but by reading eyewitness accounts by ancient and modern travelers who discover new peoples and new worlds in space. Milton invents *Paradise Lost* by integrating "empirical eyewitness reporting techniques of contemporaneous travel writing with revelations of inner, spiritual vision of a kind drawn from biblical and classical tradition" (178). In the epic, history is disclosed not through historical figurism but heroic or near-heroic acts recounted by participants or eyewitnesses, including Satan, the Son, and Michael, during a structured series of voyages that have analogies in modern journeys.

131   Diekhoff, John S. *Milton's "Paradise Lost": A Commentary on the Argument*. New York: Columbia University Press, 1946. 161 pp. Reprinted New York: Humanities Press, 1958, 1963.

Poetry's chief function, in Milton's view, is to instruct. It is related to oratory because both seek to persuade by establishing the speaker's authority (in *Paradise Lost*'s prologues, for example) and arousing the reader's various emotions toward his subject (such as

Satan's evil nature and enmity to humanity). In *Paradise Lost*, Satan never argues that his cause is good or that success will bring satisfaction. Acting the role of a rhetorician who seduces through false example, he tempts Eve, who in the separation scene fails to behave with proper submission, raising arguments from *Areopagitica* that do not apply to the prelapsarian world. When tempted, she knows right from wrong and still departs from reason; Adam falls through passion and misplaced loyalty. For God, justice is inseparable from mercy, and his providence turns permitted evil into good. *Paradise Lost*'s final books narrate and explicate the reader's world, outlining a proper way of life based on right choice, obedience, and faith.

132   Dillon, Steven C. "Milton and the Poetics of Extremism." *Milton Studies* 25 (1989): 265-83.

Paradise Lost's moments of threshold or last moments—such as book endings and characters' last words—gather force through allusion and word-play. Threshold puns evoke a materiality of language that suggests materiality has not been transcended. By emphasizing the threshold's materiality as a place of crisis or division, Milton shows where transitions become troubling. The epic is concerned with divisions and ends, repeatedly showing the process of separation and reconsolidation, expulsion and reparation. An extremist who is obsessed by ends, Milton drives off the middle. Satanic being is full, but truly to know involves leaving something out; to be in the middle is, in Milton's view, to be disobedient.

133   Dyson, A. E., and Julian Lovelock. "Event Perverse: The Epic of Exile." In *Milton: "Paradise Lost," a Casebook*, edited by A. E. Dyson and Julian Lovelock, 220-42. London: Macmillan, 1973.

Christian tragedy (or divine comedy) is transformed by the assertion of hope and controls *Paradise Lost*'s ironic effects, which are based on the three perspectives—all simultaneously present at every moment—of original perfection, perfection lost, and perfection regained. Only freedom's reality makes sense of exile and death, but it may be inseparable from evil or some temptation to independence from God, who permits hell and evil to exist as extensions of freedom itself. Heaven and hell, while eternally separate, are free in Milton's scheme to impinge on one another, and paradise cannot know its fullest potential until the serpent appears. A poem of love, *Paradise Lost* celebrates happiness and delight in all their forms. The narrator claims that Adam falls not deceived, yet he displays egocentricity and gives faulty assessments of God and Eve. Milton's theme and form exist "to salute glory from the heart of loss" (240). Approaching loss casts a shadow over paradise, but the Incarnation and Resurrection hold the promise of triumph.

134   Engle, Lars. "Milton, Bakhtin, and the Unit of Analysis." In *Reconsidering the Renaissance: Papers from the Twenty-First Annual Conference*, edited by Mario A. Di Cesare, 475-88. Binghamton, NY: Medieval and Renaissance Texts and Studies, 1992.

Milton is more dialogic than Bakhtin might indicate. Even as Milton emphasizes the necessity of monolithic unity when God is all in all, apparent dialogue emerges between God and the Son and God and Adam. Adam's request for a mate reveals the struggle between God's one authoritative voice and Adam's desire for a more fit conversational partner. Ultimately, Milton's God reveals himself as a being who uses dialogic energies to meet monologic ends.

135   Entzminger, Robert L. *Divine Word: Milton and the Redemption of Language*. Pittsburgh, PA: Duquesne University Press, 1985. x + 188 pp.

With the fall of Adam and Eve comes the fall of language, for Milton links spiritual and verbal redemption. In *Paradise Lost*, unfallen Adam gains wisdom through the dialectic between God's Word and the human words that make him the first poet rather than a spokesman for the Royal Society's advocacy of a plain, brief Edenic language. Words in Eden are used to name things (thus approximating their essences), present clear insights, and most importantly confess the creature's limited perceptions and speech. When he revolts, Satan introduces linguistic concealment, a form of secrecy that interrupts the spontaneous flow from thought to disclosure; he also puns, lies, and manipulates language by questioning the applicability of words to their referents. Because the distance between God and fallen humanity appears as a linguistic gap in *Paradise Lost*, Adam and Eve require the Son to translate their words. But grace does not restore clear and eloquent speech; rather, Michael and Adam survey the available means to convey the knowledge necessary for salvation and to address the fallen human capacity for knowing. The narrator embodies the fulfillment of the process of redeeming language because his art is redeemed by heavenly inspiration and, by using human words, he continues the revelation that God accomplishes through his Word.

136   Fallon, Stephen M. *Milton Among the Philosophers: Poetry and Materialism in Seventeenth-Century England*. Ithaca, NY: Cornell University Press, 1991. xi + 264 pp.

Centered at Milton's college, the Cambridge Platonists oppose contemporary materialist, mechanist philosophies (including the views of Descartes and Hobbes), endorsing instead "the responsibility of free choice guided by immutable moral principles" (50). Milton separates himself from these Neoplatonists by the late 1650s, having repudiated his earlier dualistic ideas and adopted animist materialism. He regards all corporeal substance as animate, self-active, and free. Based on the monist materialist assumptions of the entire epic, the angels of *Paradise Lost* are corporeal beings that Milton believes truly exist. He uses allegory to portray Sin and Death because evil has no ontological status (see entry 263); these characters are "paradoxical embodiments of privative, metaphysical evil" (187). The devils undergo a provisional, illusory descent into false ontology and false epistemology, and Satan adopts a dualism that resembles Descartes's. When the devils renounce the spirit and immerse themselves in the material, they renounce Cartesian views in favor of Hobbesian ones. The Son's victory in the war in heaven is a victory of Milton's animist materialism over the Hobbesian materialism embodied in the rebels.

137   Fish, Stanley Eugene. *Surprised by Sin: The Reader in "Paradise Lost."* London: Macmillan, 1967. xi + 344 pp. Reprinted Berkeley: University of California Press, 1971; part reprinted in *Milton: Modern Judgements*, edited by Alan Rudrum, 104-35. London: Macmillan, 1968; earlier version of part reprinted in *Milton: "Paradise Lost," a Casebook*, edited by A. E. Dyson and Julian Lovelock, 152-78. London: Macmillan, 1973; part reprinted in *Paradise Lost*, edited by Scott Elledge, 422-33. New York: W. W. Norton and Co., 1975.

Paradise Lost's subject is the reader, who is harassed because of his incorrect responses and educated about his responsibilities as a fallen person. By being deceived in good temptations, rebuked, and corrected, the reader reenacts the fall and discovers the inadequacy of his responses to literature and life. The unsettling experience of Books 1-2 leads to God's reliable, authoritative rhetoric in Book 3. But after instilling confidence in readers, God soon causes anxiety, for they are being judged. Milton presents paradise through negative apprehension—unable to give an innocent interpretation to passages about innocence, the reader sees how far he is from the state of perfection and how often he tends to remake things in his own tainted image. Because the basic pattern of "mistake-correction-instruction" (161) recurs throughout the epic, once the reader discovers his fallen self he works to repair the ruin of his first parents. The poem encourages the reader to decide whether to distort its moral structure by interpreting prelapsarian events as leading to an inevitable fall (or to a fall before the fall) or to see them as consistent with a larger moral perspective involving innocence, responsibility, and free choice. Eve falls by replacing God's law with the law of reason and empirical evidence; after she has fallen, Adam creates a dilemma—Eve or God—that is false in a God-centered universe. As the reader judges Eve's and Adam's choices, so he judges himself. See entries 121 and 163.

138   Fisher, Peter F. "Milton's Theodicy." *Journal of the History of Ideas* 17 (1956): 28-53.
        By using an act of faith united to the religious imagination and expressed in *Paradise Lost*'s final vision of justice, Milton attempts to transcend the conflict between his belief in metaphysical monism and his experience of ethical dualism. Metaphysical evil, in his view, is the state of having fallen away from virtue, defined as the knowledge of and obedience to God's will; natural evil comes from humans, not nature; and ethical evil occurs when people clash or human society acts against God. *Paradise Lost* repudiates the notions that life is tragic and that retribution is evil. Not free choice but its misuse causes evil, and Milton's later writing shows how the will can regain that freedom. Lacking a real existence, evil is an aberration that will be eliminated by the power of the good. The only existence is God or a nature consisting of infinite attributes. In the epic, Milton's metaphysics have the difficult roles of being the basis for and the example of his ethical system. By emphasizing the battle of good and evil while maintaining the metaphysical position of monism, his works present a submerged dualism.

139   Fixler, Michael. "Milton's Passionate Epic." *Milton Studies*
        1 (1969): 167-92.

If *Paradise Lost* is an argument, its devotional energy also
makes it a formal act praising the mystery of God's ways through revelation. Milton believes the poet's goal is to worship, to serve the
greater glory of God in a public act involving those readers who may
find worship a means of evangelical edification. Unlike rhetoric and
logic, poetry, in his view, is intuitive and passionate, and it thus
provides readers' closest intellectual apprehension of God and his mysterious ways. The poetic ascent recapitulates the imaginative stages in
the contemplation of beatitude and reveals an intensification of spiritual
insight. When Milton invokes Urania in Book 7, he wishes to exclude
profane readers, those who lack regenerate understanding. He offers his
poem not to damned readers, but to the community of saints and those
in between who have received sufficient prevenient grace to stand or
fall by their own will and understanding. *Paradise Lost* is "a devotional
gesture of a sacramental character" (186).

140   Frye, Northrop. *The Return of Eden: Five Essays on Milton's
        Epics*. Toronto: University of Toronto Press, 1965. viii + 143
        pp. Part reprinted in *Milton: Modern Essays in Criticism*, ed-
        ited by Arthur E. Barker, 429-46. London: Oxford University
        Press, 1965; part reprinted in *Milton's Epic Poetry: Essays on
        "Paradise Lost" and "Paradise Regained,"* edited by C. A.
        Patrides, 301-21. Harmondsworth: Penguin Books, 1967; part
        reprinted in *On Milton's Poetry*, edited by Arnold Stein, 89-
        96, 228-36. Greenwich, CT: Fawcett Publications, 1970; part
        reprinted in *Paradise Lost*, edited by Scott Elledge, 405-22.
        New York: W. W. Norton and Co., 1975.

In writing *Paradise Lost*, Milton shares his age's assumption
that an epic, which is both narrative and encyclopedic, should be an
important, patriotic poem. If an action is the expression of a free and
conscious being's energy, then there are only good acts, God is the
source of all real action, and, when they sin, Adam and Eve in fact
surrender the power to act. Because Milton associates conventional
heroism with the demonic, *Paradise Lost* is a profoundly antiheroic
poem. When the rebels in heaven refuse to understand that the Son is
their own creative principle, they deny their own origin. Just as the
conceptions of time and space are the energy and form of God's creative power, so the creation is an act of incorporating energy in form.

Paradise Lost's cosmology is divided into four realms (heaven, unfallen earth, fallen earth, and hell), with some properly imitating and some parodying others. Though hierarchies exist in the human soul and marital relationships, Milton believes the latter allow the husband only spiritual authority over the wife. Nude suburbanites, Adam and Eve have lively intellects and personalities, but no malice. As the more withdrawn character, Eve is susceptible to greed, Adam to lust. Milton is a radical or revolutionary artist.

141   Frye, Roland Mushat. *Milton's Imagery and the Visual Arts: Iconographic Tradition in the Epic Poems*. Princeton, NJ: Princeton University Press, 1978. xxv + 408 pp. 269 illustrations.
        In the eighteenth century, unlike the twentieth, readers praise Milton's visual imagination. He is exposed to a great deal of art during his Italian journey and at home, so his visual descriptions are based not primarily on nature but on the visual lexicon provided by paintings, sculptures, and mosaics. His audience's imaginative background allows him to portray the war in heaven in terms of a physical conflict, complete with armor and artillery. If the visual arts represent the demons with distorted, repulsive images, Milton gives them an external splendor and emphasizes their internal deformity. The features found in *Paradise Lost*'s description of hell, though it virtually eliminates the traditional elements, are analogous to those that appear in art. Of the various ways artists portray God—as an old man, emperor, or Jupiter figure—Milton reflects his Puritan heritage by using none, presenting him instead in synecdochic symbols. His descriptions of Eden have the same priority, details, and function as those in Renaissance landscape painting. Portrayed through sensory details, Adam and Eve reveal Milton's ideas about ideal beauty. Most of the specifics about the fall and its effects are presented similarly in *Paradise Lost* and the visual tradition.

142   Frye, Roland Mushat. "*Paradise Lost* and the Christian Vision." In *God, Man, and Satan: Patterns of Christian Thought and Life in "Paradise Lost," "Pilgrim's Progress," and the Great Theologians*, 21-91. Princeton, NJ: Princeton University Press, 1960.
        Christianity regards evil as an inferior power and a perversion of real existence. Aspiring to enjoy himself rather than God and to be-

come power without love, Milton's Satan exercises free choice and, as a symbol, presents one alternative for humanity. When Satan attacks the created order, he inflicts misery on himself, denies his own nature, and puts a curse on himself. Paralleling his fall, humanity's comes through improper self-assertion and repudiating God's image to attain deity; the evil humans experience is both an alienation from love and a denial of reason. According to Milton's justification of God's ways, the deity bears no responsibility for a free agent's choice, but—through the Son—he bears all the results that come to creatures who betray themselves. Humans need to be saved from themselves: the Atonement is an appeal for humanity to love God (for God always loves them). In the end, God perverts the perversion called evil, thus bringing good out of evil.

143   Gardner, Helen. *A Reading of "Paradise Lost."* Oxford: Clarendon Press, 1965. xii + 131 pp. 5 illustrations.

     If the attack on *Paradise Lost*'s style is a dead issue, critics now examine Milton's choice of a religious subject, narrative techniques, and success in his avowed purpose of asserting eternal providence. Milton creates an intensely dramatic universe filled with wills and energies. Though the poem concentrates on a single climax, the fall, it has an extraordinary scope in space and time. The cosmic theme of God's adversary frames the story because it occurs outside and within history, providing comparisons between angelic and human responses to obedience and repentance and showing the ideal, typical couple as both heroic and human, both tragic and exemplary. Scriptural authority limits Milton's imagination when writing about God, but he is freed by the Bible's ambiguous references to Satan and the demons.

     Elizabethan dramatic tragedy, particularly *Dr. Faustus* and the *Changeling*, presents the theme of damnation, in which a good character persists in acts against his nature and refuses to repent. A tragic figure, Milton's Satan shares many attributes of the main figures in these plays.

     John Baptista Medina, Milton's first illustrator in 1688, attempts to interpret *Paradise Lost* in visual terms, perhaps indicating how contemporaries read the poem.

144   Gilbert, Sandra M. "Patriarchal Poetry and Women Readers: Reflections on Milton's Bogey." *PMLA* 93 (1978): 368-82. Reprinted in *The Madwoman in the Attic: The Woman Writer and the Nineteenth-Century Literary Imagination*, by Sandra

M. Gilbert and Susan Gubar, 187-212. New Haven, CT: Yale University Press, 1979.

Because Milton and his epic characters constitute the misogynistic essence of patriarchal poetry, women writers come to terms with his institutionalized misogyny by devising revisionary myths and metaphors. Milton's bogey, in Virginia Woolf's view, is his cosmology, his rendering of the culture myth at the heart of western literary patriarchy. For he tells of woman's otherness or secondness, and how it leads to her demonic anger, fall, and exclusion from the gods' garden. To the female imagination, Milton and the inhibiting Father are one. Charlotte Brontë's Shirley Keeldar revises Eve into an assertive, vital character who resembles Milton's Satan, a connection *Paradise Lost* makes clear. Except for the womb of chaos, Eve's only model for maternity is Sin, who is also her double. Alienated figures, Satan and Eve are linked as artists who merely delight and as rebels against the hierarchical, oppressive status quo. Insofar as it is a demonic realm, *Paradise Lost*'s world of poetry and imagination is associated with Satan, Eve, and femaleness. Milton's Satan is like women and enormously attractive to them.

145   Gossman, Ann. "The Ring Pattern: Image, Structure, and Theme in *Paradise Lost*." *Studies in Philology* 68 (1971): 326-39.

Paradise Lost's major image is a ring pattern, which is both a circle and a ladder or chain that implies process and return. While Adam understands Raphael's account of the ring and the related issue of hierarchy, Satan knows only aspiration followed by descent and is associated with the antitype or counterfeit of the ring, the circular maze of error. Mazes, though not necessarily evil in *Paradise Lost*, become evil in the demons' wandering labyrinths of philosophical reasoning and Satan's serpentine motions when approaching Eve. The correct process is illustrated in the Son's departure from heaven to create, followed by his return, as well as the movement of light in the invocation to Book 3. Divided into three groups of four books, *Paradise Lost*'s structure reflects the ring pattern in three repeated contrasts of Satan with Christ, who is himself a ring pattern and who justifies all rings of process and return.

146   Graham, Elspeth. "'Vain Desire,' 'Perverseness' and 'Love's Proper Hue': Gender, Sexuality and Feminist Interest in *Paradise Lost*." *Critical Survey* 4 (1992): 133-39.

As a political and literary figure active during the creation of modern consciousness, Milton is an especially significant focus for feminist criticism. Although responses to *Paradise Lost*'s apparent subordination of women have varied, even those who disapprove of the epic's patriarchal values can be moved by its power. Its sublime influence is largely produced by its contradictions, whether between rationalism and eroticism, contact and separation, or sensory appeal and abstraction. The lack of fixedness that heightens unsatisfied desire in hell creates the tension necessary for reciprocity and eroticism in Eden. Whether in its invocations or treatment of angelic sexuality, the epic emphasizes openness and fluid boundaries, suggesting the possibilities of gender and sexuality, in spite of Milton's masculinism.

147   Grose, Christopher. *Milton's Epic Process: "Paradise Lost" and Its Miltonic Background*. New Haven, CT: Yale University Press, 1973. xi + 268 pp.

According to Milton's prose, a poem is the main vehicle by which the sage articulates his wisdom, it has the social function of perfecting collective understanding, it is a sensuous form of discourse, and it embodies the delight essential to the learning process. But he knows poetry shares the postlapsarian world's problems of language and epistemology. His skepticism appears in the antipoetic insight that radically human or natural images tend to become idols. Unnecessary in matters of faith, poetry is dangerous in matters of politics, polity, and worship because it speaks to the senses. In *Paradise Lost*, Milton exploits a discourse that virtually transcends the realm of poetry, using it as a vehicle to an archetypal truth and viewing it as a descriptive function of the mind as his poem images his perceptual experience. The process of speech provides the epic's structural richness and leads the author to make discoveries as the poem moves from a metaphoric style to enter the realm of human sense with its "real manner of presentation" (200). Milton emphasizes not the discursive justification he claims the poem presents but the artifice of his work and its secondary status. In the invocations, he explicates the epic's causes, dramatizing the process to make the poem work.

148   Grossman, Marshall. *"Authors to Themselves": Milton and the Revelation of History*. Cambridge: Cambridge University Press, 1987. xii + 243 pp.

Paradise Lost's opening two books show the fallen angels' exclusion from the transition from metonymy to synecdoche, the dialec-

tical transformation of difference into identity. The rebels are constituted as absolute difference. Unable to construct a social subject because he makes his will the arbiter of reality, Satan can transform the
material world only into reiterations of his own psychic economy.
Using image patterns to dramatize the process of emanation, mediation,
and return that underlie and maintain the creation, Milton's portrayal
of heaven reveals the identity of creator and creature. In Eve's account
of her creation, she points to "the divine origin of an interpersonal dialectic that gives rise to a process of self-definition distinct from that of
Satan" (83). The book of the fall is structured as a closet drama—with
its prologue and five acts that observe the unities—because Milton borrows the classical dramatic theme of the mixture of accident and fate
that seems to direct human lives. The plunge into narrative in Books
11-12, which acts as an image of the ascendancy of time over eternity,
"initiates the subjectivity of self-authorship in a fallen world" (152).

149   Hanford, James Holly. "The Dramatic Element in *Paradise
        Lost*." *Studies in Philology* 14 (1917): 178-95. Reprinted in
        *John Milton, Poet and Humanist: Essays by James Holly Han-
        ford*, 224-43. Cleveland, OH: Press of Western Reserve Uni-
        versity, 1966.
        As Milton's career progresses, Elizabethan dramatic poetry's
sensuous essence and lyrical spirit disappear from his verse, but the
dramatic tradition forms the foundation of all his poems. *Paradise
Lost*'s speeches are responsive to the situation and contain descriptions
of settings, soliloquies reveal character and form a key part of the plot,
and Adam's and Eve's words and deeds display their personalities. The
fall is presented, largely in dialogue, as a drama whose tragic irony and
hubris show the main characters' inner aspects. Significant parallels
exist between Adam and Eve's relationship and those of Macbeth and
Lady Macbeth, and Othello, Desdemona, and Iago. Satan shares certain
characteristics with Shakespeare's Richard III and Hamlet. Having intended to write an epic on dramatic themes, Milton accepts a transformation of the epic type to which his sacred matter leads him.

150   Hartman, Geoffrey. "Milton's Counterplot." *ELH* 25 (1958):
        1-12. Reprinted in *Milton: Modern Essays in Criticism*, edited
        by Arthur E. Barker, 386-97. London: Oxford University
        Press, 1965; reprinted in *Milton: A Collection of Critical Es-
        says*, edited by Louis L. Martz, 100-108. Englewood Cliffs,
        NJ: Prentice-Hall, 1966; reprinted in *Critical Essays on Milton*

from "ELH," 151-62. Baltimore, MD: Johns Hopkins Press, 1969; reprinted in *Beyond Formalism: Literary Essays, 1958-1970*, 113-23. New Haven, CT: Yale University Press, 1970.

Milton simultaneously expresses two plots to produce contrapuntal effects, particularly in *Paradise Lost*'s inset fables and similes, which magnify and diminish, show quick activity marked by a calm mood, or point to human free will and divine foreknowledge. The counterplot modulates aesthetic distance and always asserts God's imperturbability and power operating from afar.

151   Haskin, Dayton. "The Bookish Burden Before the Fall." In *Milton's Burden of Interpretation*, 183-238. Philadelphia: University of Pennsylvania Press, 1994.

In *Paradise Lost*, Milton emphasizes "the extent and degree to which Adam and Eve were involved in interpretive activities both before and after their Fall" (184). Verbal complexity and ambiguity, and the resulting interpretive difficulties, exist from the beginning. Milton privileges writing and uses the topos of the world as a book to suggest that the text called nature is largely unreadable, at least before many people appear to participate in the human construction of knowledge. Working with revelations provided by Raphael and Michael, Adam and Eve learn to construct meaning in the sort of language that is organized into narrative patterns. Milton uses Psalm 19 to read behind the creation account in Genesis; he discerns that God is a writer and that unfallen pleasures include living with interpretive difficulties. The fall intensifies the interpretive burden, as the world-as-book becomes more difficult to read. After the fall, Adam and Eve experience an interpretive breakthrough and recover the God-given ability to be "Authors to themselves" (3.122). Michael then teaches Adam to read certain material, which will be written down in Scripture, so it provides an assurance of his salvation.

152   Hughes, Merritt Y. "Beyond Disobedience." In *Approaches to "Paradise Lost,"* edited by C. A. Patrides, 181-98. London: Edward Arnold, 1968.

In *Paradise Lost*, Milton presents the prohibition as both a reasonable command (so Adam understands it) and an arbitrary test of obedience. His prose tracts often condemn implicit obedience to authority, while the epic emphasizes great acts of obedience based on reasonable explanations (by the Son and Abdiel), disobedience of reasonable principles (by Satan), and disobedience against the moral or natural law (by Eve and Adam). As a statement of the epic's theme, disobedience is inadequate—indeed the word never appears again after the invocation to Book 9. Perhaps the theme would be better articulated as God's love for humans. In Michael's lessons, Adam sees the reverse action of the vital principle Raphael taught him, according to which obedient humans improve and turn to spirit. Adam accepts the idea that destroying the fall's effects in himself will lead him to attain the happier paradise within. *Paradise Lost* is thus about the obedience that is beyond disobedience, the obedience better expressed by the word love.

153   Hyman, Lawrence W. "The Ambiguity of *Paradise Lost* and Contemporary Critical Theory." *Milton Quarterly* 13 (1979): 1-6.
       Rather than being a fault in *Paradise Lost*, ambiguity or indeterminacy is the source of its power. Milton uses ambiguity to deepen readers' imaginative experiences and to confound all attempts to derive a consistent theodicy from the epic. Pulling readers in two directions, the narrator encourages them to see a structure embodying moral principles that justify God's ways to human reason, while he also violates their attempts to make the main characters' actions fit into any coherent moral pattern: God and Satan, light and dark, and spirit and matter exist in complementary and reciprocal relationships, even as they are polar opposites. Beginning with a double response to events and characters in *Paradise Lost*, readers ultimately transcend this perspective by realizing they are being asked to judge.

154   Ide, Richard S. "On the Uses of Elizabethan Drama: The Revaluation of Epic in *Paradise Lost*." *Milton Studies* 17 (1983): 121-40.
       Milton conceives of tragedy in Elizabethan terms, according to which divine punishment answers human sin. In *Paradise Lost*, Satan plays the role of the villain revenger when deceiving Eve, but all of humanity—through the Son—will have revenge on Satan. The Elizabethan tragedy of damnation also influences Milton's portrayal of Satan, who acts at times like a stage villain and at other times like an overreacher. A tragic example of impenitence, Satan in a soliloquy in Book 4 confronts his sin and acknowledges the justice of God's punishment. Adam and Eve, on the other hand, face a potential tragedy of damnation that turns into a heroic argument, subverting the classical epic's

heroic values and celebrating the new values of penitence, patience, and redemption through martyrdom. In Book 10, as a response to Satan's tragedy of damnation, Adam and Eve are depicted in an adaptation of the comedy of forgiveness, a species of Elizabethan tragicomedy in which a reversal is effected by providential intervention. Milton retains tragicomic values in *Paradise Lost*, as well as the tragicomic action's double reversal, to inform Adam and Eve's spiritual progress.

155   Jacobus, Lee A. *Sudden Apprehension: Aspects of Knowledge in "Paradise Lost."* The Hague: Mouton, 1976. 225 pp.

As a Christian epic, *Paradise Lost* must address the issue of knowledge in all its forms, including the sensory, forbidden, proper, and revealed. If Satan's self-knowledge is distorted and Adam's is secure, Eve's tends toward self-deception. Nonintuitive knowledge in *Paradise Lost* lies in the act of judgment that occurs when reason joins or disjoins what is perceived, and the poem explores many kinds of natural knowledge or science. A unified structure, the cosmos is pervaded by divine reason, with understanding growing dimmer as one's distance from God increases. Knowledge, in Milton's view, has limits and must be handled with temperance. Though Adam and Eve have no Bible to read for revealed knowledge, Milton's poem is both biblical and the matter of revelation itself; the two angelic narrators provide various types of revelation: Raphael gives Adam knowledge and Michael repairs his reason, offers regenerative Christian assurance, and teaches him that the highest knowledge of God is useful in gaining salvation.

156   Kahn, Victoria. "Allegory, the Sublime, and the Rhetoric of Things Indifferent in *Paradise Lost*." In *Creative Imitation: New Essays on Renaissance Literature in Honor of Thomas M. Greene*, edited by David Quint, Margaret W. Ferguson, G. W. Pigman III, and Wayne A. Rebhorn, 127-52. Binghamton, NY: Medieval and Renaissance Texts and Studies, 1992.

The personification of Sin and Death dramatizes the theological indifference that is a prerequisite of free will and correct interpretation. Milton's contribution to the debate over things indifferent is to assign judgment to the individual conscience; rhetoric itself thus becomes a thing indifferent. The episode featuring Sin and Death criticizes itself by generating through Satan's narcissism forms of idolatry, violence, and rebellion. In *Paradise Lost*, allegory is a thing indifferent: it can be coercive, but it produces the intellectual obscurity necessary for true obedience. Within sublime allegory, Milton asserts both grace and free will through internalized law (reason), which can interpret the external world as text. Ultimately, language and law become things indifferent, able to close off an encounter with otherness or produce the limits and uncertainties that form the basis of ethical choice.

157   Kelley, Maurice. "The *De Doctrina* and *Paradise Lost.*" In *This Great Argument: A Study of Milton's "De Doctrina Christiana" as a Gloss upon "Paradise Lost,"* 72-191. Princeton, NJ: Princeton University Press, 1941. Reprinted Gloucester, MA: Peter Smith, 1962.

    Christian Doctrine and *Paradise Lost* contain similar ideas about God's nature and decrees, the Son, the Trinity, and the fall.

158   Kelley, Maurice. "*Paradise Lost* and the Christian Theory of History." *South Atlantic Bulletin* 37 (1972): 3-11.

    Paradise Lost is "a poetic presentation of the Christian theory of history," in which historical truths are conveyed "in the form of a Classical epic fiction" (3). Beginning with a dilemma (the origin of evil) and ending with a paradox (the fortunate fall), the Christian theory of history is linear and far more satisfactory than Toynbee's pagan cyclic theory or Marx's pagan parody of the Christian view. *Paradise Lost* follows not Calvinism but Arminianism, asserting that Christ dies for all and that God renews the human freedom of will lost at the fall. From Milton, readers can learn the value of free will curbed by responsibility, recognize that history operates under the conditions of the fall, and see providence or ethical meaning in history.

159   Kerrigan, William. *The Sacred Complex: On the Psychogenesis of "Paradise Lost."* Cambridge, MA: Harvard University Press, 1983. x + 344 pp.

    Containing the first formal temptation in Milton's art, *Comus* represents the etiology of conscience, which emerges from the conflict between external authority (law) and love focused on a distinct object (desire). In solitude, one becomes ideal by renouncing or prohibiting oneself, by allowing the figure of authority to rest within oneself. Milton's temptations typically show that what the law forbids will be salvaged in a transmuted form for the righteous. An oedipal structure contains and governs narcissistic themes in Milton's work, altering the shape of selfhood. When he tries to name the divine through the language of light in Book 3's invocation, Milton reclaims the sense in which religion and philosophy are poetry. *Paradise Lost* is an epic of genesis, devoted to firsts, primal scenes, and origins. If the ontology of the epic aspires upward, the fall as a pathogenic event reverses this movement. In *Paradise Lost*, *Paradise Regained*, and *Samson Agonistes*, Milton's Christian vision is enfolded in the symbol of home. Adam and Eve, homeless in history after losing the first paradise, gain an internal paradise and anticipate a transcendent one.

160   Kinney, Clare Regan. "Inspired Duplicity: The Multiple Designs of *Paradise Lost*." In *Strategies of Poetic Narrative: Chaucer, Spenser, Milton, Eliot*, 122-64. Cambridge: Cambridge University Press, 1992.

Despite Milton's attempts to recapture monolithic expression, multiple and multiplying plots fill *Paradise Lost*. The belated beginning of Milton's higher argument in Book 9, which ultimately seeks to transcend all fallen literary kinds, always stands in a dialogic relation to those very kinds. As a mediating narrator and a fallen human, Milton struggles to articulate a divine cosmos from a fallen perspective; through various narrators and the lyricism of Eden, he attempts to bridge the postlapsarian gap. Playing on the reader's fallen knowledge, Milton suspends the unfallen Edenic moment for as long as possible—through his choice of imagery and representations of time and space—before portraying the beginning of the fallen world. Caught between the need to clarify canonical truths and the desire to offer personal interpretations, Milton approaches *Paradise Lost* with a double vision, ultimately supplementing the tragedy of the fall with his own postlapsarian knowledge of salvation.

161   Knoppers, Laura Lunger. "*Paradise Lost* and the Politics of Joy." In *Historicizing Milton: Spectacle, Power, and Poetry in Restoration England*, 67-95. Athens: University of Georgia Press, 1994. 3 illustrations.

Examined as a story of woe that defines joy as an internal, private state, *Paradise Lost* challenges the public displays of joy that function in the royalist politics of Restoration England. With the return of Charles II, joy becomes a form of social control; it carries the promise of reward to those who publicly voice their praise, but it also

threatens dissenters with punishment. Mocking royalist faith in a restored golden age, Milton characterizes lavish celebrations and mortal
attempts to regain true heavenly joy as futile and even Satanic; Edenic
joy is private and moderated. The bacchic revelry and excess that characterize the Restoration become in *Paradise Lost* threats to the true
restoring poet, Orpheus or Milton. Paralleling the Restoration with
Satan's return to hell and humankind's fall, Milton contends that the
only true golden age is the millennium. The royalists' bacchic joy turns
out to be inherently unstable and self-subverting.

162   Knoppers, Laura Lunger. "Rewriting the Protestant Ethic:
        Discipline and Love in *Paradise Lost.*" *ELH* 58 (1991):
        545-59.

In *Paradise Lost*, Milton revises the Protestant ethic of work
and discipline, privatizing the former to make the self-disciplined subject an end commodity and using the latter to strengthen the subject
against the external manifestations of church and state. An embodiment
of the work ethic, the seventeenth-century house of correction uses
rewards and punishments to shape the process—more than the product—of rehabilitative work. The Protestant household is another disci-
plinary site; although it establishes a hierarchy of control through love
and voluntarism, it also emphasizes work process over product. *Paradise Lost* advances an internal work ethic, encouraged by supervised
labor and a divine system of rewards and punishments, but ultimately
the poem produces an obedient subject, rather than a material product.
With the fall, Adam and Eve internalize the work and discipline that
were previously forced on them, thereby subjecting themselves to a
divine authority, yet remaining an integral part of the external capitalist
economy. See entry 98.

163   Knott, John R., Jr. "*Paradise Lost* and the Fit Reader." *Mod-
        ern Language Quarterly* 45 (1984): 123-43.

Milton's "fit" or spiritually prepared reader is neither a narrowly defined sinner in need of frequent correction nor a loosely defined naive person, as some critics suggest. Rather, the reader of *Paradise Lost* has prior religious experience and maintains faith even when
faced with persecution. Milton's references to his reader point to a se-
lect group that sympathizes with his view of a reformed England, the
rule of the saints, and freedom of worship. By using the narrator's

strong controlling perspective, Milton wishes to preserve the majesty of things divine and convey God's power, so the reader's allegiance cannot be placed elsewhere. The fit reader understands the significance of responding to the poem with joy and sadness, delight and horror. A member of a community of the faithful, the reader shares in communal responses. See entries 121 and 137.

164   Kranidas, Thomas. "A View of Milton and the Traditional." *Milton Studies* 1 (1969): 15-29.

        A poem that thrives on paradox, *Paradise Lost* "contains within itself challenges of its own solidity" (15). Just as critics recognize the rhetorical orthodoxy of Milton's works, they should also see an opposing strain of caution toward and even contempt for the traditional. His prose argues that knowledge must be useful, not just ancient or supported by authority; thus he sometimes not only attacks the abuse of tradition but also displays antitraditionalism. Milton's radical metaphors simultaneously use and question tradition: following the dinner scene in Book 5 of *Paradise Lost*, in which the metaphor of physical digestion dominates, the war in heaven episode uses the metaphor of physical purgation as the body of heaven is emptied and cleansed.

165   Leonard, John. *Naming in Paradise: Milton and the Language of Adam and Eve*. Oxford: Clarendon Press, 1990. x + 304 pp.

        In *Paradise Lost*, God tests Adam's understanding of natural (prelapsarian) language, which is connected to knowledge and reason. Although Eve receives a name after the fall in Genesis, where her name is associated with sin, Milton's Adam so identifies her earlier, associating her name with life and giving it dignity. That Eve assigns any names, as she does to the flowers, is an extraordinary concession to her from a seventeenth-century perspective. Essences and names or titles are linked in *Paradise Lost*, as in the omission of the names of Nimrod, Babel, and the rebel angels, all lost when they violate their original natures. Never called Satan by his followers, the devil experiences a developing awareness of his identity and name—once Lucifer, now Satan. He finally enters his name, which means enemy or accuser, in Book 9.510-18 and acknowledges this identity in an instant of unprecedented recognition after the fall. Lucifer corrupts language to seduce the angels, who fall self-tempted because they hear and act on the ambiguities in his new vocabulary of evil. *Paradise Lost*'s multiple narrators and commentators offer varied presentations of unfallen language.

166   Lewalski, Barbara Kiefer. *"Paradise Lost" and the Rhetoric of Literary Forms*. Princeton, NJ: Princeton University Press, 1985. xi + 378 pp.

Genre choices in *Paradise Lost* place Milton's subject in culturally defined perspectives or sets of values that the poem critiques. As prophet-poets, the three narrators—the poet, Raphael, and Michael—must use the appropriate genres for their revelations and audiences, thus dramatizing "the process, the problems, and the purposes of creating divine poetry" (26). Moving from higher to lower heroic models, Satan is associated with the main varieties of epic, heroic tragedy, and romance, a decline that illustrates the perversion of all heroic values and helps readers view the heroic as a divine standard of action and speech. Milton turns to an even wider range of literary forms to portray unportrayable divine beings: multiple perspectives on God suggest his transcendence as well as the incompleteness of any single view; the Son's heroic love surpasses the heroic actions and values of epic and romance; a mixture of genres portrays the angelic community as a model for human possibility and wholeness. As the pastoral mode is used to describe Adam and Eve's prelapsarian life in Eden, it is redefined to include other genres' values—such as love, labor, and heroism—that the couple must bring together harmoniously. In Books 9-10, Milton uses Aristotelian tragedy to present the fall and Christian tragedy for its aftermath; a Christian heroic mode, defined by the fusion of several genres in Michael's prophetic narrative, governs Books 11-12.

167   Lewis, C. S. *A Preface to "Paradise Lost."* London: Oxford University Press, 1942. ix + 139 pp. Frequently reprinted; part reprinted in *Milton Criticism: Selections from Four Centuries*, edited by James Thorpe, 267-88. New York: Rinehart and Co., 1950; part reprinted in *Milton: Modern Essays in Criticism*, edited by Arthur E. Barker, 196-204. London: Oxford University Press, 1965; part reprinted in *Milton: A Collection of Critical Essays*, edited by Louis L. Martz, 40-55. Englewood Cliffs, NJ: Prentice-Hall, 1966; part reprinted in

Milton: "Paradise Lost," a Casebook, edited by A. E. Dyson and Julian Lovelock, 85-105. London: Macmillan, 1973.

As a written work with an elevated style and exceptionally solemn tone, *Paradise Lost* is a secondary epic that manipulates the reader with its complex syntax, simplicity of underlying effects, and calculated grandiosity. Milton's story of the fall, an act that consists in disobedience and results from pride, agrees with Augustine's view—that is, with orthodox Christian doctrine—and his poetic vision is based on the concept of hierarchy, which can be destroyed by tyranny or rebellion. In portraying Satan, Milton emphasizes the misery he inflicts and suffers, subordinates his absurdity, and shows he is a self-destructive liar who undergoes a progressive degradation. Not mere children, Adam and Eve are intelligent and dignified beings whom readers cannot patronize. Eve falls through pride and, when she convinces Adam to join her, commits murder; Adam falls through uxoriousness. Books 11-12 form *Paradise Lost*'s "grave structural flaw," for they provide only "an untransmuted lump of futurity" (125), in bad writing and at a crucial point in the poem. Readers who say they dislike Milton's God actually dislike God. See entries 93 and 284.

168   Lieb, Michael. *The Dialectics of Creation: Patterns of Birth and Regeneration in "Paradise Lost."* Amherst: University of Massachusetts Press, 1970. v + 262 pp.

Knowledge of truth, as Milton sees it, is forever arising from the dialectic of opposing views, which appear in dramatic events in *Paradise Lost*. Embodying productive and destructive possibilities, chaos is the center of opposition. For the fallen poet as prophet, king, and priest, creation depends on uncreation for its full expression. Only God and prelapsarian Adam and Eve fulfill the idea of an unpolluted, glorious creativity; by gardening, making love, and praying, the human couple performs a generative role analogous to God's. Beginning in the war in heaven, the process of uncreation is motivated by the Son's creation or birth as king. Union in the divine realm acts as a means of self-glorification, with God ultimately becoming all in all, but in the demonic plane it implies death and damnation. Satan's acts of pride and physical impotence parody sublime creativity. As a kind of Moses figure, he revivifies his followers in hell, but the birth he brings is simultaneously an enactment of self-destruction. The temptation and fall in *Paradise Lost* are based on the concept of generation. According to the epic's redemptive scheme, fallen humanity becomes the new chaos through which the primal image is reoriented and God achieves glory.

A creative art central to *Paradise Lost*'s creational dimension, alchemy is based on the image of the impregnating Spirit brooding on the abyss.

169   Lieb, Michael. *Poetics of the Holy: A Reading of "Paradise Lost."* Chapel Hill: University of North Carolina Press, 1981. xxi + 442 pp. 23 illustrations.
    The Christian concept of the holy, based on the New Testament appropriation of the cultic, is transformed in Milton's work to moral and finally spiritual categories. He conceives of the poet as a hierophant and oracle of the holy, a prophet who instructs by declaring God's will, and a priest who intercedes for the sinner by making sacred offerings. With its roots in Greco-Roman and Judeo-Christian thought, Milton's religiosity leads to a consecratory impulse that forms the fundamental sacrality of his work. *Paradise Lost*, a theocentric and ultimately Christocentric poem, achieves its focus and meaning through the theophany of theophanies in Book 3, a vision that permeates the epic. Fruit in *Paradise Lost* is sacred and forbidden by a God made incomprehensible and accessible through an anthropomorphic presentation. Milton associates heaven and Eden by making them divine enclosures with the characteristics of a hierophany, and mounts are theophanic centers; various Satanic structures, including Pandemonium, a hill, and hell itself, parody the pure ones. In its various forms and with the aid of the Son, the divine name reveals to imperfect humanity ways of comprehending God's existence and promises. Inexpressible and mysterious, light in *Paradise Lost* becomes a sacral phenomenon that is God's dwelling presence and the occasion for ceremonial exultation. The Old Testament ideology and contemporary view of war as a sacral event shape Milton's ideas about spiritual conflict in *Paradise Lost*'s war and temptation scenes.

170   Lindenbaum, Peter. "John Milton and the Republican Mode of Literary Production." *Yearbook of English Studies* 21 (1991): 121-36.
    Milton's literary career up to and including the publication of *Paradise Lost* in 1667 marks the beginning of the end of the aristocratic patronage system. Starting with *Comus*, Milton starts to move away from the protection offered by patronage—a process that culminates in his republican decision to educate all of England by publishing *Paradise Lost* on the strength of only his own name. Milton's slow movement away from aristocratic privilege toward republican independence finds its fullest expression in *Paradise Lost*, especially in his uneasiness over

the contemplative life. His formulation of paradise, in particular, takes on a distinctively active tone, and both before and after the fall humans are encouraged, in republican fashion, to seek truth by correcting themselves. This thematic republicanism has a counterpart in *Paradise Lost*'s publication; it locates its fit, active audience by coming into the world unadorned with the names of aristocratic supporters.

171   Loewenstein, David. *Milton: "Paradise Lost."* Cambridge: Cambridge University Press, 1993. xvi + 143 pp.
        Some of the unorthodox beliefs discussed in *Christian Doctrine*, such as *ex Deo* creation and Arminianism, are significant for an understanding of *Paradise Lost*. A poem about beginnings, Milton's epic asserts its originality in the first invocation. With its universal theme and emphasis on interior experience, it is an ambitious, prophetic poem that makes an imaginative attempt to revise the Bible and classical models. Presenting himself as both prophetic and fallen, the epic narrator shapes readers' responses to a poem that is written in a variety of styles. The portrait of Satan reveals the ambiguities of his heroic self-assertion. A courageous and charismatic military leader and a skillful rhetorician, Satan is also tyrannical, proud, and solipsistic. Milton's God is a character of emotions who struggles with his own decrees and the poem's key theological issues, particularly free will. With his independent and challenging voice, the Son embodies mercy, divine love, and voluntary obedience. The senses, human eroticism, and passion are essential to Milton's paradisal ideal; recognizing the complexity of sexual relations, *Paradise Lost* often vacillates between egalitarianism and patriarchal models. Breaking with the epic tradition, Milton makes a domestic tragedy, the fall of Adam and Eve, central to his narrative. As illustrated by various revisions or reworkings of the poem from the Restoration to the Romantic period, *Paradise Lost* exerts a powerful influence on literary history.

172   MacCaffrey, Isabel Gamble. *"Paradise Lost" as "Myth."* Cambridge, MA: Harvard University Press, 1959. vi + 229 pp. Part reprinted in *Paradise Lost*, edited by Scott Elledge, 508-12. New York: W. W. Norton and Co., 1975.
        The constant element of value in civilization's creations, myth signifies an archaic mode of experience relevant to the mind's deepest responses. Renaissance Christians believe all myths reflect the one true history of Scripture; readers must thus temporarily accept *Paradise*

Lost's myth as true. Milton uses the myth of the cyclic journey to portray humanity's movement from an original state of glory (creation) to exile (fall), and finally back to God in a restored eternal golden age (redemption). Because this myth is familiar, it promotes affirmation and recognition, using a folded structure in which various temporal threads reflect each other while being subordinated to the grand frame of eternity. Image and meaning unite in *Paradise Lost*, where the cosmos has a pyramidic shape and Milton presents a vision of rising and falling. The epic's vocabulary, limited and elevated, produces a single, simple effect of suggestive universality that supports the structure and mythic vision. Not radically figurative, the imagery, including extended similes, is also unified into the poem's pattern. When he leaves hell, Satan experiences the archetypal quest with its movement of loss, search, and return, a pattern transferred to humanity at the end of *Paradise Lost*.

173   McColley, Diane [Kelsey]. "'The Copious Matter of My Song.'" In *Literary Milton: Text, Pretext, Context*, edited by Diana Treviño Benet and Michael Lieb, 67-90. Pittsburgh, PA: Duquesne University Press, 1994.

In *Paradise Lost*, the language of divine and unfallen human characters combines mutually resonating images, sounds, metaphors, and allusions to re-create paradisal consciousness. Milton simultaneously makes many interlocking statements to help readers recognize that the mind can contain the creation and to remember its interactions "in our human callings as caretakers of the natural and cultural life of the planet that sustains us" (69). Structured after the *Te deum*, the victorious angels' hymn in Book 3.372-415 has copious matter (the Son's name), and it engages readers' contemplative faculties by overwhelming their perceptual and conceptual ones. Raphael's creation narrative in Book 7 also incorporates the prolificacy of the Word, and Milton's prosody uses the madrigalists' sensuous, kinetic, and conceptual mimicry.

174   Macdonald, Ronald R. "Milton: Traditions and the Individual Talent." In *The Burial-Places of Memory: Epic Underworlds in Vergil, Dante, and Milton*, 118-82. Amherst: University of Massachusetts Press, 1987.

A reticent poem featuring a number of reluctant speakers, *Paradise Lost* is greatly concerned with process, patience, and choice—matters requiring scrupulous deliberation. Modes of speech that charac-

ters choose (including metonymic, idolatrous, and unhistorical expression) are linked to the establishing of erroneous traditions whose
moment of origin is forgotten or suppressed and thus treated as the way
things are. Metaphor is connected to idolatry, for example, and—if one
forgets or suppresses the origin of naming and the creation—naming a
thing can degenerate into a human metaphor for creating the thing.
Hence Milton uses metaphors cautiously and precisely, purifying them
of any demonic taint and preventing them from appearing as unsuccess-
ful imitations of God's creative fiat. A fear of losing his autonomy
leads Milton to distrust traditions, which can encourage the artist to
repeat history's fossilized choices, now regarded as natural. The dangers of tradition are analogous to those of hell. Satan is characterized
by a paradoxical mingling of nostalgia and defiance; his denial of
remembering produces the repetition of an attempted return to origins.

175   McQueen, William A. "Point of View in *Paradise Lost*:
       Books I-IV." In *Renaissance Papers 1967*, edited by George
       Walton Williams, 85-92. Durham, NC: Southeastern Renais-
       sance Conference, 1968.

Milton presents the action of Books 1-2 of *Paradise Lost* from
the carefully limited perspective of the demons, distorting and height-
ening Satan's character to make him a source of dramatic conflict as a
worthy adversary of an omnipotent God. The narrator simultaneously
suggests a broader point of view without fully revealing it. At the
beginning of Book 3, God's total perspective replaces the limited view
from hell and effectively puts Satan in the proper perspective. From
this moment on, the epic's action reinforces the narrator's asides rather
than conflicting with them. *Paradise Lost*'s point of view continues to
expand gradually until it is completed in the final book. See entry 103.

176   Marjara, Harinder Singh. *Contemplation of Created Things:
       Science in "Paradise Lost."* Toronto: University of Toronto
       Press, 1992. x + 376 pp. 6 illustrations.

Neither medieval nor outdated, Milton's often conservative
scientific ideas parallel biblical ones and are also consistent with "the
framework of the postulates and beliefs that made up the system of science of his time" (ix). Milton selects his generally Aristotelian scientific ideas from contemporary opinions and uses scientific imagery and
analogies to create the physical universe of *Paradise Lost* and adapt it
to his poetic purposes. Not only does Milton fail to endorse Aristotelian

heliocentrism and ignore the implications of dualism, which he replaces with the monism that unifies his epic's universe, but he further adjusts Aristotelianism by advocating the existence of pre-creation and extra-mundane space. While using materialism to deny any split between matter and spirit, he prefers a vitalist (or animist) view of the universe to a mechanist one. When Raphael urges Adam to place limits on his curiosity and knowledge, Milton is not rejecting all sciences; rather, he rejects "the idle speculation of those who indulged in a totally ambiva-lent and therefore useless dispute" (282).

177   Martin, Catherine Gimelli. "Ithuriel's Spear: Purity, Danger, and Allegory at the Gates of Eden." *Studies in English Liter-ature, 1500-1900* 33 (1993): 167-90.
       Combining an apparent antipathy to ritual symbols with the inclusion of such seemingly sacramental instruments of truth as Mi-chael's sword, Ithuriel's spear, and Eden's gates and bower, *Paradise Lost* subverts classical allegory's poetic hierarchies and approaches the mode of mimetic representation. The epic's sacred symbols blend pure and impure, dark and light, as Milton shows that all external signs must be revalued—analyzed and tested—but not promoted into ritual symbols or demoted as mere dross. The Edenic emblems' mutual interaction and relative meaning produce a fluidity of order or an antihierarchic form of hierarchy. Unlike mimetic images, seemingly ritual instruments in *Paradise Lost* are often inefficacious, out of proportion, and drawn with sharp outlines. These symbols show that matter is subject to a variety of external and internal forces that, depending on the will's refusal or consent and the matter's degree of articulation, may be aug-mented, passively maintained, or erased. Thus, when God intervenes in creation, he primarily acts to make apparent what his creatures have already decided.

178   Martz, Louis L. "*Paradise Lost*: Poem of Exile." In *Poet of Exile: A Study of Milton's Poetry*, 79-199. New Haven, CT: Yale University Press, 1980. Reprinted 1986.
       Isolated by blindness and political circumstances, Milton writes his poem of exile, in which the poet represents humanity's individual consciousness and acts as the work's organizing center. *Paradise Lost* is structured as a double movement, for it is about destruction or loss and regeneration or hope, with alternating scenes reflecting these themes and the midpoint marking a transition between them. The plain

style meant to yield plain truth in Books 11-12 creates ironic contrasts with other conclusions in the epic tradition. Milton originally divides *Paradise Lost* into ten books to show its connections to Tasso's and Camoëns's epics, whose closing visions—of a great nation leading the world toward Christian greatness—he suggests are illusory. Journeying backward and inward, *Paradise Lost* at the end returns to its beginning. Readers might see the poem as a picture with a dark border and a bright center.

179   Martz, Louis L. "*Paradise Lost*: The Journey of the Mind."
       In *The Paradise Within: Studies in Vaughan, Traherne, and Milton*, 103-67. New Haven, CT: Yale University Press, 1964.
       Concerned with "a renewal of human vision" (105), *Paradise Lost*'s narrator turns his inward eyes toward a recovery of paradise. The opening four books, while they follow Satan's journey forward, move backward from the hell that is the reader's world to Eden's purity and then upward to the light by which the reader sees paradise and finally inward to a remembrance of the state of innocence. The epic's early style—with its foreign idioms and many allusions—is overwrought in an effort to compensate for great loss and then gradually moderated when readers reach the orderly paradisal life. Starting with the prologue to Book 9, the narrator assumes a choric role, interpreting and presenting dramatic episodes in something like a Greek tragedy. Redemptive love appears at the beginning and end of Book 10, but the middle reenacts the fallen postures of Books 1-2 and parodies the grandeur of their style. In Books 11-12, Milton loses touch with the poem's basic conception, for his voice lacks vigor when describing the effects of grace yet he presents the effects of sin with vivid horror. *Paradise Lost* is a poem with a bright center and a dark border.

180   Miner, Earl. "The Reign of Narrative in *Paradise Lost*." *Milton Studies* 17 (1983): 3-25.
       Milton conceives of genre in terms of the triad of drama, lyric, and narrative, which rules and even intrudes on the other two in *Paradise Lost*. If the lyric is appropriate to praise God and the Son, drama and narrative are the literary resources of the fallen world. Of the poem's many narrators, only God is omniscient and apparently wholly trustworthy, but his words are presented by a fallen narrator who recognizes the need for accommodation. Milton's narrator, acting as inter-

preter and relater, makes great claims for the reliability of his story; indeed, divine inspiration and assumptions about faith, grace, and regeneracy permit him to act as an inerrant narrator, though he scales down the apparent truth claims to the moral reality that is narrative's special province. As narrator, Milton follows classical patterns in terms of style and method, while he follows biblical patterns in terms of distinguishing what is true. He sometimes directs dramatic elements to his own ends, and in some other places he allows the strength of the narration to control the drama.

181   Nardo, Anna K. "Academic Interludes in *Paradise Lost.*" *Milton Studies* 27 (1991): 209-41.
        The Italian academies that Milton visits encourage broad learning, exclusively male fellowship, and wit. After he returns to England, Milton has an ambivalent view of the academies: he always describes them as ideal communities of learned men, but their aristocratic, Catholic, and intemperate nature is antithetical to his views. In *Paradise Lost*, when the devils "entertain / The irksome hours" (2.526-27) and when Raphael visits Eden, Milton reflects quite different aspects of his experience in the Italian academies. Belial's crew in Book 2 constitutes an academy, flattering their tyrannical sponsor Satan and engaging in vain philosophical discussions. Books 5-8, on the other hand, describe an idyllic academic symposium, a meal and discourse shared by male friends. Raphael and Adam discuss issues that are common topics for academic debate among the Florentines between 1500 and 1700. The domestic setting and attention to Eve's presence or absence indicate that the paradisal symposium, unlike its Italian models, does not treat the domestic and the academic as opposites and thus suffers "no segregation of gender that relegates woman to the domestic sphere" (234). Conducted in Eve's absence, Raphael and Adam's dialogue on love is left inconclusive. Their discussion reveals a flaw in the structure of all-male academic discourse that limits its ability to teach the knowledge of life.

182   Nicolson, Marjorie. "Milton and the Telescope." *ELH* 2 (1935): 1-32. Reprinted in *Critical Essays on Milton from "ELH,"* 15-45. Baltimore, MD: Johns Hopkins Press, 1969.
        More than books, the actual experience of celestial observation stimulates Milton's imagination, making *Paradise Lost* the first modern cosmic poem. His early poems give no indication that he thinks about

the new astronomy, an attitude that changes during the Italian journey, when he becomes aware of new realms of thought and vision. *Paradise Lost* contains statements about all the astronomical discoveries made since Galileo published *Sidereus Nuncius* in 1610. Like the sun and comet images, perspective in the epic reflects a sense of vast distances in space. Milton's cosmic scheme also allows for other existing worlds, a sign of the age's expanded conception of life and the universe. Contemporary telescopic astronomy shapes Milton's conception of space.

183   Nyquist, Mary. "The Father's Word/Satan's Wrath." *PMLA* 100 (1985): 187-202.
        Both *Paradise Lost* and *Paradise Regained* begin when the Father reveals himself in his Word or Son, an act that initiates a new order and a new plot as another son, Satan, is incited to rebel. By transforming himself into the Word, Milton's deity condemns himself to governing an order divided by an enemy who routinely appropriates the Word as a negative and alienating term, converting it from logos to mythos. When Satan misinterprets the Word, denies its productive efficacy, it becomes narrative. Reformed theologians interpret Eve's encounter with the serpent in Genesis as a drama of a demonic verbal assault on human faith in the Word, their dialogue revealing the stages of her progressive participation in Satan's subversive reading of the Word. In *Paradise Lost*, the bardic voice is gradually muted to initiate the movement into the recorded history of *Paradise Regained*.

184   Oerlemans, Onno. "The Will to Knowledge and the Process of Narrative in *Paradise Lost*." *English Studies in Canada* 16 (1990): 1-15.
        The epic narrator's struggle accurately to convey material inspired by God and yet develop his own original form constitutes the ultimate act of knowledge, whereby the poet's will aligns with the will of God. In an unrestricted, dynamic process, Milton comes to learn about himself and God by writing the poem and thus helping the reader internalize divine laws and experience true freedom. While Satan embodies the destructiveness of freedom apart from God's will, Christ represents the ideal of knowledge which Milton tries to achieve—he has internalized his Father's will to the point of being like, but not identical to, him. Milton's greatest attempt to unite his own will to God's is in his recounting of the fall, where Adam and Eve's most significant error

is their inability to trust patiently in God's cosmic scheme. Although Eve and Milton are set on similar courses, their ends differ; while Eve's narcissism increasingly constrains her toward the fall, Milton's apprehension of the Father's will through the narrative allows him to stand aright with God.

185   Parker, Patricia A. "Milton." In *Inescapable Romance: Studies in the Poetics of a Mode*, 114-58. Princeton, NJ: Princeton University Press, 1979.

Moments of suspension in *Paradise Lost*, such as Eve's staying or self-reflection by the pool, are pivotal, temporary threshold states of decision—of "even-ing" or evening, with a pun on Eve's name—leading up toward dawn or down into night. For the poem's characters and readers, the threshold moment of choice is implicitly a threshold of meaning in the progression from shadowy types to truth. To stay or stray in the middle realm of romance is thus to remain in the veiled world of signs, but the poem must participate in that twilight period of figural representation and its radically unstable linguistic signs. For Milton, ambiguity and metaphor are part of a process, an intervening space of trial, suspension, and interpretation; almost as often as the epic affirms the desire for resolution or conclusion, it exposes this desire as a form of temptation. At the end of the poem, Adam and Eve wander in an ambiguous twilight that is also the threshold of vision, the first step in the process of revelation. Waiting in *Paradise Lost* is a form of activity, another sign of Milton's emphasis on patience or trial rather than outcome.

186   Peter, John. *A Critique of "Paradise Lost."* New York: Columbia University Press, 1960. ix + 172 pp.

Milton's imperfectly anthropomorphic God is uneasy and defensive in Book 3, an impression the Son reinforces with his admonitory and suasive speeches. As *Paradise Lost* proceeds, readers find that God has two distinct but unreconciled personalities—sometimes merciful and loving, but usually severe and stern. The poem makes Satan interesting by asking readers to hold paradoxical views of him in suspension, simultaneously seeing him as a hero and fool. When Milton's technique becomes less subtle and Satan's deficiencies are repeated throughout the poem, they become more apparent and he loses some complexity and interest. Milton mismanages the premises on which the war in heaven is based: jealousy moves Satan to rebel, yet it appears that God, by abruptly or unnecessarily elevating the Son, wants to provoke an attack. However attractive Adam and Eve appear and however much their experience is a refined version of the readers' own, he can be disingenuous and she can be "a ninny" (93). Despite their undeniable guilt, Adam and Eve emerge in a favorable light and readers are encouraged to judge them leniently. After her fall, their speeches vindicate love's power as ennobling. If readers cannot despise the couple, then they are left concluding that only God—a self-justifying, feebly defensive character to the end—knows why they fall.

187   Quint, David. "Epilogue: From Origin to Originality." In *Origin and Originality in Renaissance Literature: Versions of the Source*, 207-20. New Haven, CT: Yale University Press, 1983.

When Satan sinks into the fountain of life at the beginning of Book 9 of *Paradise Lost*, he reenacts the sin that causes his fall and is the paradigm for all sins in Judeo-Christian theology: the denial of one's secondary status as God's creature, the desire to be original and the source of intelligibility, like God. Given the premise that God and his Word are equal, Satan reasons backward from the Word's apparently secondary status to conclude that the Father it reveals is equally secondary. He believes signification is an autonomous system arbitrarily controlled by the powers that be—and he aspires to be that power. While the Spirit the poet addresses is a source of inspiration, Satan constitutes himself as an alternate source and thus embodies a rival form of poetry that claims no authorized origin and sees all discourse as equally secondary. Not only does *Paradise Lost* denounce originality, but it demonstrates that meaning cannot be autonomous or self-created; it always depends on the divine Word's originary dispensation. Satan is condemned to imitating, though the diabolic counterfeit can interfere with the transmission of the divine original, which is exactly the problem of meaning after the fall. *Paradise Lost* thus desacralizes all books except the Bible and itself, two texts seen as original (just as Satan wants to be viewed).

188   Quint, David. "*Paradise Lost* and the Fall of the English Commonwealth." In *Epic and Empire: Politics and Generic Form from Virgil to Milton*, 268-324. Princeton, NJ: Princeton

University Press, 1993. Revised version of "Milton, Fletcher and the Gunpowder Plot," *Journal of the Warburg and Courtauld Institutes* 54 (1991): 261-68.

In *Paradise Lost*, Milton keeps alive, in disguised form, the dissenting partisan voice of his controversialist prose. Allusions to Phineas Fletcher's *Apollyonists* link the Restoration, demonic council, and Gunpowder Plot, while also connecting the Stuart Restoration and Satan's possession of the earth. By linking Adam's and Eve's psychological states to a contemporary theological dispute over assured predestination and its significance for religious politics, Milton attempts to comprehend the first sin and the deficiencies in political character that lead to the revolution's failure. Adam's profound sense of his state as creature produces a sense of inferiority in him, which is related to the Calvinist need for assurance and the contemporary English despair about their ability to govern themselves. The human plot and the divine superplot of *Paradise Lost* are structured by the opposition between epic teleology and romance deferral and deviation. Like Marino's *Adone*, Milton's epic turns toward romance and away from an epic organization of the political world.

189   Radzinowicz, Mary Ann. "The Politics of *Paradise Lost*." In *Politics of Discourse: The Literature and History of Seventeenth-Century England*, edited by Kevin Sharpe and Steven N. Zwicker, 204-29. Berkeley: University of California Press, 1987.

Critics have read *Paradise Lost* as a document of political or political disengagement. However, in keeping with Milton's understanding of heroic poetry's function and nature, the epic has a public role to play in Restoration England: using overt political thought, the poem offers "a course in political education" (206). In *Paradise Lost*, Milton's political way of handling the Bible is to seek its rational interpretation, which becomes the precedent or mode by which to judge current affairs. Based on the New Testament, the meritocracy in *Paradise Lost* endorses hierarchy as individualistic and voluntaristic; Satan advocates tyranny or frozen meritocracy. Arguing for liberty, order, and degree, Milton portrays the course of political evolution. He radicalizes the biblical account of the fall by emphasizing freedom of choice as the law of innocent and fallen humanity's being, showing that trial and change are sources of purification, and making political education turn on the amending of false linguistic usage. When Satan speaks the language of revolution, Abdiel takes it back and redefines servitude according to the proper relationship between degree and liberty.

190   Rajan, Balachandra. *"Paradise Lost*: The Uncertain Epic." *Milton Studies* 17 (1983): 105-19. Revised version in *The Form of the Unfinished: English Poetics from Spenser to Pound*, 104-27. Princeton, NJ: Princeton University Press, 1985.

By questioning the identity of *Paradise Lost*'s hero, readers for three centuries have questioned its genre and discovered two poems— the true subversive one and the establishment exercise it undermines. *Paradise Lost* is a mixed genre poem whose primary genre of epic undergoes revisionary treatment, while another genre (tragedy) subverts it by claiming primacy, a confrontation reflected in the subordinate genres. Although Milton's restructuring of the epic from ten books to twelve starts to correct the tragic weight of the first structure by emphasizing an epic of divine victories and human repentance, the final arrangement does not supersede it: the poem is suspended between the antithetical patterns. Like the human race that is its subject and audience, *Paradise Lost* seeks its identity between possibilities of tragedy and epic, of loss and restoration. Each of the poem's three main locations is associated with a genre: paradise with pastoral, heaven with epic, and hell (and fallen earth) with tragedy.

191   Rajan, Balachandra. *"Paradise Lost*: The Web of Responsibility." In *The Lofty Rhyme: A Study of Milton's Major Poetry*, 56-78. Coral Gables, FL: University of Miami Press, 1970.

Paradise Lost's images, characters, cosmography, and main ideas are structured in terms of polarities that converge on Eden, a center of decision and responsibility. By thinking herself more than sufficient to stand, Eve acts irresponsibly; Adam fails by deserting his hierarchical role. Readers are drawn to him when he wrongly chooses the lesser love over the greater, but they also judge themselves as being in error for feeling such empathy.

192   Rajan, B[alachandra]. *"Paradise Lost" and the Seventeenth Century Reader*. London: Chatto and Windus, 1947. 171 pp. Frequently reprinted; part reprinted in *Milton: "Paradise*

Lost," a Casebook, edited by A. E. Dyson and Julian Lovelock, 106-21. London: Macmillan, 1973.

Paradise Lost's ideal critic should be its ideal reader, a member of its original audience who is not necessarily erudite but knows the
Bible thoroughly, understands a system of divinity, and has read other
works on some part of the epic's action. While *Christian Doctrine* defines Milton's heresies, *Paradise Lost*'s doctrine—though consistent
with that of the prose work—subordinates them for poetic reasons. The
epic emerges from the hexameral tradition that Milton's audience
knows and he structures by redefining the chronology of events and
creating numerous correspondences among its parts. With the fall,
Adam and Eve rebel against the divine order of creation: passion rules
reason, and Adam idolizes Eve. Rather than being exclusively drab and
despairing, the poem's final books also show that the divine responses
to human depravity are mercy, justice, and grace, though Milton's last
words are pessimistic. If Satan has some admirable qualities, the
seventeenth-century reader still fears him and sees that evil perverts his
virtues. Milton creates a temporary illusion in which Satan is admirable
in poetic terms; eventually, however, readers condemn him when the
moral context of heavenly values comes to the foreground. Clear,
forceful, and simple, *Paradise Lost*'s style is not dramatic or derived
from the stage.

193   Raleigh, Walter. "*Paradise Lost*: The Scheme" and "*Paradise
       Lost*: The Actors. The Later Poems." In *Milton*, 77-125 and
       126-74. London: Edward Arnold, 1900.

Paradise Lost may deal with the largest theme, the fortunes of
the human race, and present a vast setting, but its focus on Adam and
Eve does not concern modern readers. Not a national document that
records contemporary ideas, *Paradise Lost* presents the intellectual and
imaginative schemes Milton imposes on the age. "The *Paradise Lost*
is not the less an eternal monument because it is a monument to dead
ideas" (85). As the poem proceeds, Milton finds himself serving Satan.
The metaphysical, the spiritual, the mysterious—none has a place in
this epic, yet the poet senses that his theme is intensely abstract and
unreal.

The essence of Milton's heresies is basing the universe on political rather than religious principles. Thus his God, a character who
expresses his will through law, is "a Whimsical Tyrant" (130). *Para-*

dise Lost's epic value comes from Satan's character and achievements. Adam, on the other hand, is sententious; drawn to the more important and ideal character of Eve, Milton resents his own susceptibility to feminine charm. Although he handles abstract thought pedantically, the power of his style emerges in descriptions of epic characters.

194   Readings, Bill. "'An Age Too Late': Milton and the Time of Literary History." *Exemplaria* 4 (1992): 455-68; "Postscript: It's a Fair Cop." *Exemplaria* 4 (1992): 489-92.

Paradise Lost is characterized by a temporal difference, which marks the beginning of literary history—the conception of literature as a lost historical object in need of restoration. By making literature an object of history, Milton gives writing a displaced relationship to time. Readers can see *Paradise Lost* as an object that they create through their conception of themselves as subjects; even as they attempt to master the knowledge of their own ruin, they alienate themselves from a history which would allow them to be subjective. Literary history, though not invalid, is blinded by the historical consciousness (of otherness) that arises after the poem finishes; readers are expelled from time as Adam and Eve are expelled from Eden. By voicing what is inherently mute and repeating what is supposedly original, *Paradise Lost* erases the fall from itself. Ultimately, historical consciousness remains outside but is revealed by the epic's poetic discourse.

Despite Eve's prelapsarian mixing of the speakable and unspeakable, she does not truly initiate the opposition between speaking and muteness that sets history in motion because she belongs more to the realm of shadow than substance. Her confusion of image and its representation should awaken readers to their own illusory position in the poem.

195   Reesing, John. "A Poem About Loss" and "An Essay for the Tercentenary of *Paradise Lost*." In *Milton's Poetic Art: "A Mask," "Lycidas," and "Paradise Lost,"* 53-68 and 71-86. Cambridge, MA: Harvard University Press, 1968.

As the meanings of three key words—"loss," "death," and "wrath"—are transformed throughout *Paradise Lost*, the ideas and emotions associated with them change. Loss and death (or Death) initially appear in hell, but death, in Adam's view, comes to mean extinction. When Michael articulates it for Adam, the theme of redemption radically alters the significance of these words. As these key words are transformed and the closing book presents a joyous revelation, the poem narrates "Milton's comforting vision of man's cosmic predicament" (68).

By revising *Paradise Lost* from ten books to twelve, Milton emphasizes its midpoint and division into halves, as well as echoes and contrasts between Books 6 and 12. Late in the poem, Adam chooses to reenter the spiritual life by associating himself with Abdiel and his heroic traits of patience, acceptance, and dependence on God.

196   Reichert, John. *Milton's Wisdom: Nature and Scripture in "Paradise Lost."* Ann Arbor: University of Michigan Press, 1992. i + 296 pp. 3 illustrations.

Milton finds Wisdom approachable and accessible through God's creation. Wisdom in the Bible and in *Paradise Lost* is closely associated with light, the Son, and the Father, and it is considered God's creating force. The two books of Wisdom—nature and Scripture—give the epic its organizing principles, particularly as each of the three structural groupings (Books 1-2, Books 3-10, and Books 11-12) moves "from a preoccupation with nature to a preoccupation with the Word" (51). Various characters attempt to go through this process, including Satan, the narrator, and Adam and Eve, whose fall is characterized by the failure of memory. Eve seeks a parodic form of wisdom, while Adam forsakes it. Their conversion in Book 10 follows the Puritan meditative pattern that begins with attendance on the ministry of the Word and finding the conviction of sin; when Adam and Eve call for divine assistance, they find an internal promise of salvation. As fallen creatures, they need new instruction and new wisdom.

197   Reist, John S., Jr. "'Reason' as a Theological-Apologetic Motif in Milton's *Paradise Lost*." *Canadian Journal of Theology* 16 (1970): 232-49.

Like the Cambridge Platonists, Milton borrows from Plato and shares the humanistic reverence for right reason, but his thinking reveals a tension between readers' impurity and their ability, with education, to repair the first parents' ruins. He seeks to justify God not to vindicate him (an unnecessary act) but to show reason's role in the story of creation and redemption. Sin, as *Paradise Lost*'s broad scheme demonstrates, is unreasonableness. Reflecting God's mind, the rational and orderly creation nearly denies real freedom, so Milton turns to the Greek tragic scheme to portray Satan's and Adam's falls. Adam sins not by seeking knowledge but by an act of pure disobedience as he defies order, forgets God, and tries to gain individuality. The forfeiture of reason is not part of Adam's punishment.

198   Robertson, David. "Soliloquy and Self in Milton's Major Poems." In *Of Poetry and Politics: New Essays on Milton and His World*, edited by P. G. Stanwood, 59-77. Binghamton, NY: Medieval and Renaissance Texts and Studies, 1995.

Before Milton's age, soliloquies appear in dramatic works to report off-stage events, disclose and deliberate plans for future action, and reveal a character's innermost feelings and thoughts. The nine soliloquies in *Paradise Lost* form a pattern. Most of Satan's five soliloquies portray the internal act of repressing positive feelings "to create the Satanic self he feels his public role demands" (65). Adam and Eve, who soliloquize before actually biting the fruit and falling, present soliloquies that are also concerned with the creation of new selves, often duplicitous and sinful. The despair and blaming of another that characterize Adam's second soliloquy appear in the opening soliloquy of *Samson Agonistes* and in Mary's soliloquy in Book 2 of *Paradise Regained*. However, Jesus's two soliloquies in the brief epic show intensive soul-searching and a mixture of doubt and confidence, as he recognizes a gap between what he feels himself to be and the public role he is expected to assume.

199   Rollin, Roger B. "*Paradise Lost*: 'Tragical-Comical-Historical-Pastoral.'" *Milton Studies* 5 (1973): 3-37.

An "encyclopedic drama-epic" (4), *Paradise Lost* is most successful when it adheres to the three genres of drama (tragedy, tragicomedy, history play) and least successful when it deviates from them. Though it is contained by the epic form, the large framework, the history play of the Son of God, contains and unifies Satan's tragedy and Adam and Eve's pastoral tragicomedy. Satan pays dearly for becoming a realist, and his tragic plot is in a complementary relationship with Adam and Eve's plot. By viewing *Paradise Lost* in terms of dramatic forms, one sees the three plots' catastrophes contained in Books 10-12. As the preeminent hero of the Bible—and thus, for Milton, of history—the Son is the hero of a history play about power that reveals a tension between God's reason manifested as order and human or Satanic passion manifested as disorder. The narrator, the only character whose role remains consistent in all three plots, acts as a stage manager by providing exposition, setting moods, and explicating the moral aspects of events. He participates in the drama of the epic poet's victory, in which he dramatizes the art of writing by making himself the hero and *Paradise Lost* the sign of his success.

200   Rosen, Alan. "The Monomachia Sequence in *Paradise Lost.*"
        Studies in English Literature (Tokyo) 65 (1989): 159-74.
        Milton's six monomachia scenes (single combat between powerful and fearless opponents) in the first half of his epic form an interconnected sequence, whose themes and drama cumulatively express a meaning greater than the sum of its parts. The three scenes leading up to the war in heaven begin with Satan's encounter with Death, in which Milton departs from tradition by emphasizing the hideous nature of the confrontation. The second monomachia scene, in which Satan and Gabriel meet in Book 4, is more gradual, describes Satan's fear, and emphasizes the battle of intellects and the beginning of an indictment of war. Abdiel initiates the third combat by challenging Satan in Book 5—a confrontation distinguished by its broad nature and lack of physical arms. The next monomachia scene, again between Abdiel and Satan, brings the poem's first physical blow—which ironically falls on Satan—and a release of dramatic tension. Violence and power escalate in the fifth scene, where Satan's fight with Michael echoes the first confrontation and emphasizes the external nature of strength. Reversing conventions of strength, number, and even the destructive nature of power, Milton concludes his sequence with the Son's rout of the rebel angels in Book 6, including enough comparisons with the first monomachia scene to finish where he started.

201   Rumrich, John Peter. *Matter of Glory: A New Preface to "Paradise Lost."* Pittsburgh, PA: University of Pittsburgh Press, 1987. xii + 208 pp.
        Milton bases his ideas of glory on the Hebrew word *kabod*, meaning a great reputation or a substantial entity's very being; in the Old Testament, it refers to God's being or its manifestations in creatures. According to the Homeric idea, glory means reputation, honor, charisma, or excellence. The New Testament word for glory, *doxa*, stresses the recognition of glory by others and the fact of glory (that is, truth or God's being). In *Paradise Lost* and in his life, Milton unites the Old and New Testament meanings in the expression of glory as a principle of existence, while reserving the Greek senses for the heroic

excellence linked to death and the desire for immortal fame. Chaos is the material basis of God's power, and glory is both the very end or final cause of creation and the intervening struggle by which the merely possible of chaos becomes the fully actual of end time. A metamorphic epic, *Paradise Lost* argues that Adam and Eve enhance their status as creatures and actualize the glory of their resemblance to God by physically assuming his *kabod* through love and proper nutrition. As Satan and his offspring show, hate and malnutrition lead to shame, death, and loss of *kabod*. The goal of creation, to give God glory by revealing him as fully as possible, is better met in a fallen world than in an unfallen one.

202   Sauer, Elizabeth. "'Barbarous Dissonance' and Multivocality in *Paradise Lost.*" *English Studies in Canada* 19 (1993): 263-89.

Rather than encouraging a regression toward one uniform voice and government, represented by Nimrod, Milton's epic promotes a mixed republican government made up of diverse voices. *Paradise Lost* itself enacts the process of forming conversation from cacophony (striving for but never achieving univocality), especially through the narrator, who must create the epic in spite of dissonant voices. In response to royalist supporters who seek to suppress divergent voices and liken a stable monarchy to a beehive, Milton uses the ant (emmet) to validate his support for a multivocal commonwealth. He reworks the account of Babel to condemn monarchy, illustrate the difference between secular and spiritual fame, explain the democratic nature of multivocal communication, and describe inner aspirations toward truth. In offering alternatives to monarchy, Milton stresses the creativity and diversity that come from obeying God's will; the parliamentarians' hypocrisy and self-interest contribute to Milton's disillusionment with his own cause. Without returning to an Edenic language, he celebrates and expands the possibilities of multivocality.

203   Schiffhorst, Gerald J. "'My Advent'rous Song': *Paradise Lost.*" In *John Milton*, 68-149. New York: Continuum (Frederick Ungar), 1990. 3 illustrations.

By choosing western culture's fundamental story, presenting a vast stage and encyclopedic subjects, and turning to his predecessors' words while insisting that *Paradise Lost* is superior because it is based on God's Word, Milton creates a new concept of the epic. He redefines heroism by assigning its traditional attribute, physical valor, to Satan and showing the true heroism of love and humility in the Son. While Milton's grand subject demands an elevated style, the poem's multiple styles distance readers from its transcendent events.

In a book-by-book commentary, Schiffhorst summarizes *Paradise Lost* and provides an introductory discussion of every significant character and episode.

204   Schoenfeldt, Michael C. "'Among Unequals What Society?': Strategic Courtesy and Christian Humility in *Paradise Lost.*" *Milton Studies* 28 (1992): 69-90.

"Milton regularly diffracts the experience of *Paradise Lost* through the prism of human manners" (69), which resemble those used in Renaissance courts and English churches. Echoing views that the revolutionary Milton holds, Satan and the rebels abjure a system of religious and political worship that exacts deference, yet their pretensions to liberty are deflated by irony. Satan's "God-like imitated State" (2.511) announces the deific ambitions that lurk beneath his libertarian rhetoric and hints at the political subjugation for which heaven can serve as a model. He can adopt a strategically submissive posture when it suits his agenda, thus revealing the aggressive potential of a superficially submissive demeanor. The politics of this courtly pattern inverts the earthly hierarchies that Christianity proclaims—the exaltation of the self produces humility; the humiliation of the self produces exaltation. Adam's conduct with his heavenly superiors embodies an epitome and a reproof of courtly behavior. Milton portrays the fall as a social breach whose effects also appear in a social context. *Paradise Lost* promises but does not participate in a democratic universe in which monarchy will be no more and God and humanity will be united.

205   Schwartz, Regina M. *Remembering and Repeating: Biblical Creation in "Paradise Lost."* Cambridge: Cambridge University Press, 1988. ix + 144 pp. Reprinted Chicago, IL: University of Chicago Press, 1993.

Paradise Lost presents chaos as a threatening and destructive region lacking the divisions that sanctify creation. Like Satan, with whom it is associated, chaos is evil, lawless, and boundless. As an area of ambivalence or potential, it is in a state of indecision—hardly a neutral role in a poem concerned with choice. A fallen chaos issues in creation, just as the fall of Adam and Eve leads to the creative act of redemption. Knowledge in *Paradise Lost*, as Raphael teaches Adam, is laudable if it celebrates creations and thus furthers the process of creation. With Satan as an example of the voyeur who presumptuously seeks hidden knowledge, Milton confronts his apprehension that the poet's own inquiries may be forbidden. His poem is created and threatened like the universe, as the struggle between chaos and creation informs his subject and poetic process. Indeed, the epic is imperiled especially when he describes creation, for he wonders whether he can do so unblamed and whether language has the power to dispel chaos and be answerable to the muse. Language that promises creation discharges the debt for creation, the greatest of all gifts. *Paradise Lost*'s repetition of creation is both a ritual by which it renews and redeems as well as a goal by which it comes to rest in silence—in another repetition of creation or beginning. See entries 254 and 259.

206　　　Schwartz, Regina [M.]. "Rethinking Voyeurism and Patriarchy: The Case of *Paradise Lost*." *Representations* 34 (1991): 85-103.

　　　　The nature of the gaze in *Paradise Lost*—where one is not only watching but being watched—can go far toward weakening patriarchy and recognizing the inherently unstable nature of victimization. A challenge to voyeurism (and the source of power it represents) is introduced by the simile comparing Satan's shield to the moon. As voyeur and aggressor, Satan manipulates Eve (exhibit and victim) to become a voyeur herself in a process where speculation is incorrectly assumed to be sadistic, because a look outward ultimately becomes a narcissistic look inward. It is difficult to use voyeurism as a basis for polarized power in *Paradise Lost* because everyone is being watched by someone else, and those apparently most free from prying eyes—God, the narrator, and the reader—actually look at extensions or images of themselves that are further distorted by perspective. Ultimately, the gaze that dominates the epic is the narrator's own; not exactly a victim, the blind poet is an active exhibit who is illuminated for the purpose of seeing.

207　　　Schwartz, Regina M. "The Toad at Eve's Ear: From Identification to Identity." In *Literary Milton: Text, Pretext, Context*, edited by Diana Treviño Benet and Michael Lieb, 1-21. Pittsburgh, PA: Duquesne University Press, 1994.

Paradise Lost explores "the permutations of identification, imitation, and identity" (3), as shown by various characters and even language itself. Wanting to portray the ontological category of identity as more trustworthy that the epistemological category of identification, Milton shows how Eve fails to recognize her identity; Adam carefully distinguishes identity from the identification Eve mistakenly makes of herself with her image in the pool. The Father and Son also show a substantial identity, and God is substantially expressed in his creation. Yet the unity of the universe's ontology leads to the fall. Because Adam does not feel distinct from Eve, his will cannot be distinct from hers. Weakening the will of others, Satan acts as a hypnotist and master-interpreter in a transference relationship with Eve. In their relationships with God, however, characters have the real freedom to choose to submit their will to his, even to identify their will with his. Transference is "the master trope for Milton's poetic practice" (18-19), as the reader consents to the narrator's knowledgeableness and the dynamics of identification that he establishes.

208   Sharon-Zisser, Shirley. "Silence and Darkness in *Paradise Lost*." *Milton Studies* 25 (1989): 191-211.

Paradise Lost's presentation of light and dark imagery uses two traditions: the Platonic equates darkness with evil and ignorance, and the *theologia negativa* associates it with silence. Only by combining these two traditions can Milton emphasize both the negative and positive aspects of silence and darkness in their nonliteral significations. Darkness is an attribute of hell and chaos as well as an external correlative of hell's epistemological state. In the created world, however, silence is self-destructive and darkness functions as a vehicle of order because it always appears with an agent of reason. *Paradise Lost* is a speech act, the obverse of silence, that moves toward justifying God's ways to man and restoring humans to their proper vocation.

209   Shaw, William P. "Milton's Choice of the Epic for *Paradise Lost*." *English Language Notes* 12 (1974): 15-20.

Milton chooses the epic genre for *Paradise Lost* because it allows him to include tragedy. Disagreeing with Aristotle, who finds tragedy the more inclusive genre, Italian commentators set the precedent for Milton by favoring the mixture of the two genres. The tragic form lets him isolate and emphasize Adam's temptation and fall, events that most nearly fit tragedy's form and substance: the tragic hero faces a tragic choice with cosmic implications; this episode observes the three unities; and its tone is didactic and sublime. Milton assumes that the epic genre includes and transcends all others.

210   Shawcross, John T. *With Mortal Voice: The Creation of "Paradise Lost."* Lexington: University Press of Kentucky, 1982. x + 198 pp.

As the author of *Paradise Lost*, Milton associates himself with God the creator and the poem with God's creation. Inspiration, God's breathing of the life-giving force into the poet, which Milton often portrays with metaphors of sexual intercourse, leads to enlightenment and creation. The Son's ascent to defeat Satan in Book 6 is the poem's structural climax, and Milton's subject is thus "man in the Christian world, a world which will end with Judgment Day and the resurrection of the dead" (28). If the epic is concerned with the loss of paradise, its basic theme is love. Satan is the prototype antihero, Adam and Eve are protagonists in the drama of life, and the Son is the exemplary or prototype hero. Perhaps the reader is the hero. The poem's original division into ten books creates bipartite, pyramidic, and numerological structures. With its cyclic pattern, the myth of return implies birth, growth, death, and rebirth in Milton's poem, while the linear myth of exodus involves moving through stages and reaching God. *Paradise Lost* is unified by its imagery, metaphors, and patterns of individual words. When he wrote *Paradise Lost*, Milton gave it intermittent attention from 1640 to about 1655 and closer attention in about 1655-58 and 1661-65.

211   Shullenberger, William. "Wrestling with the Angel: *Paradise Lost* and Feminist Criticism." *Milton Quarterly* 20 (1986): 69-85.

Instead of being resisting readers of Milton, women can find in his poetry "the promise of authority and identity, the possible blessing of imaginative life" (69). A radically self-critical text, *Paradise Lost* addresses the blind spot of its female antagonists by encouraging and supporting feminist interpretations. Satan represents a critique of the oppression that haunts patriarchal thinking, while Milton uses the portrait of God to acknowledge the provisionality of the metaphor of the Father, creating a character who questions all authority that sacrifices human liberty and who thus empowers others. The Son embodies the maternal thought of a loving, self-giving concern with relationship to overcome death. An epic of domestic heroism and human activity, *Paradise Lost* shows Eve as having existential fullness and an imaginative life. The relationship of Adam and Eve presents the concepts of superiority and inferiority as relational and progressive; Milton reveals that the language of power inadequately accounts for the reciprocities of love. Not a heroic revolutionary, Satan is actually a self-absorbed terrorist and dictator.

212   Shumaker, Wayne. *Unpremeditated Verse: Feeling and Perception in "Paradise Lost."* Princeton, NJ: Princeton University Press, 1967. xi + 230 pp.
        An "enormous 'tell-me-why' story" (6), *Paradise Lost* brings together the universe as a divine narrative and strikes readers where they are ontologically and racially vulnerable. Because of Milton's style and the epic's rationality, readers take his myth seriously. Along with descriptions of people and things, the poet frequently provides a statement of their attitudinal qualities or the conclusions one should draw from the descriptions. In *Paradise Lost*, animism appears in rhetorical figures and perhaps in the author's view of the creation. Adding no new information because Milton's sensibilities are not dissociated, synecdoche and metonymy reinforce the affective bias toward a character or location. His visual imagery is general when presenting the background and precise when sketching in the foreground. The creation and debates between Raphael and Adam are conveyed to readers as sound; the temptation scene and its effects are portrayed through somatic perceptions. In Books 11-12, Milton sacrifices visual development for the sake of brevity, though he fully presents Adam's affective reactions.

213   Stapleton, Laurence. "Perspectives of Time in *Paradise Lost*." *Philological Quarterly* 45 (1966): 734-48.
        While time is measured differently outside the visible world, in heaven it is an order or motion of events. Milton presents time as definite in various settings to achieve verisimilitude and a monumental effect in the depiction of events or as indefinite to create an impression of limitlessness or disorder. In the descriptions of events in paradise, particularly in the final four books, definite indications of time stress continuity and causality. The use of specific temporal markers during Raphael's visits connects his mission to Adam's daily experience, advances the succession of events, and greatly increases Adam's aware-

ness of the past. Michael's narrative brings together immediate time, which Adam lives in, and cosmic time, which governs the course of all events.

214   Steadman, John M. *Epic and Tragic Structure in "Paradise Lost."* Chicago, IL: University of Chicago Press, 1976. xi + 189 pp.

Milton is an Italianate Englishman in terms of his critical orientation, for he views classical literature and defines his poetic theory from an Italian perspective. Retaining the heroic poem's formal motifs and devices, *Paradise Lost* invests them with Christian matter and meaning. The poet rejects the martial theme and narrative of triumph in favor of an argument that stresses the hero's sin and defeat. In *Paradise Lost, peripeteia* must be defined as reversal (or change in fortune), the main one occurring at the moment of crisis when Adam and Eve fall from felicity to infelicity. *Anagnorisis* or recognition, another crucial Aristotelian part of the fable, is relevant in many scenes, including the fall, Satan's meeting with his offspring, and Adam's regeneration and learning of his redeemer. Defined as both suffering and its causes, *pathos* could include speeches of lament as well as a character's physical or spiritual pain, all presented to arouse pity and fear. Milton uses the epic marvelous to arouse wonder, particularly by divine or demonic agency. *Paradise Lost* accommodates a tragic temptation episode to an ideal of the epic form, whose decorum Milton maintains and subverts.

215   Steadman, John M. *Milton's Epic Characters: Image and Idol.* Chapel Hill: University of North Carolina Press, 1968. xiii + 343 pp. Earlier version of part reprinted in *Milton: Modern Essays in Criticism*, edited by Arthur E. Barker, 467-83. London: Oxford University Press, 1965.

Conceived as an imitation of reality, *Paradise Lost* portrays heroic virtue as revealed in *ethos* or character. In Adam, Satan, and the Son, Milton presents contrasting patterns of heroic virtue: Satan is a spurious hero who acts as a foil for the Son, the perfect divine image, essential form of heroic virtue based on humiliation and a ministry of redemption, and agent of human heroism. *Paradise Lost* and *Paradise Regained* emphasize the literal loss and recovery of beatitude or felicity in the happy state of perfection. Part of the epic tradition, the values of warfare, conquest, and revenge are demonic, and Satan is a heroic idol, a magnified version of the ancient pagan heroes who lack sanctity and

use force and fraud to gain their own glory on earth. The devils embody the ideas of illusion, mendacity, and sophistry. In the demonic
council, they practice deliberative oratory, arguing the merits or demer-
its of a plan—that is, persuading and tempting—rather than exploring
reality. Milton alters the timing of Satan's sudden metamorphosis into
serpent form in Book 10 to link it with his transgression in Eden, reduce the infernal victory to its true dimensions, and remove any remaining illusion of heroism in his character.

216   Stein, Arnold. *Answerable Style: Essays on "Paradise Lost."*
       Minneapolis: University of Minnesota Press, 1953. ix +
       166 pp. Reprinted Seattle: University of Washington Press,
       1967; part reprinted in *Milton: Modern Essays in Criticism*,
       edited by Arthur E. Barker, 264-83. London: Oxford Univer-
       sity Press, 1965; part reprinted in *Milton: A Collection of
       Critical Essays*, edited by Louis L. Martz, 148-55. Englewood
       Cliffs, NJ: Prentice-Hall, 1966; part reprinted in *Milton's Epic
       Poetry: Essays on "Paradise Lost" and "Paradise Regained,"*
       edited by C. A. Patrides, 92-120. Harmondsworth: Penguin
       Books, 1967.
       Both a tragic hero and an absurd villain, Milton's Satan has an
erratic awareness of his main flaw (pride) and maintains a sense of
purpose by relying on his responsibilities as leader. This role traps him,
creating a restricted course of action that amounts to a loss of outward
freedom, just as pride takes away his inward freedom. As part of a
complex metaphor, the war in heaven is dominated by physical, psychological, and intellectual ridicule and grotesqueness, excesses that
strain the narration and turn the battle into a mock-epic event. In hell,
the dominance of Satan's will and imitative, materialistic fashioning of
a new heaven counterpoint the powerful effects of achievement and
defiance. Readers approach the sensuous yet orderly garden, portrayed
as the image of an archetype, through its perplexing wilderness and
from Satan's point of view, which carries the experience of the first
fall. While the external entrance of evil is inevitable in *Paradise Lost*,
only its internal victory over the will—a self-temptation—makes the loss
enormous. The creation of Eve is a responsible action for Adam, yet
the metaphor he grants her creates him in her image. Though Eve is
tempted to fall, two characters who react to her in similar ways, Adam
and Satan, fall by self-temptation. The style of Milton's epic accepts
the requirements of the highest genre, including cosmic and domestic

drama, patterns of conflict in the description and narration, organization
of sounds that shape meaning, and many levels of diction.

217   Summers, Joseph H. *The Muse's Method: An Introduction to
        "Paradise Lost."* Cambridge, MA: Harvard University Press,
        1962. 227 pp. Reprinted Binghamton, NY: Center for Medie-
        val and Early Renaissance Texts, 1981; part reprinted in *Mil-
        ton: A Collection of Critical Essays*, edited by Louis L. Martz,
        183-206. Englewood Cliffs, NJ: Prentice-Hall, 1966; part re-
        printed in *Milton's Epic Poetry: Essays on "Paradise Lost"
        and "Paradise Regained,"* edited by C. A. Patrides, 179-214.
        Harmondsworth: Penguin Books, 1967.

Milton is concerned with movements in a spatial and temporal
world, movements that appear in large patterns of creation, sin, and
redemption; in images of rising and falling; and, as Adam and Eve's
morning hymn proclaims, in the rhythms of Edenic daily life. All of
the poem's motions are associated with the "two great Sexes" that
"animate the World," and sexual union (for unfallen angels or Adam
and Eve) and its perversion (the demons' narcissism, Satan's incestuous
relationship with Sin, fallen Adam and Eve's lust) are central to
Milton's vision. The change from ten books to twelve emphasizes Abdiel's role as the one just man at the epic's center and clarifies the
structural distinction between creation's magnificence and Adam's
recollections and questions, and between the world destroyed with the
flood and the world restored with Noah's covenant. In Book 9, Adam
abandons his authority and reason, and the fall shows that "sin is the
result of a failure in love and a failure to perceive the reasons for the
love of God" (150). The concluding books appear to offer insufficient
comfort for Adam, but they combine reassurance and bleakness, forcing him and the reader to face the world with a sense of responsibility.

218   Tillyard, E. M. W. "The Later Poems: *Paradise Lost*." In
        Milton, 201-51. London: Chatto and Windus, 1930. Revised
        edition 1967. Part reprinted in *Milton Criticism: Selections
        from Four Centuries*, edited by James Thorpe, 178-210. New
        York: Rinehart and Co., 1950.

Paradise Lost's real subject is the state of the author's mind
rather than the professed subject of the drama in Adam's and Eve's
hearts. Because Milton is vague and contradictory about the first cou-

ple's roles and motivations, the fall episode cannot bear the weight he places on it. The poem argues that Eve falls because of sensuality and Adam because of female charm, but her ruin actually comes from triviality of mind and his from that weakness and gregariousness. In terms of conscious meaning, Milton associates Christ with reason and creation, Satan with passion and destruction. However, his unconscious meaning is apparent: Satan best expresses the heroic energy of Milton's mind; the poet can manage only a cold intellectual belief in the incarnate Christ; the state of innocence is at variance with the human mind's primal needs, so Milton cannot view Adam and Eve as happy; and his pessimism emerges from a lack of sincere faith in the millennium. The construction of *Paradise Lost* is further upset when Satan provides the positive statement of its meaning, while Adam and Eve, limited to inactive virtues, can give only the negative statement.

219   Tillyard, E. M. W. *Studies in Milton*. London: Chatto and Windus, 1951. viii + 176 pp. Frequently reprinted; part reprinted in *Milton: A Collection of Critical Essays*, edited by Louis L. Martz, 156-82. Englewood Cliffs, NJ: Prentice-Hall, 1966; part reprinted in *"A Maske at Ludlow": Essays on Milton's "Comus,"* edited by John S. Diekhoff, 43-57. Cleveland, OH: Press of Case Western Reserve University, 1968; part reprinted in *Milton: "Paradise Lost," a Casebook*, edited by A. E. Dyson and Julian Lovelock, 122-28. London: Macmillan, 1973.

To make the immediate transition from innocence to sin is impossible in a complex narrative, so Milton "resorts to some faking" (10): he attributes to unfallen Adam and Eve feelings that are incompatible with their sinless state. They fall in stages before the fall, and there is no plain beginning of postlapsarian life. In the temptation scene, Eve's passions and intellect sway her will, while Adam's intellect is dormant and his will subordinated to passion for Eve. Disobedience, in Milton's view, means breaking the natural order God prescribes. The poem's real crisis, which is not Eve's eating of the apple but the reconciliation of Adam and Eve, receives the fullest structural emphasis. Adam is *Paradise Lost*'s active hero; Satan is initially tragic and ultimately tyrannical and perverted to ill. Rather than being final and static, Adam and Eve's prelapsarian life in paradise is a temporary honeymoon before the serious business of propagating the planet.

220   Toliver, Harold E. "Complicity of Voice in *Paradise Lost*."
        Modern Language Quarterly 25 (1964): 153-70.

Paradise Lost reveals the difficulty of communicating among levels (angelic, pre- and postlapsarian human, demonic, and so forth), each having a decorum that reflects that of the others. From these contrasting modes, Milton must eventually fashion a human decorum—his voice as a Christian poet—that encompasses the range of fallen experience and is composed of a dialectic of good and evil. The decorum of hell follows a repeated pattern of approaching consummation, in debates or philosophical speculation, for example, only to reach a dead end before returning to wander through the labyrinth again. Unfallen Adam and Eve use celebrational modes of love to worship and name other aspects of the creation, processes that work immediately and reach their goal of discovering divine immanence all around and within the couple. But there is a potential deficiency in human conversation. Though Raphael's discourse widens the distance between God and humanity, it is crucial to Adam's definition of his prelapsarian role and the definition of postlapsarian style. The narrator must shape the ultimate human style out of the fallen experience of forlorn wandering, searching for genuine light among many false lights.

221   Waldock, A. J. A. *"Paradise Lost" and Its Critics*. Cam-
        bridge: Cambridge University Press, 1947. vii + 149 pp.
        Frequently reprinted; part reprinted in *Milton: A Collection of
        Critical Essays*, edited by Louis L. Martz, 77-99. Englewood
        Cliffs, NJ: Prentice-Hall, 1966; part reprinted in *Milton's Epic
        Poetry: Essays on "Paradise Lost" and "Paradise Regained,"*
        edited by C. A. Patrides, 74-91. Harmondsworth: Penguin
        Books, 1967.

Milton does not recognize some of the difficulties posed by his theme because he misconceives his own relationship to it and overestimates his belief in it. He is thus trapped by his theme, a predicament readers can avoid by recognizing the important distinction between what they read (the events in the poem) and what he wishes them to read into it (the author's commentary). Eve's fall, for example, is not one act of pride, as Milton insists, but a sequence of perhaps four or five phases. With Adam's fall, the narrative's climax, rifts begin to open in the poem: when he learns of Eve's sin, Adam reacts with and falls because of love, not—as the poet wants readers to believe—because of female charm. The narrative material is out of Milton's control; readers know that Adam's decision is correct and they are supposed to condemn him for it. With this dilemma at its center and no way of making an intelligible transition from a state of innocence to sin, the poem breaks apart. There is a similar discrepancy between readers' sympathetic reaction to Satan and the poet's repeated attempts to portray him as laughable or neutralize his speeches with intrusive commentary. Nor can God's self-justifications succeed in making readers suppress their view of him as a nervous, insecure character who is vindictive, hypocritical, and unamiable at best. Unconscious meanings reveal a great deal about this epic because "the *Paradise Lost* that Milton meant is not quite the *Paradise Lost* that Milton wrote, for the *Paradise Lost* that he meant was, in a strict sense, unwritable" (143).

222   Webber, Joan Malory. "The Politics of Poetry: Feminism and *Paradise Lost.*" *Milton Studies* 14 (1980): 3-24.
        Milton breaks ground, however awkwardly and imperfectly, when he raises issues involving women's rights and importance. In *Paradise Lost*, he layers the biblical epic's form and content with complexities and ambiguities that subvert their traditions. No defender of a static patriarchal order, God relinquishes power and is in process toward full realization of the higher state imagined in the genderless images of light. Milton prepares for the patriarchal tradition's demise, when all things will finally be united in God. Heaven is a realm of both sexes, though they are not contraries, where fertility abounds. Reflecting every female potentiality that a Renaissance epic writer and Christian humanist could conceive of, Eve is associated with both inspiration and the demonic; she and Adam are different but spoken of in language that implies absolute equality. *Paradise Lost*, unlike most epics, is a domestic work that uses marriage not as a goal but as its main subject and theme. Although Milton does not present a division of labor for Adam and Eve, she is more at home in paradise, has more comprehensive responsibilities, and rightly becomes preoccupied with the problem of their chores. Satan is the epic's patriarchal, domineering character, a proponent of hierarchy and a reactionary rebel who despises change. In *Paradise Regained*, Jesus repairs the damage Adam and Eve do to the self while combining the qualities distinguished in their creation.

223   Weisberg, David. "Rule, Self, Subject: The Problem of Power in *Paradise Lost.*" *Milton Studies* 30 (1993): 85-107.
        Paradise Lost's transitional quality "lies in the gap between its representations of power and human autonomy and its own . . . theorization of those representations" (85). In Book 1.209-18, Satan is

portrayed as a dominated subject whose actions are greatly influenced but not caused by another's actions. When questioned by Uriel in a confrontation over specific forms of knowledge in Book 3, however, the disguised Satan acts on his own body to transform himself under the influence of but without any domination from heaven. Discussing his creation, the prohibition, and the punishment, Adam sees himself as part of a relation in which he perceives the possibility of change. For Adam, making his will concur to his being (or becoming an "I") is also a process of becoming the governed subject of an external will or power. *Paradise Lost* invests its characters and structures its narrative acts with such forms of subjectivity as contestation, questioning, self-knowledge, and the dialogic internalization of a listening presence.

224   Widmer, Kingsley. "The Iconography of Renunciation: The Miltonic Simile." *ELH* 25 (1958): 258-69. Reprinted in *Milton's Epic Poetry: Essays on "Paradise Lost" and "Paradise Regained,"* edited by C. A. Patrides, 121-31. Harmondsworth: Penguin Books, 1967; reprinted in *Critical Essays on Milton from "ELH,"* 75-86. Baltimore, MD: Johns Hopkins Press, 1969.

In *Paradise Lost* and *Paradise Regained*, Milton's similes—particularly those applied to Satan—use traditional humanistic materials with an ironic disparity that devalues classical virtue and emphasizes the theme of Christian renunciation. The pastoral, for example, dramatizes the momentary adequacy but final inadequacy of natural goodness, which needs to be redeemed by Christian authority. Often suggesting multiple relationships rather than single comparisons, Milton's similes frequently define the recurrent dialectic of the conflict between energetic evil and immutable good. Instead of fusing classical and Christian materials, Milton reverses them in an act of moral absolutism that insists on Protestant values and renounces all others.

225   Wilding, Michael. *Milton's "Paradise Lost."* Sydney: Sydney University Press, 1969. 128 pp.

An anti-narrative poem because its events are never in doubt, *Paradise Lost* relies instead on echo, parallelism, cross-reference, and ironic prolepsis. If readers view Satan as the hero, they must recognize that Milton repudiates the traditional concept of heroism as an ambiguous combination of the noble and the corrupt. Presented as a magnified human potentate, God, unlike the Son, seems tyrannical, defensive, petty, egotistic, and in some way perhaps responsible for the fall. By creating a bigger and better war than appears in any classical work, Milton derides the convention of military grandeur. To make innocent Adam and Eve interesting, Milton develops their psychological naturalism and emphasizes their sexuality as well as their other drives dealing with hunger, thirst, and the need for stimulation or exploration. Each character's fall is portrayed as a tragedy of disobedience, followed by human dignity because the couple returns to God. Paradise is lost, but Adam and Eve are not. Admired in the eighteenth century, given Satanist readings in the nineteenth, and met by anti-Miltonists in the twentieth, *Paradise Lost* has stylistic variety and many facets.

226   Wilkes, G. A. *The Thesis of "Paradise Lost."* Melbourne: Melbourne University Press, 1961. 42 pp.

Not primarily concerned with the fall and the theme of obedience, *Paradise Lost* deals with the larger pattern of the celestial cycle— the war in heaven, creation, fall, and subsequent human history. The opening two books present the demons' side of a contest and their values, whose flaws become clearer when set in the poem's wider perspective. While God's statements about the fall in Book 3 are logically just and rational, his foreknowledge and omnipotence make him appear unsympathetic until readers see him turn evil to good by forgiving or creating. That Adam falls because of selflessness in love does not refute the epic's thesis about asserting eternal providence. Rather, the episode shows the collision of God's and Satan's orders, providence's temporary defeat, and in its aftermath the victory of good, of God's design. In *Paradise Lost*, the fall is fortunate.

227   Woodhouse, A. S. P. *"Paradise Lost*, I: Theme and Pattern" and *"Paradise Lost*, II: The Elaboration of the Pattern."* In *The Heavenly Muse: A Preface to Milton*, edited by Hugh MacCallum, 176-207 and 208-91. Toronto: University of Toronto Press, 1972. [*"Paradise Lost*, I" is an alternative version of "Pattern in *Paradise Lost*," *University of Toronto Quarterly* 22 (1953): 109-27.]

More than just an epic, *Paradise Lost* is also a theodicy that turns to the order of grace to justify God's ways in that realm and the order of nature. Adam is the poem's defeated protagonist, Christ its victorious protagonist in the war in heaven and hero in the act of redemption, and Satan its antagonist. The poem's central lines, which describe the appearance of Christ's chariot, provide the large context of Satan's first defeat as a symbol of his final one, which puts the tragic nature of the fall into the perspective of a divine comedy.

With his pagan, self-centered heroism, Satan perverts the God-centered heroism that is *Paradise Lost*'s standard, just as hell perverts the order of heaven. The invocation to Book 3 presents the patterns of spiritual light's triumph over darkness and of darkness as a positive force in disguise. Eden reflects heaven's order, and Adam and Eve freely accept God's authority. In Book 9, Milton returns to the main setting and characters of Book 4 and to the pattern established in Eve's dream. The final books place the tragic fall in the perspective of a much larger divine comedy.

228   Wright, B. A. *Milton's "Paradise Lost."* London: Methuen, 1962. 210 pp.

Paradise Lost presents a total view of life as seen in the catholic faith of seventeenth-century Christendom, a rationalistic view that accounts for Milton's failure in portraying a self-justifying God. According to the epic, God is all, and there is no distinction between the material and spiritual. Milton insists that Adam and Eve's prelapsarian love is normal and innocent, and though he believes in a hierarchy, his view of marriage gives the woman more dignity than do most of his contemporaries. Not difficult or idiosyncratic, the diction of *Paradise Lost* is rather straightforward for its period; the syntax is Latinate but not unusual in terms of English usage. Carefully connected to the narrative, the similes might be considered "transposed descriptions" (95). In the war in heaven episode, Milton satirizes warfare in general as disorder enters the poem's pattern and foreshadows what will occur on earth if Satan succeeds. Rather than falling before the fall, Adam and Eve reveal tendencies that lead them to respond to temptation by sinning. In Books 11-12, poetic interest remains strong as Michael covers material essential to the argument, yet it cannot be brought into the action.

PART III:

PARADISE LOST

10. THE NARRATOR, HIS INVOCATIONS, AND HIS MUSES

229   Adelman, Janet. "Creation and the Place of the Poet in *Para-dise Lost.*" In *The Author in His Work: Essays on a Problem in Criticism*, edited by Louis L. Martz and Aubrey Williams, 51-69. New Haven, CT: Yale University Press, 1978.

The process of writing implicates Milton in *Paradise Lost*'s subjects—creation, imitation, image making, and inspiration. Both good and evil characters create reflections and imitations throughout the epic, indicating that all events are shadowy types of one authentic event. Even God uses reflections when he creates a universe that is a shadow of himself, a universe reflected by the imitative structure of Milton's poem. The poet thus imitates God's act of creation by analogy to convey spiritual truths through narrative's shadowy form. Various sources of inspiration, including the poet's muse and Satan as an alternative muse at Eve's ear, suggest that Milton's inspiring spirit, and his imitative poem, seems Satanic. As his invention and attempt to communicate unrevealed matters, *Paradise Lost* is implicated in the desire for forbidden knowledge associated with the fall. Though the muse's presence acts as a guarantee against the Satanic model, the poet must deny his own authorship. His invocations show both certainty of the muse's aid and fear that he, not she, is the poem's only author. Eve poses the same temptation for Adam (and for herself) that Sin poses for Satan and the poem poses for the author—the temptation to self-love or idolatry (the substitution of one's own created image for the universe God created).

230   Berry, Boyd M. "Melodramatic Faking in the Narrator's Voice, *Paradise Lost.*" *Milton Quarterly* 10 (1976): 1-5.

In some episodes, *Paradise Lost*'s narrator injects melodrama when the scenes are not at all melodramatic. He deludes the reader and then denies the delusion when he introduces Satan's fights with Michael and Gabriel, Satan's confrontation with Death, the demonic council's reaction to Beelzebub's speech, and the Father's call for a volunteer to redeem humankind. Each event's outcome fails to meet the melodramatic expectations the narrator arouses. Readers thus lose faith in his credibility and must rely on their own judgment.

231   Chambers, A. B. "Wisdom at One Entrance Quite Shut Out: *Paradise Lost*, III.1-55." *Philological Quarterly* 42 (1963): 114-19. Reprinted in *Milton: Modern Essays in Criticism*, edited by Arthur E. Barker, 218-25. London: Oxford University Press, 1965.

By arguing that there are two kinds of light, physical and celestial, and two sets of eyes, the body's and the mind's, the invocation to Book 3 establishes Milton as a divinely inspired poet who can understand God and explain his actions. Milton agrees with Plato that mortal sight leads to wisdom, but the poet, deprived of that faculty, turns to the mind's eyes and prays for illumination by celestial light. Thus Books 1-2 contemplate infernal regions, while Book 3 moves upward to view heaven and God. All eyes are suddenly united, as are all lights, and vision and beatitude and wisdom. With the fall, the image of sight is inverted to become an entrance for sin.

232   Cirillo, Albert R. "'Hail Holy Light' and Divine Time in *Paradise Lost*." *JEGP: Journal of English and Germanic Philology* 68 (1969): 45-56.

To assert eternal providence in the temporal design of a poem, Milton blurs sequential distinctions and reconciles two lights—the offspring of heaven first born and the eternal beam—in the single radiance of eternity. Time in *Paradise Lost* flows from God to the material world and back to his eternity. Light moves from its essential or uncreated form in God to become material light, while Christ unites essential and material light and time and eternity. *Paradise Lost*, inspired by holy light, is acted out in time as a part of eternity. In Book 3's invocation, the poet presents a metaphor for eternity as he goes through the inner light of divine inspiration to approach God, the essential light. This passage summarizes the epic's temporal pattern, as does the dialogue between the Father and the Son, who is eternity incarnate in time. Milton's invocation to light conflates time and eternity under the single aspect of eternity.

233   Ferry, Anne Davidson. *Milton's Epic Voice: The Narrator in
       "Paradise Lost."* Cambridge, MA: Harvard University Press,
       1963. xv + 187 pp.
    Paradise Lost's events and characters are presented in the
context of a narration by a narrator whose unique visionary powers
make the world of prehistory available to mortal imaginations. A poetic
device or invention, *Paradise Lost*'s narrator uses the invocations to
define readers as sinners who need help to transcend their fallen nature;
with bird and light imagery, he describes himself as a blind sinner who
has received illumination and is thus of humankind yet distant from
them, a role that determines his tone and point of view. The narrator's
didactic comments, similes, and style control readers' responses to the
entire poem, and his syntax, metaphor, word-play, and diction satisfy
the demands of his personality and sacred argument. Speaking scriptural language, the narrator and prelapsarian Adam and Eve convey a
metaphysical vision of a united creation that is shattered with the fall.
Emphasized with repetition and circle imagery, *Paradise Lost*'s structure imitates and helps readers see the form of a divinely unified world.
The poetic device of contrast imitates the destruction of that unity.

234   Fixler, Michael. "Plato's Four Furors and the Real Structure
       of *Paradise Lost*." *PMLA* 92 (1977): 952-62.
    Adapting the Platonic model, Milton describes poetry as a
channel of grace moving in a divine cycle that begins with an outside
force inspiring the poet and ends beyond the reader's heart and mind.
Plato's four furors, containing a model for the movement of poetic
energy, provide the structure for the sequence of invocations in *Paradise Lost*. The *furor poeticus* is followed by raptures identified with
Apollo, Dionysus, and Eros, a pattern assimilated into the Christian
mystical scale of ascent: the soul's awakening, purification, illumination, and apotheosis. As the narrator proceeds through these stages in
the four invocations, love stands at both the bottom and the top of the
scale that shapes the poem. This vertical, spatial pattern is complement-
ed by the horizontal and temporal narrative one.

235   Flinker, Noam. "Courting Urania: The Narrator of *Paradise
       Lost* Invokes His Muse." In *Milton and the Idea of Woman*,
       edited by Julia M. Walker, 86-99. Urbana: University of Illi-
       nois Press, 1988.

Satan's incestuous relationship with Sin is evidence of his "manipulative masculinity" (86), and Adam attacks Eve with misogynistic platitudes in Book 10. Condemning these attitudes, *Paradise Lost*'s narrator avoids antifeminism as he appeals to Urania with metaphors that link inspiration and sexuality. His allusion to four ancient poet-prophets in Book 3 evokes their association with the complex relationship of inspiration, light, and sexuality, though their blindness creates ironic tensions. Prophecy's dangers and Thamyris's interest in sex with his muse are sublimated into a Homeric emphasis on inspiration, in which sexuality is integrated into the spiritual mode of Urania's celestial light.

236   Gregory, E. R. "Three Muses and a Poet: A Perspective on Milton's Epic Thought." *Milton Studies* 10 (1977): 35-64. 5 illustrations. Reprinted in *Milton and the Muses*, 94-124. Tuscaloosa: University of Alabama Press, 1989.

When Milton's poems refer to Calliope, he considers her the general representative of poetry. Clio is the giver of poetry, the muse of history and glory, and the guardian of lustration and the few who perform or record heroic deeds. Although Clio has as much claim as Calliope to the title of epic poetry's muse, she disappears from Milton's verse after the early 1640s because he cannot reconcile her values with those of Christianity. *Paradise Lost*'s opening invocation calls to two distinct figures, the heavenly muse (Urania) and the Spirit, just as in Book 3 Milton refers to the same muse and holy light as different beings. Urania is an intermediary through whom grace, as it is relevant to this epic, can be conveyed. The muse of heavenly things, Urania is connected in literature and iconography with the antiheroic posture Milton embraces in *Paradise Lost* and *Paradise Regained*. She reveals God's wisdom through art, particularly divine poetry, while the inspiration of pagan prophecy and heroic verse is Clio, whom Milton rejects.

237   Hardison, O. B., Jr. "Written Records and Truths of Spirit in *Paradise Lost*." *Milton Studies* 1 (1969): 147-65.

As Protestant doctrine and *Paradise Lost*'s invocations state, the Spirit inspires the writer of sacred texts and leads devout readers to understand them. The epic's opening associates the spirit in the heart with the Spirit that presides over the creation, which Milton figures in terms of sexual imagery. Just as the creation of the cosmos involves two principles, the Spirit giving the seed and matter or chaos being impregnated by it, so in poetic creation the Spirit and writer participate in a union. Milton's depiction of the creation compromises between the organic theory and the main concepts expressed in Genesis. Furthermore, he links unfallen human sexuality to the erotic principle and creative process that form the cosmos, for they are all fertile and cyclic, moving from heaven to earth and then returning to God.

238   Hughes, Merritt Y. "Milton and the Symbol of Light." *Studies in English Literature, 1500-1900* 4 (1964): 1-33. Reprinted in *Ten Perspectives on Milton*, 63-103. New Haven, CT: Yale University Press, 1965.
       Scholars have recently recognized various metaphoric designs in *Paradise Lost*, including its light and dark imagery. The invocation to light in Book 3 is indebted not to Robert Fludd's theories but to Augustine, the many commentaries on his work, and hexameral literature.

239   Hunter, William B., Jr. "Milton's Urania." *Studies in English Literature, 1500-1900* 4 (1964): 35-42.
       The invocation to holy light in Book 3 of *Paradise Lost* is addressed to the Son, to whom Milton also speaks in the invocations to Books 1, 7, and 9. Associating Urania with light, the poet asks for inspiration from the Son—and thus from his source, the Father to whom he is subordinate. In his invocations, Milton prays for the heavenly Spirit's help in the form of the Father's power and virtue manifested in the Son as holy light, Spirit, and Urania.

240   Hunter, William B. [Jr.], and Stevie Davies. "Milton's Urania: 'The Meaning, Not the Name I Call.'" *Studies in English Literature, 1500-1900* 28 (1988): 95-111. Reprinted in *The Descent of Urania: Studies in Milton, 1946-1988*, 31-45. Lewisburg, PA: Bucknell University Press, 1989.
       Milton's muse is a multiple figure, presented in different combinations and with different emphases in the invocations to Books 1, 3, and 7. While each of these invocations appeals to the whole threefold unity of God, the first addresses each member of the Trinity individually, the second focuses on the Son, and the third emphasizes the Holy Spirit or Urania. In the sequence of its invocations, *Paradise Lost* thus embodies a structural representation of the Godhead's wholeness. The Spirit acts as the necessary medium of communication with

a transcendent God as well as the vehicle through which he gives grace. According to some traditions, the Spirit is associated with the feminine gender and a mother principle in the deity, an identity Milton explores in the invocation to Book 7, where he unites the Hebraic Wisdom and the Hellenistic Urania. In *Paradise Lost*, Urania is a poetic refraction of the Spirit and, in her association with Wisdom, a symbol of the creating Logos.

241   Lifson, Martha. "The Mediating Muse of *Paradise Lost*: Guide to Spiritual Transformation." *Notre Dame English Journal* 13 (1981): 45-60.

Containing the essential confessional part of all autobiographies, *Paradise Lost*'s invocations stop narrative time, refer back to creation, focus on the despairing poet's re-creation, and look ahead to the reader's participation in the process. Milton's muse is capable of supreme mediation and reveals "the possibility of an eternal present and communion with God" (46); she shows readers that the story of Adam and Eve's creation, fall, and redemption is their story. With the muse's help, the narrator, who initially identifies himself with darkness and chaos, undergoes a number of spiritual transformations so he can eventually share the divine energy and imagine creating a poem. The muse is ancient and nocturnal, embodying unconscious and primitive urges. Like other autobiographers, the speaker in *Paradise Lost*'s invocations concentrates on those characteristics of himself that he wants to reject and those that are goals he wishes to attain. The muse mediates between different times, places, and moral states as she gives the speaker guidance.

242   Lord, George de F. "Milton's Dialogue with Omniscience in *Paradise Lost*." In *The Author in His Work: Essays on a Problem in Criticism*, edited by Louis L. Martz and Aubrey Williams, 31-50. New Haven, CT: Yale University Press, 1978. Reprinted in *Classical Presences in Seventeenth-Century English Poetry* with an essay on *Paradise Regained* as "Milton's Translation of Epic Conventions," 55-83. New Haven, CT: Yale University Press, 1987.

Establishing a unique epic role as man and poet of omniscience, Milton leaves the mark of his personality everywhere in *Paradise Lost*, particularly in the invocations that explore his function as the heavenly muse's collaborator and instrument. He must reconcile his fallen condition and obligations as a Christian with his grand aspirations, which are connected to his very subject—the first sin of aspiring to divine knowledge. To show he understands the risks of his enterprise, Milton elaborates on analogies between his own ambitions and Satan's. Milton balances the autobiographical or subjective and the impersonal or objective impulses. The poetic act has Satanic potential, but *Paradise Lost* is the author's vehicle for deliverance through a chastening and humbling of the self that lead to an exaltation in the love and service of God.

243   Mollenkott, Virginia R. "Some Implications of Milton's Androgynous Muse." *Bucknell Review* 24 (1978): 27-36. Special issue *Women, Literature, Criticism*, edited by Harry R. Garvin.
        If Milton's muse initially appears to be masculine and is identified with the female Urania only in Book 9, the opening invocation describes this figure in androgynous terms, including the word "brood" (that is, hatch and breed or impregnate). Furthermore, the poet portrays his celestial patroness Urania in Book 9 as hardly distinguishable from the celestial light (the sun or Son) in Book 3's opening theophany, a connection that casts the Son as a female. Nor is Milton reluctant to describe himself in a passive, stereotypically female role in his relationship to the patroness who spiritually impregnates him each night. His androgynous imagery for inspiration and the Trinity is derived from the Bible and literary tradition, and it removes anthropomorphic traits from God. Because this imagery's egalitarianism threatens the Judeo-Christian tradition's patriarchal assumptions, Milton cannot fully face the implications of the feminine element in his unconscious.

244   Mulder, John R. "The Lyric Dimension of *Paradise Lost*." *Milton Studies* 23 (1987): 145-63.
        Rather than assuming consistency and certitude in Milton's principles throughout his life and works, readers should experience *Paradise Lost*'s interplay of narrative perspectives as an opportunity for making choices and a process of "surrendering to the absence of human certainties" (147). The four invocations reveal a double pattern of affirmation and denial by which Milton reenacts his overweening aspiration in order to recant it. He thus avows and disavows his character, goals, and accomplishments. The opening invocation gives the epic a

lyric frame, reinforced by the invocations to Books 3 and 7, which focuses on the act of writing the poem as its first great event. Beginning with Satan because his condition resembles the narrator's, the epic tells of the poet's salvation and ends by illustrating his kinship with Adam. In Book 9's prologue, the narrator uses exposition instead of apostrophe as he addresses neither the muse nor the readers but himself. His character and conduct reenact the strife between heaven and hell, and his attempt at justification must ultimately fail.

245   Reesing, John. "Miltonic Sensibility in *Paradise Lost*." In *Milton's Poetic Art: "A Mask," "Lycidas," and "Paradise Lost,"* 107-19. Cambridge, MA: Harvard University Press, 1968.

Speaking more than one-third of *Paradise Lost*, the narrator sometimes uses a neutral tone of unemphatic expression, particularly when he wants to contrast his voice to a character's speech, but often his pace is fast. God, on the other hand, has the poem's slowest voice, which always sounds the same—imperturbable and quiet. Milton's responsiveness in *Paradise Lost* is flexible and varied, for the poet creates a range of modes to portray the many characters, both good and bad, who amaze him.

246   Revard, Stella P[urce]. "Milton's Muse and the Daughters of Memory." *English Literary Renaissance* 9 (1979): 432-41.

Milton's muse is associated not only with the Holy Spirit but with her sisters of Greek antiquity because of her gender, haunts and habits, and relationship with her poet, a mystical communion that establishes and sustains his dedication to the poetic vocation. In *Paradise Lost*, Urania is closely linked to Hesiod's muses, who are also divinely begotten and sing to delight their father-god. Like Urania, Hesiod's muses teach him to sing at night, giving him a religious experience and initiating him as a humble poet whose status is elevated only because of their visit, command to sing, and gift of the knowledge of the past and future. Hesiod's experience resembles the Homeric and Hebraic ordination of the prophet-priest, a cultural combination Milton uses when invoking his muse. While denying literal authority to pagan myth in calling for Urania's meaning rather than her name, he still lets the myth stand next to the Christian account and thus cast its poetic truth. By claiming to be inspired by his muse, Milton follows other Renaissance authors in trying to restore poetry to the place of honor it held in antiquity as a divinely inspired art and the poet to his position as a moral and religious voice in society.

247   Riggs, William G. *The Christian Poet in "Paradise Lost."* Berkeley: University of California Press, 1972. x + 194 pp.

Milton uses *Paradise Lost*'s main characters and events to reflect on his own sense of himself as a Christian poet. By asking readers to compare the portraits of the poet and Satan, Milton acknowledges that writing this poem is a presumptuous act but one he hopes is not caused by self-glorifying pride because, unlike Satan, the poet submissively voices the need for divine aid. He insists on his pious intentions and exposes his poetic role's Satanic potential. If his narrative of the state of innocence—its creation, loss, and recovery within—is exemplary for readers, it is particularly a warning for the poet as our fallen representative in the epic, who must be vigilant about Edenic life's main concerns: proper and improper intellectual aspiration, an awareness of limits and one's place, obedience to and glorification of God, and art's proper use and source. By allowing the angelic narrators Raphael and Michael to dominate a large portion of *Paradise Lost*, Milton suggests that a Christian poet's pattern and song have angelic precedents. Decorum governs Raphael's bombastic narrative of the war in heaven and Michael's simpler style in Books 11-12. Though God's remoteness and self-sufficiency make him inimitable for the poet, Milton finds an ideal pattern in the Son: both are active agents of the Father's will who obey and depend on God and act as mediators, prophets, creators, and redeemers.

248   Rollin, Roger B. "Milton's 'I's': The Narrator and the Reader in *Paradise Lost*." In *Renaissance and Modern: Essays in Honor of Edwin M. Moseley*, edited by Murray J. Levith, 33-55. Saratoga Springs, NY: Skidmore College, 1976.

By gradually developing the narrator as a dramatic character throughout *Paradise Lost*, Milton eventually shows him to be the protagonist of one subplot. This narrator asks only that readers listen to his great argument; that they should act is merely implied, in part because the ego-function of reality testing is suppressed when reading. If readers identify with literary characters, however, our mythic consciousness is expanded, as with the heroic narrator, a father figure, guide, and god whose actions approach the marvelous. The narrator insists that his poem has its genesis in dreamlike states, so the epic itself embodies some of the qualities of dreams. Generating characteristic unconscious fantasies, including those of phallic assertiveness and omnipotence of thought, is a key part of the process of reading Milton's poem. For readers to respond positively to *Paradise Lost*, they must manage the primal emotions and unconscious fantasies that come with the reading experience and synthesize all or part of their characteristic adaptation or defense structure. Readers create wish-fulfillment fantasies of themselves and find that the poem does indeed have meaning.

249   Shawcross, John T. "The Poet in the Poem: John Milton's Presence in *Paradise Lost*." *CEA Critic* 48-49 (1986): 32-55.
        The biographical interpretation of poetry, while useful as a foundation, produces a one-dimensional reading and a flat poem. But an examination of the poet in the poem—that is, those elements in the work "that indicate a poetizing mind behind it" (37), including language, imagery, structure, and sound effects—reveals what is consciously placed in the work to create various meanings. In *Paradise Lost*, Milton announces his presence through the oxymoron and metaphor of the burning lake, for example, which contains multiple external and internal allusions, and through a large pyramidic structure whose apex is the plains of heaven in Book 6. The poet further displays his presence and craft by using numerology and verbal echoes. In the twentieth century, negative commentary about *Paradise Lost* is frequently misinformed or based on invalid criteria, and the writing of many modern poets shows signs of Milton's presence.

250   Sims, James H. "The Miltonic Narrator and Scriptural Tradition: An Afterword." In *Milton and Scriptural Tradition: The Bible into Poetry*, edited by James H. Sims and Leland Ryken, 192-205. Columbia: University of Missouri Press, 1984.
        With the Spirit's help, *Paradise Lost*'s narrator struggles to distinguish what can be presented as truth (that which follows scriptural tradition) from falsehood or mere opinion. He rejects traditions that contradict scriptural texts and, by presenting many alternatives, encourages readers to believe they can make similar wise choices. Although God sets boundaries to human knowledge, curiosity is not evil; Milton insists that believers have the freedom to inquire into God's truth using sound hermeneutical principles and reason guided by the Spirit.

251   Stein, Arnold. *The Art of Presence: The Poet and "Paradise Lost."* Berkeley: University of California Press, 1977. ix + 190 pp.

Paradise Lost's narrator is not an individual engaged in human relationships but a dedicated poet-prophet who conceals and reveals his presence. Because Milton believes poetry can re-create the original state of human perfection, he has no nostalgia when addressing the issues of freedom and destiny. In the garden, Adam experiences trials of merit, usually at the hands of a benevolent God, through which he begins to prove his birthright as his perfection evolves. The poet is also tested, particularly in terms of his inspiration's truth and his action's merit. Using novelty in style and subject matter, Milton creates multiple effects, double perspectives, and a rhetoric of surprise. Dominating *Paradise Lost*, the poet's presence reveals or withholds information, identifies with various characters, and shapes our perspective in every episode.

252   Sundell, Roger H. "The Singer and His Song in the Prologues of *Paradise Lost*." In *Milton and the Art of Sacred Song*, edited by J. Max Patrick and Roger H. Sundell, 65-80. Madison: University of Wisconsin Press, 1979.

Paradise Lost's invocations form a coherent poem by themselves, with their own voice, progression, themes, and purpose. After the first one raises three main subjects, each of the rest, while covering all three, develops a single theme: the poet (Book 3), muse (Book 7), and poem (Book 9). The invocations to Books 1 and 7, marking the poem's beginning and middle, pose epic questions and use a formalized manner of initiating the narrative. When the narrator calls for inspiration in Book 3, he asks no epic question and speaks to holy light rather than his muse. Book 9's prologue contains no invocation. Neither Milton nor the editorial narrator, the voice in the prologues is instead a formulaic, almost mythic figure who moves from cautious confidence to presumption, and then from apprehensiveness to tested, regained confidence. During the poem, the epic speaker becomes "the figure of a Christian whose service is singing," an act that is an adventurous, ultimately successful trial of his virtue (71).

For other studies of Milton's narrator, invocations, and muses, see entries 67, 73, 114, 118, 180, 184, 199, 293, 309, and 398.

11. BOOKS 1-2

253   Achinstein, Sharon. "Milton and the Fit Reader: *Paradise Lost*
        and the Parliament of Hell." In *Milton and the Revolutionary
        Reader*, 177-223. Princeton, NJ: Princeton University Press,
        1994.
        By drawing on the parliament of hell tradition that emerges
around 1640, specifically its portrayal of Satan, Milton irreversibly
connects allegory and political expression—an act designed to train his
fit readers. As depicted by royalists writing in the parliament of hell
genre, Satan first represents the origin of sects, then parliament itself,
and finally specific members of parliament. With the Restoration, royalists interpret the previous years as the struggle of good and evil,
thereby buttressing their belief that cosmic order is mirrored in political
order and that the relationship between signifier and signified is fixed.
Although *Paradise Lost* uses conventional royalist imagery, Milton
remains loyal to the spirit of the revolution, giving his signs multiple
interpretations and thus emphasizing reader responsibility. He claims
that, through reading the allegory of history and *Paradise Lost*, individuals can make the transition from perplexity to apprehension of the
truth. Because perfect language is lost to fallen humanity, Milton's fit
readers must attempt to decipher the truth in the midst of the world's
darkness.

254   Adams, Robert M[artin]. "A Little Look into Chaos." In *Illus-
        trious Evidence: Approaches to English Literature of the Early
        Seventeenth Century*, edited by Earl Miner, 71-89. Berkeley:
        University of California Press, 1975.
        In between immutably, eternally good heaven and immutably,
unremittingly evil hell is Milton's chaos, a realm of struggle and
change from which God created the entire cosmos and to which the
creation will revert at the end of time. Chaos assists Satan in his journey and, in the war between him and God, paradoxically expands its
empire when God subtracts from it to form hell, earth, and heaven. Because chaos contains seeds of light and darkness, it occupies an ambiva-

lent place in the cosmic war. Present or potentially present throughout *Paradise Lost*, chaos is an image of evil as essential weakness located in a position of neutrality between good and evil. As a proponent of disorder, though, chaos may be beyond good and evil in moral terms. While God and Satan sit on equal and opposite thrones, one character balanced against the other, the final books contain the metaphorical reassertion of the power of chaos in the cosmos, including planetary shifts, climatic changes, and human history's turbulence. After the fall, the inner lives of Adam and Eve are similarly chaotic. See entries 205 and 259.

255   Benet, Diana Treviño. "Hell, Satan, and the New Politician." In *Literary Milton: Text, Pretext, Context*, edited by Diana Treviño Benet and Michael Lieb, 91-113. Pittsburgh, PA: Duquesne University Press, 1994.

The demonic council in *Paradise Lost* defines alienation from God and dramatizes a second fall to emphasize the justice of God's treatment of sinners. Portraying oppositional politics and a radical moral struggle, seventeenth-century pamphlets often describe Satan as a politician who leads a council and becomes immersed in English affairs. Milton casts him as "an avatar of the self-made politician achieving prominence in England during the period from 1642-60" (102). This kind of leader, unlike a hereditary monarch, gains ascendancy and maintains power by merit, talent, and the support of followers. Like the oppositional politics of Milton's epic, the governance of hell is thoroughly agonistic.

256   Bennett, Joan S. "God, Satan, and King Charles: Milton's Royal Portraits." *PMLA* 92 (1977): 441-57. Reprinted in *Reviving Liberty: Radical Christian Humanism in Milton's Great Poems*, 33-58. Cambridge, MA: Harvard University Press, 1989.

In *Eikonoklastes*, Milton's interpretation of King Charles I's monarchy is consistent with his portrayal of Satan's tyranny in *Paradise Lost*. The image of the sun—for royalists, a symbol of the king's absolute rule, but for others a sign of arrogance in which the king tries to make himself God—links Charles and Satan as false rulers or false suns that do not shine with the light given to them. Both Charles and Satan curse weakness and worship strength, even if it is separated from virtuous qualities. Just as Charles claims to defend the people's freedom, so

Satan says he rebelled to secure freedom for his followers. Neither individual adheres to law, which alone has the power to liberate. Abdiel is the true Miltonic revolutionary. In Milton's portraits, Satan and Charles use rhetoric to enslave their followers, substituting prerogative for God's law.

257   Borris, Kenneth. "Allegory in *Paradise Lost*: Satan's Cosmic Journey." *Milton Studies* 26 (1990): 101-33.

In *Paradise Lost*, Milton appropriates and redevelops heroic-romantic allegory to portray Satan's cosmic flight as a figurative investigation of tendencies to err and their implication in evil and sin. Satan's inadequacies as a flier satirize intellectual excesses, and Milton's reductive treatment of his journey mocks intellectual ascents. By pointing to the emptiness of Satan's pretensions, Milton satirizes his "titanic audacity" and deflates his "distended notions of self-reliance" (115). Besides dealing allegorically with difficulties and conditions of intellect compromised by sin, Satan's journey ironically expresses a mental state that cannot go anywhere because it always brings the depths of hell. If the individual's relationship to God is appropriate, Milton favors intellectual enterprises, as Raphael, the narrator, and the regenerate Adam and Eve reveal. *Paradise Lost*'s final books redefine the ascent of enlightenment as a humble acceptance of metaphysical mystery.

258   Brodwin, Leonora Leet. "The Dissolution of Satan in *Paradise Lost*: A Study of Milton's Heretical Eschatology." *Milton Studies* 8 (1975): 165-207.

Rather than presenting the orthodox idea that Satan and the damned are condemned to eternity in hell, Milton in *Paradise Lost* suggests that this is a Satanic doctrine and instead professes the heretical view of the dissolution of Satan, those he perverted, and hell. But the creation cannot be annihilated, according to Milton's materialism, so from the conflagration will come new heavens and earth. Thus hell in *Paradise Lost* is not a place of humanity's eternal punishment but the fallen angels' mortal abode. By believing the erroneous view that spirits cannot perish, Satan reveals the limitations of his knowledge. *Paradise Lost*'s qualified warnings of eternal torment do not deter some characters from disobeying God, but Milton includes them to criticize the idea that the fiction of this torment needs to be preserved as a deterrent to sin. With respect to suicide, however, he appears to believe in the deterrent value of eternal torment. The heroic code's basic evil is apparent in Satan's death-oriented values and the demons' association with the giants in *Paradise Lost*'s discussion of Enoch in Book 11. Milton's views on hell correspond to those of the Socinians.

259   Chambers, A. B. "Chaos in *Paradise Lost.*" *Journal of the History of Ideas* 24 (1963): 55-84.

Milton's depiction of chaos is connected to Plato's concept of space as a receptacle in which the demiurge creates visible copies of eternal forms. Resenting the loss of empire to a newly created world, chaos is God's enemy who shares with Satan the hope that the universe can be returned to confusion. Although Milton is unclear about the time and manner of the origin of chaos, his cosmos comes into existence in four stages: a "material" God; "incorporeal," passive matter (perhaps Milton's ancient night) logically but not actually distinct from God; "corporeal" chaos; and ordered matter. In *Paradise Lost*, chaos foreshadows the condition that Satan finds eternally his: alienated from God, internally at war, destructive. See entries 205 and 254.

260   Engel, William E. "The Experience of Death and Difference in *Paradise Lost.*" *Milton Studies* 28 (1992): 185-210. 3 illustrations.

In the textual system of *Paradise Lost*, Death functions "in ways analogous to 'differance'. . ., as a kind of unrepresentable otherness which both constitutes and threatens the possibility of conceptualization" (187). Personified and distanced from what is usually understood by personification, Death evokes an image of the human undone and overcome by death; it is both an other and an image of humans after they have ceased to be. In his portrait of Death, Milton fuses potentially discordant iconographic traditions to show the insufficiency of any one of them to suit his larger polemical and poetic design. Like various printed representations of Death, Milton's character evokes a series of seemingly incompatible images that turn back on themselves and turn readers back on themselves and their mortality. Milton's rhetorical portrait of Death takes into account its implied future passing; like humans and like death, Milton's Death "always carries its death within itself" (207).

261   Fiore, Amadeus P., O.F.M. "Satan Is a Problem: The Problem of Milton's 'Satanic Fallacy' in Contemporary Criticism." *Franciscan Studies* 17 (1957): 173-87.

Paradise Lost's twentieth-century critics distinguish between an aesthetic response to Satan's point of view and a moral response to the theological concept of him. Exposing himself through his own words, Satan uses the language of pride and ironic heroism. That a character of such great intellect embraces contradictions and poor logic makes his tragedy even greater. He is not the epic's hero but instead a fool throughout.

262   Foley, Jack. "'Sin, Not Time': Satan's First Speech in *Paradise Lost.*" *ELH* 37 (1970): 37-56.
Satan's first speech reveals a great deal about his personality and present condition, often in ways that he does not intend or that will not become clear until later. Similarities between the devil and the narrator start to appear, particularly in terms of self-assurance and arrogance. The narrator has created this character for this moment, isolating him and his words on stage as he delivers his first speech as Satan. But the character bungles the job by expressing uncertainty and ignorance in a nearly mock-heroic speech. When he starts to see the truth of his predicament, he finds refuge in nostalgic, deceitful, and finally euphemistic words as he tries to avoid coming to terms with his fall, Beelzebub, and their new home. By floating in flames, unconscious after his defeat, Satan parodies the Spirit moving on the waters in Genesis and the creative Word in John.

263   Gallagher, Philip J. "'Real or Allegoric': The Ontology of Sin and Death in *Paradise Lost.*" *English Literary Renaissance* 6 (1976): 317-35.
Milton expects readers to accept his narrative as the most literal account of cosmic history available and thus to see Sin and Death as real—that is, physical and historical—though they always have a figurative level. The fall and its aftermath illustrate the allegorical use of the conceptual contents of events involving Sin and Death, as they enter the human realm not just literally but also morally and psychologically. In his description of Sin's cephalic parthenogenesis, Milton turns to Hesiod's *Theogony* to critique its cosmogony and reconstruct the myth, thus showing how the Greek distortion of it came to be. Agreeing with the patristic repudiation of Hesiod, Milton believes that the Greek poet, inspired by Satan, tells a true story but confuses its details. The implication of Hesiod's myth of Athena's birth from Zeus's head is that to beget (or commit) sin is not sin but wisdom. If Satan passes himself off as Zeus in this story, readers see that certain Greek myths

are the devil's prevaricated autobiography. See entry 136.

264   Griffin, Dustin. "Milton's Hell: Perspectives on the Fallen."
       Milton Studies 13 (1979): 237-54.
       The multiple perspectives on Satan's followers in Books 1-2
of *Paradise Lost*—they are anonymous and then individualized, godlike
and then damned, spiteful and then harmlessly comic—create a proleptic image of humanity's postlapsarian condition. Rather than allowing
readers to pass an easy judgment on the demons, Milton calls forth
ambivalent responses so readers explore their relationship with the
fiends, whose predicament and moods are recognizably theirs. Some of
the epic similes initially distance the rebels by associating them with
biblical characters, but these images of evil are brought home because
later human patterns recapitulate biblical history. Though Milton unde-
niably disapproves of the demons, he generates sympathy for them because readers must be aware of their fallen responses and thus armed
against sin.

265   Hamilton, G. Rostrevor. *Hero or Fool? A Study of Milton's
       Satan*. London: George Allen and Unwin, 1944. 41 pp.
       In the abstract, readers conceive of Satan as an evil power be-
cause of their preconceptions about him; in their imaginations, they see
him as the enemy but also as a mixture of good and evil, heroism and
folly. Milton shares this double view, for the author is both a stern
moralist and an imaginative writer. Fortunately, in *Paradise Lost* Milton the poet is far greater than Milton the moralist: he creates a Satan
who is courageous in words and deeds, yet heroic qualities do not make
an evil character fully admirable. However, an imaginative failure in
drawing the omnipotent God contributes to readers' assessments of
Satan's heroic and formidable qualities. Milton's Satan is a character
of tragic and selfish pride, a darkened and perverted hero, but he is not
a fool.

266   Hardison, O. B., Jr. "*In Medias Res* in *Paradise Lost*." *Mil-
       ton Studies* 17 (1983): 27-41.
       Acting as narrators, various characters introduce material from
Paradise Lost's inclusive plot, which begins with the Son's exaltation
and ends with the Last Judgment, into the unifying dramatic plot that
tells of the particular action of the fall. But Milton does not present

Books 1-3 through surrogate narrators or subordinate this material to the dramatic plot. The episodes in Books 1-2 are not based on Scripture or literary tradition, and they create confusion about the identity of the poem's hero—that is, about whether *Paradise Lost* glorifies Satan or narrates Adam's trials. At an early stage in his thinking about a work on the fall, Milton apparently chooses to begin with the opening of the dramatic plot when Satan delivers the soliloquy in what is now Book 4.32, which suggests that he was viewing the fall in terms of an Elizabethan tragedy, particularly the revenge play. In the Trinity manuscript's four outlines, however, Milton prefers a classical structure's opening to that of the revenge play. Finally beginning his epic at none of these points, he starts *in medias res* with Satan in hell, stressing that there are two valid perspectives, demonic and divine, and that the former appears threatening and significant. Satan is thus portrayed—perhaps too successfully—as a credible example of evil.

267   Hughes, Merritt Y. "'Myself Am Hell.'" *Modern Philology* 54 (1956): 80-94. Reprinted in *Ten Perspectives on Milton*, 136-64. New Haven, CT: Yale University Press, 1965.
        Hell in *Paradise Lost* is a physical place outside the universe, yet Milton also constructs the moral and psychological hell that classical authors and the Neoplatonists describe. While Satan displays some stoic qualities, which the epic criticizes, his character is based on the tradition of Christian thinking about the psychology of evil.

268   Hughes, Merritt Y. "Satan and the 'Myth' of the Tyrant." In *Essays in English Literature from the Renaissance to the Victorian Age*, edited by Millar MacLure and F. W. Watt, 125-48. Toronto: University of Toronto Press, 1964. Reprinted in *Ten Perspectives on Milton*, 165-95. New Haven, CT: Yale University Press, 1965.
        In *Paradise Lost*, Satan is the archetypal tyrant, the destroyer opposed to God's orderly cosmos who is associated with Turkish tyrants and Virgil's Turnus, but not with King Charles or Cromwell. Milton makes Satan an example of reason's surrender to passion and the deception of self and others that follows. Though he is not the poem's hero, Satan is still an antitype of the hero and a great tragic figure, an idol placed in contrast to God and Milton's ideal of the true orator.

269   Hunter, William B., Jr. "The Heresies of Satan." In *Th'Up-
        right Heart and Pure: Essays on John Milton Commemorating
        the Tercentenary of the Publication of "Paradise Lost,"* edited
        by Amadeus P. Fiore, O.F.M., 25-34. Pittsburgh, PA: Du-
        quesne University Press, 1967. Reprinted in *The Descent of
        Urania: Studies in Milton, 1946-1988*, 56-62. Lewisburg, PA:
        Bucknell University Press, 1989.
        A heretic and the source of heresies, Satan expounds certain
views—such as fatalism, polytheism, and a lack of belief in God's omnipotence and omniscience—without indicating to the reader that they
are unorthodox. In *Paradise Lost*, Satan never alludes to the Son's existence, an omission that recalls the heresy of monarchianism or the rule
of a single god rather than a triune Godhead. The events of *Paradise
Regained* show that Satan believes in dynamic, not modalistic, monarchianism, which further denies the Son any individual existence or divinity, a view Milton shares.

270   Law, Jules David. "Eruption and Containment: The Satanic
        Predicament in *Paradise Lost*." *Milton Studies* 16 (1982): 35-
        60.
        Satan's punishment in *Paradise Lost* is the radical freedom that
comes when God removes all opposition and constraint, leaving the
devil unable to fill the enormous physical and rhetorical space permitted
to him. Critics and the loyal angels fail to understand that Satan's
energies are compromised when extended, that divine constraint would
make Satan heroic, his energy victorious. Restraint stimulates growth,
as in Eden's vegetation, yet Satan interprets everything in terms of
containment as a negative force and eruption as a positive one. Though
Satan vows to defy God's will, he accomplishes everything he sets out
to do without ever resisting or contradicting the providential plan.
Boundaries continually recede beyond Satan, condemning him to the
freedom of forever wandering and extending himself in indeterminate
geographical and rhetorical realms. In *Paradise Lost*'s universe, only
God is uncircumscribed and requires no boundaries to define his identity. For all other beings, containment provides form and meaning.

271   Low, Anthony. "The Image of the Tower in *Paradise Lost*."
        Studies in English Literature, 1500-1900 10 (1970): 171-81.
        With Pandemonium in Book 1 and Babel in Book 12, *Paradise
Lost* begins and ends with buildings that mark the culmination of evil's

drive to rival God and create its own reality. Both buildings parody the constructive power of good, particularly in their symbolism of upward aspiration, which parallels Satan's pride. Like other upward movements in the poem, Babel's sinful striving to rival God is humbled in the tragedy of its fall and the comedy of its presumption. Pandemonium is treated more seriously, however, particularly by being associated with the tragedy of worldly striving to accumulate wealth and build splendid but corrupt cities. Heaven, too, is described with tower imagery but the context defines its legitimacy as the unfallen archetype that the others parody. Outside heaven, the tower image is usually a symbol of human glory, ambition, and transience, and only once—when it describes the sun's position—does it appear in a purely positive way. In *Paradise Lost*, the tower image is both an ambivalent and a unifying symbol.

272   McAlister, Caroline. "Milton's Monstrous Moral Interlude and Dramatic Decorum in Book II of *Paradise Lost.*" *Criticism* 33 (1991): 491-502.
        The tragicomic interlude of Book 2 in which Satan encounters Sin and Death illustrates Milton's positioning of the devil and his cohorts on the margin of his sacred epic, thereby mocking and debasing them. Milton defines an interlude as a drama that grows out of popular appeal, often mixing genres and morals without a clear resolution. Seventeenth-century interludes are characterized by sibling rivalry and ridiculous quarreling among the Vices, just as Satan's meeting with his family descends from a potential heroic clash to a comic awareness of God's belittling eye. The interlude in Book 2 has an ultimately redemptive function: it reminds readers of their vulnerability to sin, stands as a contrast to the true heroic values of Books 11-12, and clarifies Milton's own views on good and bad drama.

273   McQueen, William A. "'The Hateful Siege of Contraries': Satan's Interior Monologues in *Paradise Lost.*" *Milton Quarterly* 4 (1970): 60-65.
        At the beginning of crucial books in *Paradise Lost*, Milton emphasizes Satan's presence with a limited point of view that deliberately distorts his actions. He thus appears as a serious adversary of God, a view that a wider perspective reveals to be false. Books 4 and 9 present Satan's initial dominance through interior monologues—soliloquies and asides—that always occur in paradise and in close proximity to Adam and Eve but that reveal his isolation because no one hears

them. Readers perceive the victims from the destroyer's unique perspective, which increases dramatic tension. By adjusting the poem's scope to the confines of a single tormented consciousness, the soliloquy in Book 4 makes Satan more commensurate with his human adversaries. Indeed, as his next monologue indicates, he is more human than they are and more like the reader. With each speech, the demon's antipathy toward humans increases, as does the sense of menace he conveys. His speeches contain some material that contrasts with Adam and Eve's statements and some that parallels them.

274   Martin, Catherine Gimelli. "Self-Raised Sinners and the Spirit of Capitalism: *Paradise Lost* and the Critique of Protestant Meliorism." *Milton Studies* 30 (1993): 109-33. Revised in *Spokesperson Milton: Voices in Contemporary Criticism*, edited by Charles W. Durham and Kristin Pruitt McColgan, 31-46. Selinsgrove, PA: Susquehanna University Press, 1994.

Although the devils in *Paradise Lost* define a model of the Protestant ethic that features a dualistic split of humanity into elect and reprobate, both Milton and Marx "condemn it as the price of an alienation that must be overcome" (110). Milton disagrees with the mainstream Protestant ethic that believes in meliorism and thrives on accumulating surplus value, views that Michael leads Adam to see as erroneous. Early in the epic, the meliorist Satan endorses the ideas of the rebel angels' fortunate fall and of something approaching Calvinist election for them. Satanic meliorism consistently produces nihilism for his followers, as the demonic council illustrates. If Moloch proposes a scheme that is too obviously fatalistic and Belial one that is too blatantly self-deluding to appeal to the others, Mammon shares and improves on their delusions by voicing a meliorism that is tenable only on the basis of Calvinist dualism. Milton's poem overturns the mainstream Protestant ethic by criticizing the melioristic conviction that, for the elect, ultimately all is best.

275   Musgrove, S. "Is the Devil an Ass?" *Review of English Studies* 21 (1945): 302-15.

Because readers assume from the start that Satan is evil, Milton does not have to prove it; rather, he needs to show Satan acting in accordance with that preconception. The seemingly glorious demon of Books 1-2 thus fits as only a very deceptive part of the complete portrait. Without allowing themselves to be dazzled for the entire poem, readers should confess that, as unregenerate beings, they recognize some grandeur in Satan's early actions in hell. But evil can seem magnificent only in a false context such as hell, not against heaven's true light. Satan's degradation begins at the gate of hell, where readers learn of his incestuous behavior and see his undignified conduct with Sin and Death, and continues throughout the epic. In his soliloquies, he shows not just that he is a liar but that he believes his own lies, which places him in a less than magnificent role. Even his portrait in the rebellion, early in *Paradise Lost*'s chronology, contains intellectual inconsistencies and nothing to distinguish him from other prominent angels. In Book 9, all that remain are Satan's boundless misery and the evil that grows more predominant in him. He recovers some of his glory in his final appearance, returning to hell only to have even the illusion of magnificence removed when the demons turn to serpents. See entries 167 and 284-85.

276   Pecheux, Sister M. Christopher. "The Council Scenes in *Paradise Lost*." In *Milton and Scriptural Tradition: The Bible into Poetry*, edited by James H. Sims and Leland Ryken, 82-103. Columbia: University of Missouri Press, 1984.
        The Old Testament's tradition of the divine council influences *Paradise Lost*'s council scenes. In the demonic councils, the fallen angels' description as gods corresponds to the primitive biblical tradition in which Yahweh presides over an assembly of the lesser gods. The epic's four infernal councils show Satan gradually discarding the pretense of democracy and fully adopting the role of tyrant. Heavenly councils in *Paradise Lost* reflect the scriptural tradition of a forum in which God declares his orders to messengers who transmit and execute them. If Milton's heavenly councils reveal joy and spontaneity, in hell the participants feel uncertainty and fear. The biblical tradition evolves to admit prophets to the council, a role *Paradise Lost*'s narrator assumes when he receives special illumination. See entry 288.

277   Rebhorn, Wayne A. "The Humanist Tradition and Milton's Satan: The Conservative as Revolutionary." *Studies in English Literature, 1500-1900* 13 (1973): 81-93.
        Usually expressing himself in political metaphors, Satan describes his action as a rebellion against tyranny and an exaltation of liberty over servility. He believes in hierarchy but not in its dependence on God, who he says rules only by fate or custom. As an upholder of

this established order and his place in it, Satan is a conservative whose view of merit parodies Christ's true merit. Satan's conservatism is the antithesis of Christian humanism, for he sees heroism and merit not as Christian virtues but as the triumph of heroic self-assertion. Where Christian humanism defines inherited social position as meaningless, Satan feels great pride in his presumed place in heaven and starts a conservative revolution to defend the old ways and structure that existed before Christ was exalted by merit. Satan is not in fact a revolutionary.

278   Rosenblatt, Jason P. "'Audacious Neighborhood': Idolatry in *Paradise Lost*, Book I." *Philological Quarterly* 54 (1975): 553-68.

The narrator's complaint against idolatry (1.387-91) is based on antitheses derived from 1 Corinthians 6.14-17, in which Paul insists on the separation of light and darkness, believer and infidel, in order to attain union with the divine. Satan's awareness of the terrible difference between present and past is emphasized by antitheses that illustrate the separation of hell from heaven and expose his malice. The demonic catalogue shows threats of violence, contamination of the holy by the profane, and the effects of ignoring Paul's advice not to become yoked to demons disguised as idols. Both the demonic catalogue and the fall derive from Milton's Pauline thinking, expressed in the *Doctrine and Discipline of Divorce*, concerning marriage, demons, and idols.

279   Schanzer, Ernest. "Milton's Hell Revisited." *University of Toronto Quarterly* 24 (1955): 136-45.

In *Paradise Lost*, each character's mental and geographical realms are closely connected. The movement from the center (God) to the periphery (self), for example, parallels the movement from mental heaven or paradise to mental hell, an isolated, marginal region as removed as possible from heaven's light. Created in a state of evil, hell consists of ordered matter even as its fierce extremes and storms make it resemble chaos. The rebels' minds are similarly chaotic because passion rules them and they are divided between their former angelic condition and new diabolic one; they are interested in order only in its perverted state, which produces tyrannical rule and a united, disciplined army pursuing evil and hoping to defeat good. Best illustrated by Satan, hell's mental state is characterized by the endless celebration of the self, an increasingly feeble intellect, and a reluctance to face unpleasant facts. Numerous parallels between regions emphasize contrasts between heaven and hell as well as the demons' attempt to turn their new realm into a mock heaven. The microcosmic hell of Satan's mind is a very close replica of the macrocosm of hell.

280   Shullenberger, William. "Satan's Death Trip." *Milton Quarterly* 27 (1993): 41-48.
        Satan remains unredeemed because he chooses an identity apart from God, and therefore apart from the source of repentance and salvation. When God exalts Christ over the angels, he defines true identity as coherence with his own being. Satan rejects this connectedness by making himself a function of his own will, exemplified by his isolated dialogue (soliloquies) and self-destructive relationship with Sin and Death. Equally vexed by God's paternal authority and maternal generosity, Satan continually revives the moment of his expulsion through a repetition compulsion that drives him to perpetual aggression, especially toward the source of God's desire, Christ. Satan's ultimate goal is not to triumph but to be destroyed; however, his immortality frustrates his longing to fulfill the death instinct. Ultimately, Satan hopes that by destroying humankind and provoking God, he will cause the promised bruise to occur, thereby allowing him to be destroyed without repenting.

281   Stavely, Keith W. F. "Satan and Arminianism in *Paradise Lost*." *Milton Studies* 25 (1989): 125-39.
        As Milton's God outlines his Arminianism in Book 3 of *Paradise Lost*, it applies even to Satan, who is damned not because he must remain the source of evil (a Calvinist view) but because he will do so. Individual freedom and an autonomous will, though they can be misused, are central to Arminianism, and Milton further describes the obligations of perceptual freedom. Satan exercises this interpretive freedom when he sees the stairs that resemble Jacob's ladder in Book 3: the passage invites Satan to enter heaven's gate through repentance and faith (for the stairs are a type of Christ) and prophesies his defeat; Satan must make the interpretive choice between these views. When he lands on the sun, he receives an even better spiritual opportunity as well as another omen of his defeat. But as the divine offering increases in clarity and generosity, the demonic rejection increases in malignancy. In *Paradise Lost*'s Arminian philosophy, God never withdraws the possibility of reconciliation and repentance.

282   Steadman, John M. "The Idea of Satan as the Hero of *Para-dise Lost*." *Proceedings of the American Philosophical Society* 120 (1976): 253-94.

The debate about Satan's role as *Paradise Lost*'s hero is the oldest and possibly the most persistent of many controversies concerning the poem, with critics usually arguing extreme positions of execration or veneration of this character. But the issue is far more complex, for Milton plays various meanings of heroism against each other. As a partly conscious pretense, Satan creates his own heroic image—a lie, idol, and perversion of true heroism—whose validity depends on the fallacious criteria of traditional epic poetry. But this image is as ambiguous as the nature of heroic virtue. Until about the 1950s, critics perceive inadvertent contradictions in Satan's personality, a view replaced by the calculated dialectic of contraries that recent critics find. Milton presents Satan in a sequence of seemingly inconsistent dramatic images, interspersed with moral commentary and retrospective or proleptic allusions, leaving the reader to interpret and reinterpret this character from many perspectives. Satan is finally "a sort of moral zombie" (291) who degenerates and whom Milton degrades.

283   Steadman, John M. "Milton's Rhetoric: Satan and the 'Unjust Discourse.'" *Milton Studies* 1 (1969): 67-92. Reprinted in *Milton and the Paradoxes of Renaissance Heroism*, 111-35. Baton Rouge: Louisiana State University Press, 1987.

Milton distinguishes between true and false rhetoric on the basis of the speaker's moral purpose. A true sophister, Satan uses rhetoric to deceive, so he never reveals his true character or moral purpose, and Milton's editorial comments provide accurate assessments by undercutting his personality. Rather than being degraded in *Paradise Lost*, the supposedly heroic Satan of the opening books is already degraded, though he uses false heroism to disguise his condition. To distinguish Satan's real from his feigned intent, readers must see that his different types of speeches—soliloquies, conversations with Beelzebub and others, and public addresses in battle or council—have different value as evidence. Thought or *dianoia* plays a prominent role in Milton's epics because of the temptation motif's importance to their arguments. As the verbal battles between just and unjust discourse reveal in *Paradise Lost*, opposition brings logical contraries into sharp focus.

284   Stoll, Elmer Edgar. "Give the Devil His Due: A Reply to Mr.
        Lewis." *Review of English Studies* 20 (1944): 108-24.
        C. S. Lewis is wrong in *A Preface to "Paradise Lost"* (see
entry 167) to call Satan ridiculous and absurd, for in hell he displays
a kind of heroism and defiance triumphing over defeat. Given the
nature of his adversary and the need for a demonic motive and point of
view, Satan's lies are dramatically appropriate. And he is provoked—however slightly—by God, who produces the sense of injured
merit to which defiance and despair are responses. Satan is not *Paradise Lost*'s hero but its main character because of his speech, bearing,
place, and active role in the story. Like the loyal angels, the rebels are
subjected to a denigrating process that turns the heroic into the mock-
heroic. Yet the demons display the attributes of courage, patience, and
resolution; Satan feels remorse for his actions and pity for his victims.
Adam and Eve commit the sin of disobedience, not—as Lewis believes—uxoriousness and murder, respectively. Satan, his followers,
Adam, and Eve are all more interesting after their falls because they
become limited within the bounds of Milton's and the reader's comprehension. See entries 275 and 285.

285   Stoll, Elmer Edgar. "A Postscript to 'Give the Devil His
        Due.'" *Philological Quarterly* 28 (1949): 167-84.
        Unwilling to enter into *Paradise Lost*'s dramatic situation,
many critics devalue Satan's daring, compassion for his fellows, and
pity for his victims. Readers must sympathize, though unequally, with
both God and Satan. In his poetry, Milton cannot help but warm up to
Satan as "the first and greatest of Protestants, of Independents, of
Dissenters" (172). Because the poem's hero, humanity, is innocent and
ignorant, Satan must monopolize the action until the fall, leaving
Milton the poet and Milton the moralist somewhat in conflict. The poet
tells the story of the angels' fall, in which demonic song, architecture,
and debates closely resemble their heavenly counterparts. The moralist
tells of Satan's degeneration and the retribution demanded by theological and poetic justice. By attributing classical heroic qualities to Satan,
Milton does not discredit pagan heroes; rather, he shows how Satan
overshadows them. See entries 167, 275, and 284.

286   Stollman, Samuel S. "Satan, Sin, and Death: A Mosaic Trio
        in *Paradise Lost*." *Milton Studies* 22 (1986): 101-20.

The allegorical figures of Sin and Death, and their encounter with Satan, act out Milton's antinomian view of the Mosaic law as an obstacle to attaining Christian liberty. Forming a Mosaic trio, the infernal trinity reveals the consequences of perpetuating the law. Satan is a parodic Moses figure who enacts both the Mosaic law and the type of Moses as liberator, mediator, and lawgiver; as a caricature of and engendered by the law, Sin and Death establish Satan in his role of typing the law. Satan expropriates the typological relationship of Moses and Jesus, and of the law and the Gospel, to thwart its development and thus destroy humanity. The concept of a Mosaic trio helps clarify such issues as Satan's leadership role, Sin's transformation from fair to foul, and the construction of the bridge from hell to earth. With the abrogation of the law, according to Milton, only Satan supports the Mosaic law and human traditions.

287   Toliver, Harold E. "The Splinter Coalition." In *New Essays on "Paradise Lost,"* edited by Thomas Kranidas, 34-57. Berkeley: University of California Press, 1969.

The fallen and loyal angels are defined by their different styles and responses to divine manifestation, which drive the rebels into their own self-glorifying plots and the celestial host closer to the center. Substituting a political style for homage to truth, Satan still uses that homage to create an epic program of supposed restoration uniting a nation of heroes. Though *Paradise Lost*'s God is permissive, the divine ironic plot will reverse the Satanic one. Enlightenment, actually a form of suspicion for Satan, is revealed as enlightened self-interest. The members of the splinter coalition he leads tighten their political bond by using rationalization. Exhibited first in his treatment of Beelzebub and later of Eve, Adam, and finally Christ in *Paradise Regained*, Satan's method is to encourage a seemingly self-initiated action that would place them in a position of partitioning themselves and declaring the devil's centrality. Satan splits the creation's monism into an incurable dualism. The cosmos changes from pastoral (untested heaven) to parody (the rebellions of Satan and Eve) and finally to a higher synthesis (paradise restored).

288   Wittreich, Joseph. "'All Angelic Natures Joined in One': Epic Convention and Prophetic Interiority in the Council Scenes of *Paradise Lost*." *Milton Studies* 17 (1983): 43-74.

As shaped by the model of Revelation, the purifying and subsuming form of prophecy absorbs Milton's epic undertaking and adjusts
the epic's conventions. The inward movement of epic toward the
spiritual life signals a convergence of epic and prophecy, one genre's
conventions being modified under pressures exerted by the other. In
Paradise Lost's demonic and heavenly council scenes, Milton interior-
izes and psychologizes an epic convention to make it responsive to
prophecy's demands. Each council scene, occasioned by and responsive
to a prophecy fulfilled or about to be fulfilled, begins and ends in the
mind of the main character, Satan or God, that it exteriorizes and
fragments into component parts. In the Old and New Testaments, as in
Milton's portrayal of Satan and God in their councils, each character
is initially a multiplicity that becomes a unity only to be differentiated
by way of anatomizing evil or good in its constituent parts. Milton
inverts the traditional sequence of epic conventions—beginning with a
descent into hell, for example, and only then turning to a debate—to
challenge them and focus on the interior life. See entry 276.

289   Wooten, John. "The Metaphysics of Milton's Epic Burlesque
        Humor." *Milton Studies* 13 (1979): 255-73.
        Paradise Lost presents two realms—the fallen world and the
comic universe of Christian promise—in an uneasy balance that produces a burlesque vision of absurdity and that Milton asks readers to
transcend as believers in a divine comedy. Various juxtapositions create
burlesque discords mixing humor, awe, horror, and farce. The descriptions of the limbo of vanity and chaos contain tragic solemnity as well
as burlesque absurdity, a building up of expectations and a letdown that
results in a satiric debunking or ridicule accompanied by grim laughter.
Metaphysical buffoons in a philosophical comedy, Sin and Death receive a burlesque treatment because of the reader's anxiety about the
meaning of a world order that contains such absurd realities. Milton's
God brings uneasiness into the poem when he uses a combination of
divine anger and divine laughter to describe Sin and Death's arrival on
earth. While God's perspective is unified, burlesque records a division
in the fallen perception of reality.

Other studies that examine Books 1-2 are identified in entries 64, 89,
148, 156, 175, and 181.

12. BOOK 3

290   Arnold, Marilyn. "Milton's Accessible God: The Role of the
       Son in *Paradise Lost.*" *Milton Quarterly* 7 (1973): 65-72.
       Milton's remote God of heaven is made accessible to humans
through the Son, who acts as God of earth but not of heaven. A judge
whose laws condemn from afar, God is anxious to be cleared of responsibility for the angels' and humans' falls, so he turns to the Son as
mediator, redeemer, and vehicle through which people can accept punishment. In *Paradise Lost*, the Son always acts in God's name and is
usually adorned with his power and glory. He embodies the loving aspect of the Father's personality, establishing a bond between heaven
and earth when Christ descends to live as a man and die for humanity's
redemption.

291   Bauman, Michael. *"Paradise Lost."* In *Milton's Arianism*,
       203-318. Frankfurt am Main: Peter Lang, 1987.
       As Arian documents, *Christian Doctrine* and *Paradise Lost*
generally agree in their portrayal of the Son. The invocation to Book
3 of the epic addresses holy light—suggesting God's ubiquity, purity,
and truth—not the muse or the Son identified as Urania. Perfect and
thus immutable, true divinity does not belong to the Son, because he
grows in prestige and character, a process of development consistent
with the Arian doctrine of his mutability. The Father and Son are equal
in their enthronement in the highest bliss, but Milton never mentions
equality of their persons or their oneness of essence. He is an Arian
and *Paradise Lost*, besides being "steeped in anti-Catholicism" (290),
advances Arian views because Milton believes them. Before the discovery of *Christian Doctrine*, some of Milton's early readers insist that
Paradise Lost contains heresies.

292   Bennett, Joan S. "Milton's God: Creativity and the Law." In
       Reviving Liberty: Radical Christian Humanism in Milton's

Great Poems, 59-93. Cambridge, MA: Harvard University Press, 1989.

God rules in *Paradise Lost* primarily by virtue of his power to create, and the rebels fall because they proudly will not admit this power's significance. Yet God's goodness dictates that he cannot subject his creation to contraries, such as disorder, lies, or evil. As the Psalms indicate and as Adam learns, God's observable physical order, the creation, contains and describes the moral order and leads a rational creature to understand it. Milton seeks an English government modeled on God's government of the creation—that is, on the rule of law to which the ruler is accountable. In *Paradise Lost*, divine and human beings retain their freedom by acting in accordance with the laws of their natures. Adam, like the English people after the execution of their king, must work toward understanding God's ways. When tempted by Satan, Eve becomes confused about the relationship between God's goodness and power. Abdiel and Michael understand that each event or outcome is part of the providential scheme that prepares for the next effort, which leads to another event or outcome.

293   Cook, Eleanor. "Melos Versus Logos, or Why Doesn't God Sing: Some Thoughts on Milton's Wisdom." In *Re-membering Milton: Essays on the Texts and Traditions*, edited by Mary Nyquist and Margaret W. Ferguson, 197-210. New York: Methuen, 1987.

God speaks, God composes, but God does not sing. He is the Word or Logos, usually considered the language used of men; he is rarely the Song or Melos, part of the feminine mode of discourse. An activity appropriate for a created being, a poet's singing thus lacks a relationship by analogy with the speaking that is proper for a creator. As Proverbs 8.22-31 illustrates, however, Wisdom, as an agent of creation and part of the Godhead, rejoices in song. During the temptation and fall in *Paradise Lost*, Eve parodies Wisdom's pleasure and, with Adam, is implicated in the violation of Wisdom. The potential discord between Adam and Eve involves the Word as Adamic Wisdom (associated with love and reason) or as Song (associated with Urania and Wisdom). Milton's poetry contains both a hierarchical harmony, in which song must be governed by reasonable wisdom, and a sisterly harmony, in which humans and God use true song and play to re-create themselves continually.

294   Danielson, Dennis Richard. *Milton's Good God: A Study in Literary Theodicy*. Cambridge: Cambridge University Press, 1982. xi + 292 pp.

Avoiding the premise that from its beginning the universe exists in a metaphysically evil state, Milton's theodicy—particularly in *Paradise Lost*'s description of chaos and narrative of creation—asserts the goodness of God and the matter he creates from himself. Milton denies dualism, enhances God's freedom and omnipotence, and presents a deity who states many Arminian positions. While divine agency accounts for good and human agency for the evil of sin, humankind is free to reject the offer of grace and use the innate power to sin or to accept it and use the power given by God to avoid sin. In many of his works, such as in Book 3 of *Paradise Lost* when God justifies himself, Milton presents the foundation of his theodicy, the free will defense. He endorses the incompatibilist model of free will, harmonizing it with the free will defense, a soul-making theodicy, which appears in Adam and Eve's Edenic life and holds that humanity comes to perfection through free choice. Full of "Theodical repugnancies" (205), the paradox of the fortunate fall has no place in Milton's epic. The foundation and conclusion of Milton's theodicy are the same: God's goodness.

295   Empson, William. *Milton's God*. London: Chatto and Windus, 1961. 280 pp. Revised edition 1965. Reprinted Cambridge: Cambridge University Press, 1981; part reprinted in *Milton's Epic Poetry: Essays on "Paradise Lost" and "Paradise Regained,"* edited by C. A. Patrides, 157-78. Harmondsworth: Penguin Books, 1967; part reprinted in *Paradise Lost*, edited by Scott Elledge, 478-90. New York: W. W. Norton and Co., 1975.

As "an impressive example of one of the more appalling things the human mind is liable to do" (revised edition, 13-14), *Paradise Lost* presents a Satan whose plan for humanity is the same as God's—a fortunate fall. Satan initially believes in his cause, believes God is an envious usurper; one must feel horror at a God who eventually degrades Satan. Because Milton sees God as ineffable and the opening chapters of Genesis as thus not literally true, he must present a very grim portrait of the Father and place him on trial with all the other characters. To drive the rebel angels into greater evil, God wants to give them the false evidence that he is a usurper, so readers join Satan in feeling the force of the temptation that produces his fall. A harsh and arbitrary character who enjoys malignant jokes, God parodies legalistic behavior to justify a privileged few in his very unattractive heaven. Milton makes the strongest case possible for Satan, Adam, and Eve, and he believes God needs to be defended.

296   Fallon, Stephen M. "'To Act or Not': Milton's Conception of Divine Freedom." *Journal of the History of Ideas* 49 (1988): 425-49.

Milton adopts neither the Cambridge Platonists' view that "God acts of necessity according to his nature" nor Hobbes's view that there are "no limitations on God's free choices" (425). Though Milton agrees with the former concerning human free will, God's immutable perfection raises the issue of whether, if his goodness always leads him to act for the best, he is compelled to act in this one way, the best way. *Paradise Lost* does not attempt to subordinate God's will or wisdom. Distancing his God from necessity and chance, Milton, like Aquinas, argues that God is free to express his goodness in a variety of ways, following "a priori standards of goodness in ordering the free gift of creation" (439). The term "significant freedom" describes the liberty Milton's God has to choose among equal good alternatives.

297   Fixler, Michael. "All-Interpreting Love: God's Name in Scrip-ture and in *Paradise Lost*." In *Milton and Scriptural Tradition: The Bible into Poetry*, edited by James H. Sims and Leland Ryken, 117-41. Columbia: University of Missouri Press, 1984.

When the word "all" in *Paradise Lost* becomes "All" or "All in All," it designates God's transcendence, partakes of the enigmatic quality associated with his names in the Bible, and is associated with the Son's identifiable name and function as Love, another name with an enigmatic quality. God's various names range from clear to obscure so they can be accommodated to a character's (and reader's) purity or fallenness. The worship of God in *Paradise Lost* involves the knowl-edge of his nature as manifested through his names. Though faith is the epic's explicit argument, love, presented through the devotional mode, also becomes evident when the poet narrates and joins in the angels' choral worship of God. In this passage in Book 3, "all" delimits the bounds between God's knowable attributes and their absoluteness, which humans cannot know; this word also celebrates the aspect of God that is the Son's identity as mediator or Love. The angelic hymn, like the entire epic, is both doctrine and devotion, and the Son's divine name signifies the poem's extended argument. When Adam asks God's name and expresses social and sexual insufficiency, the Father addresses only the latter issue because it involves Adam's ignorance of the divine name of Love. Wisdom is necessary to fulfill the narrator's and Adam's capacity for creative love.

298   Flesch, William. "The Majesty of Darkness." In *John Milton*, edited by Harold Bloom, 293-311. New York: Chelsea House, 1986. Revised version in *Generosity and the Limits of Authority: Shakespeare, Herbert, Milton*, 223-71. Ithaca, NY: Cornell University Press, 1992.

Paradise Lost dramatizes a series of misinterpretations of God in order to make a great claim for poetry as the only human endeavor adequate to this epic's deity. By nobly surrendering a name or title that invests him with God's image, Lucifer-Satan shows a less iconic and more admirable understanding of the deity than do the other angels, while idolatrously attempting to rival his invisibility and inaccessibility. The only difference between God and Satan is one of degree, according to every angel (particularly Raphael, whose view resembles Satan's) except Abdiel, who recognizes a radical discontinuity between the highest angels and the Son, an interpretation not encouraged in heaven. Adam and Eve share the limited, Platonic view of God that Raphael promotes, and their fall is fortunate because it enables a much deeper understanding of God, including a sense of the discontinuity between finite intelligences and an unknowable deity. Book 9's invocation asserts that the fall also produces poetic affect, a concept Milton celebrates and laments, for he shares with Satan a better understanding of God. The real God does not and cannot appear in *Paradise Lost*; the poem's portrayal of him is an emanation constructed for the angels' limited knowledge.

299   Gilbert, Allan. "Form and Matter in *Paradise Lost*, Book III." *JEGP: Journal of English and Germanic Philology* 60 (1961): 651-63. Reprinted in *Milton Studies in Honor of Harris Francis Fletcher*, edited by G. Blakemore Evans et al., 43-55. Urbana: University of Illinois Press, 1961.

When Milton shifts *Paradise Lost* from drama to epic, he retains much of the romance and martial spirit that the invocation to Book 9 apparently rejects. As the choice for his great argument, the fall of Adam and Eve decides humanity's fate and personifies the conflict between light and darkness. When Satan journeys toward earth, he hopes to thwart God by destroying humans, an act of apparent freedom that carries out the divine will and shows God's justice in the ultimate triumph of good. The Father and Son look down at Satan as he travels, creating a dramatic situation that reinforces the theology presented in the heavenly council. The divine dialogue in Book 3 negates Satan's seduction of humanity before it occurs. In order to turn the Father and Son into participants in an epic, Milton must describe them anthropomorphically: God behaves like an earthly ruler, the Son like a prudent courtier. The God of *Paradise Lost* may be stern and tyrannical, but he expresses contemporary views and as a poetic character he is not an object for ethical judgment.

300   Hamilton, Gary D. "Milton's Defensive God: A Reappraisal."
        Studies in Philology 69 (1972): 87-100.

        In Book 3 of *Paradise Lost*, God adopts a defensive tone to counter those aspects of seventeenth-century Calvinism that Milton and others find inconsistent with their understanding of God's goodness. Where Arminians see a God of love, Calvinists see a God of power who shows his glory by arbitrarily saving some people and damning others. Arguing for the Arminian view, Milton's God shows Englishmen how to avoid the obstacles the dominant Calvinist theology places in the way of appreciating divine benevolence and mercy. As a character who explains the Father's positions and makes choices of his own free will, the Son reinforces Book 3's Arminianism.

301   Huckabay, Calvin. "The Beneficent God of *Paradise Lost*."
        In *Essays in Honor of Esmond Linworth Marilla*, edited by
        Thomas Austin Kirby and William John Olive, 144-57. Louisi-
        ana State University Studies, Humanities Series, no. 19. Baton
        Rouge: Louisiana State University Press, 1970.

        A positive alternative to Satan and his destructive course of discord and stoic autonomy, God in *Paradise Lost* is a constructive power of order and good. Indeed, he is goodness itself. Readers see and interpret God from several perspectives: when he appears as a character, when the narrator comments on him, when even the rebel angels admit his enormous magnitude, when the loyal angels refute Satan's views and explain God's ways, and when Adam and Eve are created by and communicate with him. The composite picture that emerges is of a beneficent force, a character who uses evil to bring forth good.

302   Hughes, Merritt Y. "The Filiations of Milton's Celestial Dia-
        logue (*Paradise Lost*, III.80-343)." In *Ten Perspectives on
        Milton*, 104-35. New Haven, CT: Yale University Press,
        1965.
        The celestial dialogue contains a hint of the allegorical debate
among the four daughters of God over fallen humankind's fate, though
Milton's episode features not Justice and Mercy but the distinct persons
of the Father and the Son. By defining these two parts of the Godhead
as opposites, critics deny the Son's free will and demonstrations of faith
in his Father's mercy. Milton's God is open to persuasion and not
cruel; at the end of the dialogue, his will and his Son's are united, their
characters established as coequal.

303   Hughes, Merritt Y. "Milton's Limbo of Vanity." In *Th'Up-
        right Heart and Pure: Essays on John Milton Commemorating
        the Tercentenary of the Publication of "Paradise Lost,"* edited
        by Amadeus P. Fiore, O.F.M., 7-24. Pittsburgh, PA: Du-
        quesne University Press, 1967.
        Integrated into the narrative through the very different allegory
of Jacob's ladder, Milton's allegory of limbo includes historical elements that link it thematically to the visions of future history—particularly the giants and the builders of Babel—in Books 11-12. In *Paradise Lost*'s limbo, Empedocles, who sought to achieve deification
through death, illustrates the indulgence in the vain human hope of
fame. Another suicide, Cleombrotus, also reveals the evil effects of the
pagan philosophers' false wisdom. As in Ariosto's *Orlando Furioso*,
part of which illuminates Milton's limbo, the satire is directed at eccle-
siastical venality. Milton's limbo is also connected to the meadow of
the vision of Er in Plato's *Republic*. See entry 304.

304   Huntley, Frank L. "A Justification of Milton's 'Paradise of
        Fools' (*P.L.* III.431-499)." *ELH* 21 (1954): 107-13.
        Apparently digressive or offensive in its anti-Catholicism, the
limbo of vanity episode begins with a vulture simile and marks the
midpoint of Satan's journey to earth. He is alone, yet he will not
remain so if his mission succeeds and he later populates this location.
Filled with satire and grotesquery, the passage looks forward to others
who pause on journeys, even as readers see the future crowd—Satan's
victims—moving backward from earth to this plain. The central imagery here is of hypocrisy and monstrous birth; the main sin is pride. See
entry 303.

305   Lewalski, Barbara K. "Generic Multiplicity and Milton's Lit-
        erary God." In *A Fine Tuning: Studies of the Religious Poetry
        of Herbert and Milton*, edited by Mary A. Maleski, 163-86.
        Binghamton, NY: Medieval and Renaissance Texts and Stud-
        ies, 1989.
Milton tries to justify God by using a vast array of generic
conventions and literary forms, each designed to emphasize a particular
quality and thus hint at the infinite complexity of the deity. Drawing on
the Bible's multiple interpretations of God, Milton suggests God's
transcendence through various generic perspectives, ultimately indicating that all literary accommodations, even *Paradise Lost*, are inadequate. The council in heaven, which focuses on divine love, transcends
and reverses several literary forms, including epic, romance, mystery
and morality drama, and tragicomedy. The Father, speaking with the
Son or Adam, also relies on various kinds of discourse to create true
dialogue. Of all the attributes assigned to God, Milton most strongly
emphasizes heroic love, energetic creation, and the ability to educate
through dialogue.

306   Lieb, Michael. "Milton's 'Dramatick Constitution': The Celes-
        tial Dialogue in *Paradise Lost*, Book III." *Milton Studies* 23
        (1987): 215-40. Revised version in *The Sinews of Ulysses:
        Form and Convention in Milton's Works*, 76-97. Pittsburgh,
        PA: Duquesne University Press, 1989.
A fully realized being, Milton's God engages readers and demands that they struggle with him, just as he struggles with himself in
the drama of the Godhead's personalities. As the Trinity manuscript
suggests, the dialogue in heaven is structured as a five-act drama with
a comedic action resolved by the assertion of the fortunate fall. The
dialogue in heaven shows a reconciliation between the Father and the
Son only after shifts in mood and tone as well as authentic conflicts
between and within these characters. Wrestling with his theology, God
justifies his own ways to himself, and the Son questions the Father's
goodness and greatness in a spirit of contentiousness that pervades the
Old Testament. Milton radicalizes the dialogue in heaven.

307   Lieb, Michael. "Reading God: Milton and the Anthropopa-
        thetic Tradition." *Milton Studies* 25 (1989): 213-43.
The concept of anthropopatheia defines God's nature not only
as "an anthropomorphic presence but as a passible being" (213), and
it considers whether he experiences emotions and how they may pro-

vide keys to his personality and readers' understanding of it. Dismissing the concept of anthropopatheia but accepting the idea of divine passibility, Milton in *Christian Doctrine* explains that, in Scripture, God accommodates or authors himself in an act of self-revelation; as interpreters of the Bible, readers must pursue a hermeneutics of intentionality to know him. The God of *Paradise Lost* experiences a full range of emotions that constitute essential attributes of him, not rhetorical maneuvers that make him the product of an anthropopathetic perspective. As the author of all being and meaning, God may be inaccessible but he enables readers to conceptualize him, primarily through the Son.

308   Low, Anthony. "Milton's God: Authority in *Paradise Lost.*" *Milton Studies* 4 (1972): 19-38.
        Predisposed to dislike all forms of authority, modern readers are not receptive to God's real personality in *Paradise Lost*. But Milton carefully distinguishes natural authority from the postlapsarian arbitrary forms that displace the divine universal order and its criterion of natural excellence. No person, Adam learns, has natural authority over another, though he does not see that sin forces humans to live in imperfect states and obey rulers, as long as they are reasonably just. Milton believes absolutely in God's goodness and total authority; in *Paradise Lost*, he represents perfect justice, beneficent power. Because he can speak in no other way, God sounds stern, powerful, and without humility, though his range of tone is fairly wide. While readers recognize that the Son embodies divine love, they fail to note that he always points to its source in the Father, whose character is defined by his Son and actions, particularly creative ones. During Adam's temptation, human love conflicts with divine love and withers because it is deprived of its source of being, God.

309   MacCaffrey, Isabel G[amble]. "The Theme of *Paradise Lost*, Book III." In *New Essays on "Paradise Lost,"* edited by Thomas Kranidas, 58-85. Berkeley: University of California Press, 1969.
        Paradise Lost's focus on God's treatment of humans shifts in Book 3 to an emphasis on how they can come to know God. In this book's invocation, the narrator leaves behind temporal limitations and leads into an overview of the world from the divine perspective, and the dialogue in heaven further conveys the distinction between human and divine understanding. God's speech to his creatures is his way of presenting the truth one cannot learn only by studying the creation.

Because the divine dialogue's material contains doctrine in debate form and shows God's foresight, it is meant to be heard by the mind's ear and thus its style carries no sensuous implications. If Book 3 deals with humanity's knowledge of God, the limbo of vanity episode and Satan's career show misguided efforts to take the heavenly kingdom. When this book rejoins Satan's journey, *Paradise Lost*'s normal mode of vision returns.

310   MacCallum, Hugh [R.]. *Milton and the Sons of God: The Divine Image in Milton's Epic Poetry*. Toronto: University of Toronto Press, 1986. x + 325 pp.

In the Bible, Milton's epics, and *Christian Doctrine*, the idea of divine sonship applies to God the Son, all believers (through the Son), and all humans because they are created in God's image. The Spirit frequently signifies not the third person in the Trinity but the Father's power and virtue, and the Son appears consistently as the Father's subordinate, who in Book 5 of *Paradise Lost* receives an elevated status in God's image or manifestation. When the Son offers to sacrifice himself for humanity, his redemptive role is inseparable from his divine nature, for he shows a development into the perfect image of the Father. Created in God's image and developing with the labor of choice through reason, unfallen Adam and Eve learn to evaluate the self, God, and everything else that expresses God. Through revelation, Adam learns of Christ, but his regeneration shows that God is the ultimate object of faith and one can proceed toward recovery without explicit knowledge of Christ as the source of its benefits. After the fall, Adam and Eve continue to grow, moving from repentance to natural renovation and then, with Michael's guidance, to saving faith and its promise of eternal life. They are engaged in the process of regaining God's image, and there are analogies and a continuity between the pre- and postlapsarian learning processes.

311   Miller, George Eric. "Stylistic Rhetoric and the Language of God in *Paradise Lost*, Book III." *Language and Style* 8 (1975): 111-26.

In *Paradise Lost*, speaking style defines moral distinctions between characters. Though there is little scriptural authority for God's speeches in Book 3, Milton uses an abundance of rhetorical figures— particularly balance, repetition, and word-play—"to establish the authoritative illusion, to signal the internal coherence, the rationality, that is God" (116). Despite the complex use of rhetorical ornamentation, God's plain style creates the illusion of coherence and clarity. See entries 24 and 425.

312   Murrin, Michael. "The Language of Milton's Heaven." *Modern Philology* 74 (1977): 350-65. Revised version in *The Allegorical Epic: Essays in Its Rise and Decline*, 153-71. Chicago, IL: University of Chicago Press, 1980.

Milton protects *Paradise Lost*'s scenes in heaven from a literalist reading and makes allegory impossible by inventing a special language derived from the Bible. His portrayal of God is especially indebted to the manifestation at Mount Sinai in Exodus; the Son's chariot comes from Ezekiel; and the source of heavenly ritual is Revelation. When he describes heaven, Milton uses similes to assert difference rather than likeness. Because heavenly terms refer to each other and similes here explain the known by pointing to the unfamiliar, they do not clarify the setting but instead remind readers that they have entered a self-contained world whose unknown language they cannot interpret. Milton's iconoclasm, his refusal to create images of even the true God, denies him the use of traditional analogical language, including allegory. Adopting prophetic techniques, he attempts to translate vision literature directly into epic narrative.

313   Nuttall, A. D. "*Paradise Lost.*" In *Overheard by God: Fiction and Prayer in Herbert, Milton, Dante and St. John*, 83-111. London: Methuen, 1980.

By giving the Father a speaking style governed by human precedent, Milton does not allow readers to mistake divine speech in *Paradise Lost* for God's real or probable thoughts. Milton shows an "ostentatious coarseness" and a "declaratory impulse" (86) by dealing directly with the character of God rather than veiling him in obscurity. Just as Adam's questions for Raphael reflect the author's curiosity, so the angel's responses, which rebuke and indulge his pupil's curiosity, show both Milton's confidence about his learning and an awareness of his limitations. His use of the doctrine of accommodation is complex, for the poet claims to describe a semblance that literally exists—God's personality, for example—yet he qualifies and contradicts this position. Much of the epic avoids accommodation, however, and belongs to the higher, unconfined order of metaphysical thought. Milton's myth presupposes exactly what it tries to explain (the existence of sin), which forces the narrative's explanatory structure to crumble. God must be the author or joint author of evil, the procurer of Satan's, Adam's, and Eve's falls. The story Milton chooses espouses Satan's cause, and God ends up being indefensible.

314   Patrides, C. A. "The Godhead in *Paradise Lost*: Dogma or Drama?" *JEGP: Journal of English and Germanic Philology* 64 (1965): 29-34. Reprinted in *Bright Essence: Studies in Milton's Theology*, by W. B. Hunter, C. A. Patrides, and J. H. Adamson, 71-77. Salt Lake City: University of Utah Press, 1971.

Although *Christian Doctrine* is a subordinationist document, *Paradise Lost* maintains the Godhead's unity and generally does not distinguish between the Father and the Son. But the epic contains discrepancies, as the Son is sometimes the apparently equal manifestation of the Father and at other times not his equal. The latter view occurs only during their verbal exchanges, satisfying the narrative's requirement for drama; the former view occurs primarily when members of the Godhead engage in action outside heaven, thus answering the demands of dogma with a portrayal of a unified Father and Son. That the demons in hell never refer to the Son further suggests that Milton has dramatic purposes for introducing a distinction between members of the Godhead.

315   Samuel, Irene. "The Dialogue in Heaven: A Reconsideration of *Paradise Lost*, III.1-417." *PMLA* 72 (1957): 601-11. Reprinted in *Milton: Modern Essays in Criticism*, edited by Arthur E. Barker, 233-45. London: Oxford University Press, 1965; reprinted in *Paradise Lost*, edited by Scott Elledge, 468-78. New York: W. W. Norton and Co., 1975.

Offering a sharp contrast to the demonic council, *Paradise Lost*'s dialogue in heaven conveys drama rather than dogma, defining God's nature as total being, an identity that makes the near tonelessness of his first speech appropriate. This passionless, logical voice encourages the Son's compassionate tone and argumentative stance. Some of the heavenly dialogue's drama is produced by the Son's lack of omniscience: he does not know that the death he volunteers to undertake will not be final; he must trust the goodness of the omnipotent Father. In reconciling his immutable moral law and his Son's trusting offer, God can adopt a loving, warm tone. His final statement no longer emphasizes humanity's redemption but instead the exaltation of the Son, who grows to virtual equality with the Father.

316   Shoaf, R. A. "'Our Names Are Debts': Messiah's Account of Himself." In *Reconsidering the Renaissance: Papers from the Twenty-First Annual Conference*, edited by Mario A. Di Cesare, 461-73. Binghamton, NY: Medieval and Renaissance Texts and Studies, 1992.

By accounting himself human before God, Christ reveals the manhood that separates him from but also saves the Father. Like language itself, Christ must go into debt (with God) to receive merit and meaning. Milton views writing itself as an account, formed for and because of his audience; readers' expectations form the debt he must pay. Christ's request for manhood becomes a moving appeal because, even as he takes responsibility for human errors, he allows himself to become indebted to all people by taking the name of humanity.

317   Waddington, Raymond B. "Here Comes the Son: Providential Theme and Symbolic Pattern in *Paradise Lost*, Book 3." *Modern Philology* 79 (1982): 256-66.

God's eye at the beginning of Book 3 is not an anthropomorphic representation but a figurative emblem that expresses his function, which is further symbolized in the image of the sun. If the eye of heaven suggests the sun, their figural interplay asserts eternal providence by revealing God's design, as manifested in the Incarnation of the Son or the risen sun. God foresees and benevolently orders, just as the sun sees all, regulates the world, and provides light, heat, and life. Because the distinction between the Father and the Son in *Paradise Lost* is merely a matter of accommodation, their dialogue in Book 3 makes explicit for human understanding what is implicit in the invocation: the providential eye, both the eye of God and of the world, reveals its plan for humanity's redemption through the Son's Incarnation as the world's light. The rest of Book 3 clarifies the subjects of Christ's agency, the actions that call for his intervention, and the form of that intervention.

318   West, Robert H. *Milton and the Angels*. Athens: University of Georgia Press, 1955. ix + 237 pp.

To account for what occurs without human agency and demonstrate God's administration of the universe, angelology is a living, very flexible study during Milton's age, though Protestants minimize all intermediaries between God and humans. The mature Milton believes in angels but is unwilling to go beyond scriptural authority and into theological speculation about such hidden matters. In *Paradise Lost*, his study of angelology, if not his precise sources, is evident. Not just machinery, as in other epics, Milton's angels have roles as characters. Much of the angelology in *Christian Doctrine* and *Paradise Lost* is orthodox, agreeing with the Bible or the views of Puritan angelologists. While Milton is indifferent to the science of angelology, the epic's heresies—including angelic digestion and love-making—address larger thematic and doctrinal matters by defining the similarities between heavenly and earthly life or the role of sexuality in each realm.

Other studies that examine Book 3 are identified in entries 21, 24, 33, 65, 97, 175, 231-32, 276, and 288.

13. BOOK 4

319   Anderson, Douglas. "Unfallen Marriage and the Fallen Imagination in *Paradise Lost.*" *Studies in English Literature, 1500-1900* 26 (1986): 125-44.

Milton conceives of paradise as unfallen marriage, which is shaped by his accommodation of hell, heaven, and paradise to the reader's fallen imagination. While hell is presented literally and heaven through hierarchies, paradise is treated figuratively because it is the most complex region in *Paradise Lost*. An open and vulnerable place, paradise is very demanding, as it conveys the final relationship between God and his creation, in which all barriers will vanish. The fallen reader's concepts of parent, child, and spouse are tested when Milton portrays the relationship between God and Adam, as well as Eve's creation from Adam's rib.

320   Bell, Ilona. "Milton's Dialogue with Petrarch." *Milton Studies* 28 (1992): 91-120.

Paradise Lost blends admiration of and a challenge to Petrarch, for "Milton represents Petrarchan love as the obverse and test of paradisal love" (92). While Petrarch's Laura is generally silent, enigmatic, and inaccessible, Milton's Eve is outspoken, practical, and at ease with her own body. A Petrarchan relationship between man and woman is characterized by absence and frustration, but Adam and Eve experience full satisfaction. Beginning in Eve's first moments of existence, God takes charge of her education, symbolically names her, and divinely authorizes her independent subjectivity and desire. The traditional Petrarchan woman, on the other hand, is objectified and supposed to mirror her lover's desires and thoughts. In an act that redefines love from the female point of view and undoes the assumptions of Petrarchan love, Eve eagerly yields to Adam because God teaches her to seek her own joy and because she finds Adam more physically appealing than herself. As Satan's relationship with Sin shows, he has "pseudo-Petrarchan" desires (106), and he is a committed Petrarchan love poet. After they sin, Adam and Eve assume the speaking style of self-absorbed Petrarchan lovers, emerging from isolation and misery through conversation and empathy. *Paradise Lost* uses Petrarchan imagery to reject Petrarchan ideology. See entry 336.

321   Blackburn, Thomas H. "'Uncloister'd Virtue': Adam and Eve in Milton's Paradise." *Milton Studies* 3 (1971): 119-37.
        Neither impure from the beginning nor incapable of choosing evil because they lack free will, Milton's Adam and Eve possess a knowledge of good and evil long before the fall. They are informed, sophisticated, and—until the climactic moment in Book 9—innocent, meaning they have committed no sinful act. Characterized not by an increase in knowledge, the fall marks a shift in the mode of one's knowledge of good and evil: before the fall, good is an actuality and evil a potentiality; after the fall, good recedes and becomes a potentiality, while evil is known as an actuality. Michael's narrative reveals how good and evil cleave together as twins in the postlapsarian world. Though knowledge in Eden implies knowledge by experience, from God's perspective the same knowledge poses no problem in heaven, where evil, from the moment of actualization, is turned to good. Unfallen or fallen humans cannot gain knowledge in this way.

322   Brooks, Cleanth. "Eve's Awakening." In *Essays in Honor of Walter Clyde Curry*, 281-98. Vanderbilt Studies in the Humanities, 2. Nashville, TN: Vanderbilt University Press, 1954. Reprinted in *Milton: Modern Judgements*, edited by Alan Rudrum, 173-88. London: Macmillan, 1968; reprinted in *A Shaping Joy*, 349-66. New York: Harcourt Brace Jovanovich, 1971.
        Created as a mature, perceptive person with a powerful intellect, Eve shows a sensitivity to beauty when gazing at her reflection in the lake. As Adam will have to do at *Paradise Lost*'s climax, she must choose between images. Milton's Eve "recapitulate[s] the whole process of the child's growing up and transferring the affections to the other sex" (353). When Adam is created, he seeks his maker's name and his own image, which God provides with Eve. The nature of the fall is implied in Adam's and Eve's creations. After eating of the fruit, a choice Eve makes based on pride and Adam makes based on selfishness masked as love, they gain self-consciousness.

323   Clark, Ira. "Milton and the Image of God." *JEGP: Journal of English and Germanic Philology* 68 (1969): 422-31.
        Far from being selfish, Milton's egotism is based on a sense of humanity's divinity and worth. God's image in *Paradise Lost* and the prose evokes the cycle of human perfection, fall, and potential regeneration through the recovery of the divine image. Formed like God, Adam and Eve have infinite worth, but their creation in the divine image foreshadows their fall as Adam recognizes his uniqueness and both characters see too much of God in her. The fall leads to a reduction of humanity's resemblance to the creator, as Michael teaches Adam, along with the lesson that belief in Christ's sacrifice leads to recovering God's image.

324   Coffin, Charles Monroe. "Creation and the Self in *Paradise Lost*." *ELH* 29 (1962): 1-18. Reprinted in *Kenyon Alumni Bulletin* 20 (1962): 11-17.
        Paradise Lost describes the relationship of the human and the divine outside secular history (before the fall) and within it, in the individual's personal and public life. In the epic's opening lines, Milton presents the pattern of the human-divine relationship in terms of "association, dissociation, and preparation for reassociation" (2). Because humans receive free will, they cannot lose or surrender their identity; when God, the "All" from whom all the multiplicity of particulars proceeds, merges with those particulars to become "All in All," everyone's identity is transformed yet not lost. Adam is alone when created, but he has a good rapport with heaven. Then his experience of nature develops and he undergoes the unsteady, complex process of self-realization accompanied by a sense of dependence and limitation. A more independent creature, Eve is in the precarious position of being "the supreme human particular emerging from creation's individuating process" (15). Adam and Eve must recognize their mutual interdependence to resolve the defective unity of self.

325   Daniells, Roy. "A Happy Rural Seat of Various View." In *"Paradise Lost": A Tercentenary Tribute*, edited by Balachandra Rajan, 3-17. Toronto: University of Toronto Press, 1969.
        Though walled in, *Paradise Lost*'s Eden seems open and provides its residents with a variety of landscapes; though open to visitors,

the garden is always orderly without being rigid and protective of
Adam and Eve's privacy. Adam looks not out from Eden but up to the
heavens, which enclose him without producing claustrophobia. Before
the fall, Adam and Eve form a charmed circle that Raphael strengthens
by explaining Eden's place in cosmic, moral, and temporal terms. With
the single exception of Raphael, Adam and Eve talk to no other angel
and only to each other before the fall. The garden's external beauty has
a correlative in the minds of Adam and Eve, an inner paradise that
gives their personalities meaning.

326   Davies, Stevie. "Milton." In *The Feminine Reclaimed: The
        Idea of Woman in Spenser, Shakespeare and Milton*, 175-247.
        Lexington: University Press of Kentucky, 1986.

        If various women, including Milton's first wife and daughter,
sabotage his patriarchal authority, his major characters use woman as
a scapegoat who receives the blame for all kinds of cosmic darkness.
This is a sign not of Milton's misogyny but of his thwarted idealism.
When Adam curses Eve, he knows her source is himself, yet he wants
to divide the wholeness of God-given human nature in the futile act of
divorcing male from female. *Paradise Lost* does not endorse this ugly
view. Woman in Milton's work is the source of enlightenment and confusion, as the invocations reveal by exploring the feminine as the elusive counterpart of the poet's own nature. An evolving figure, the female muse offers the stigmatized poet protection, infinite love, and an
archetype of a maternal role. Just as the epic's first image of the muse
incorporates both male and female, so the poet discovers that he, his
God, and the creation are all bisexual. Milton eventually finds an exact
affinity with the feminine. Contrary to his professed aim, *Paradise Lost*
reconciles contraries as it honors the bond of nature that is humanity's
life line to the feminine.

327   Duncan, Joseph E. *Milton's Earthly Paradise: A Historical
        Study of Eden*. Minneapolis: University of Minnesota Press,
        1972. ix + 329 pp.

        In describing paradise and Adam and Eve's life, Milton fol-
lows Genesis while freely expanding it and uses the classical idea of a
golden age or paradise, both considered pagan distortions of sacred
truth. While some early Christian commentators treat paradise as an
allegory, later eastern church fathers believe in it as a literal, historical
setting. Protestant writers of the Renaissance prefer rational, historical

accounts and argue that the flood destroys paradise. Both the law and the Gospel, according to Milton and Genesis 3.15, are revealed to Adam who, with Eve, also receives a conditional covenant of grace that extends to their descendants. Projecting his ideals back to a lost paradise, Milton emphasizes the individual's liberty in marriage, society, and worship. His paradise is simultaneously mythic and real, and it has a typological relationship to the celestial paradise.

328   Ferry, Anne [Davidson]. "Milton's Creation of Eve." *Studies in English Literature, 1500-1900* 28 (1988): 113-32.
        When he creates Eve, Milton must work with or around Genesis and the most authoritative New Testament interpretations of it, particularly the epistles of Peter and Paul. Milton distinguishes the sexes and has Adam created first, while modifying the Pauline interpretation by bringing Eve closer to her divine creator and stating that she shares sovereignty with Adam. Milton's Eve provides solace not servitude, cheerful conversation not a subordinate's silence. Before the fall, Milton thus "acknowledge[s] scriptural definitions of woman's nature and place, while elevating Eve above them to a stature that would make her a fit companion for Adam in marital conversation" (122). When Adam describes his feelings toward Eve, Raphael responds with Paul's view of woman's relation to man, which Adam corrects by insisting that marriage is a union of minds or souls. Milton's treatment of the fall, unlike traditional misogynistic renderings, balances sorrow and anger for both Adam and Eve. Confronted with their sin in Book 10, however, Adam is deviously self-exonerating and Eve is humbly penitent, an unscriptural, unbalanced presentation that makes Eve spiritually superior to Adam. Throughout *Paradise Lost*, Milton rescues her from the place that inescapable biblical authority assigns to woman's nature.

329   Froula, Christine. "When Eve Reads Milton: Undoing the Canonical Economy." *Critical Inquiry* 10 (1983): 321-47. Reprinted in *Canons*, edited by Robert von Hallberg, 149-75. Chicago, IL: University of Chicago Press, 1984.
        Feminist perspectives pose a radical challenge to the politics of canon formation and the very idea of the canon. An archetypal scene of canonical instruction, Eve's story of first waking in *Paradise Lost* tells about consigning her authority to Adam and through him to God, and then to the poem and finally to the ancient patriarchal tradition. But

she also recalls an origin innocent of patriarchal indoctrination when she stares in the pool, a moment the narrative presents as narcissistic. By leaving the watery image, Eve abandons her self, which she soon cedes to Adam by becoming his mirror and shadow, illustrating both how canonical authority converts believers from their own authority to a supposedly higher one and how patriarchal culture imprints itself on women's and men's minds. Eve internalizes the speeches and values of her mentors (the voice and Adam), speaks the views of the patriarchal authority, and reads it as the only one that exists. With the fall, she is punished for desiring experienced rather than mediated knowledge—that is, for reading outside the bounds of the cultural and poetic authority. At his birth, Adam projects an invisible God who institutes a hierarchy to compensate for the disparity he feels between himself and Eve. Both of these birth scenes reveal that "the repression of the mother is the genesis of Genesis" (337), a repression the poet participates in by transforming and silencing his female muse as he invokes the God of creation.

330   Frye, Northrop. "The Revelation to Eve." In *"Paradise Lost":*
        A Tercentenary Tribute, edited by Balachandra Rajan, 18-47.
        Toronto: University of Toronto Press, 1969.
        The relationship of unfallen Adam and Eve allows the male
only spiritual authority over the female. In the fallen world, the relationship between genders operates by analogy with the prelapsarian
one, with social supremacy replacing the spiritual. Requiring an object,
pride leads Adam to idolize Eve, and Eve to indulge in self-worship.
Milton associates the male principle in nature with sky, sun, wind, and
rain, the female with earth, moon, caves, waters, and flowers. One can
view nature in sensuous terms or, as Milton prefers, as an intelligently
created order, to which the poet in the ascent of eros looks for revelations of providence. In *Paradise Lost*, Eve receives two dreams—one
from Satan, a fantasy based on appetite, and the other from God, a
revelation of a serpent's defeat by a redeemer descended from her.

331   Giamatti, A. Bartlett. "Milton." In *The Earthly Paradise and*
        the Renaissance Epic, 295-355. Princeton, NJ: Princeton Uni-
        versity Press, 1966.
        Because Eden in *Paradise Lost* reflects everything within
Adam and Eve, it includes not only their innocence and perfection but
also their potential for change. Milton must describe innocence while

preparing for sin, a double perspective captured by the Satanic style's hints, implications, and allusions. Eden has traditional garden motifs, but beneath the surface other elements prepare readers for the fall: excessive comfort and pleasure and a lack of vitality, direction, and purpose. While readers know Adam, Eve, and their garden are perfect, allusions to sinful couples and gardens raise doubts. Most of the sinister echoes surround Eve, who is associated with sensuality, narcissism, and aspiration. Just as the theme of appearance (illusion or art) and reality (truth) is relevant to the first couple and Eden, so it is an explicit part of the fall. Adam and Eve first lose their garden spiritually, leaving an internal landscape of despair.

332   Grossman, Marshall. "Servile/Sterile/Style: Milton and the Question of Woman." In *Milton and the Idea of Woman*, edited by Julia M. Walker, 148-68. Urbana: University of Illinois Press, 1988.
        Though he has everything, Adam asks for company, so woman enters the creation in *Paradise Lost* as a lack that contains and sums up all. Adam is unable to see only one thing in Eden, a circumstance that changes when his rib becomes visible and he partakes with himself. But he cannot contain this other who is and is not himself; rather than holding her in his eye, he is drawn to her. The subjectification of Adam leads to the subjection of Eve because he is anxious about the autonomy of a creature who contains him. She is to be for Adam, but when she is for herself she is excessive. Though created to be an image for Adam, Eve first encounters her own image, which she is and which partakes with her. A voice draws her away with the promise of changing her name from the generic "woman" to "Mother of the human Race," a title she can fulfill only by investing her desire in Adam, whose image she is, and multiplying that image in their descendants.

333   Guillory, John. "From the Superfluous to the Supernumerary: Reading Gender into *Paradise Lost*." In *Soliciting Interpretation: Literary Theory and Seventeenth-Century English Poetry*, edited by Elizabeth D. Harvey and Katharine Eisaman Maus, 68-88. Chicago, IL: University of Chicago Press, 1990.
        In *Paradise Lost*, gender exists in relation to the master discourse of hierarchy, and it destabilizes that hierarchy only when interacting with alternative discourses, particularly the economic and scientific. In his account of creation and of humanity's first clothing, Milton

attempts to capture a gendered pre-oedipal moment, in which his (and the reader's) fears of fatherly judgment are delayed by a feeling of total motherness. When Adam and Eve question the workings of the universe, they initiate an economic discourse about different gendered modes of existence; to find a motive in their curiosity is to force a theological reading where none exists. As the movements of the cosmos collapse as an adequate theological justification of Eve's subjection, no single discourse emerges to uphold the gender hierarchy. Moving from the superfluous to the supernumerary, *Paradise Lost*'s apparently retrograde trajectory points to its eternal struggle with conflicting discourses.

334 Huntley, Frank L. "Before and After the Fall: Some Miltonic Patterns of Systasis." In *Approaches to "Paradise Lost,"* edited by C. A. Patrides, 1-14. London: Edward Arnold, 1968.
The pattern of systasis, or the dialectical union of two complementary opposites, forms an ideal third thing greater than the sum of its parts. In *Paradise Lost*, Milton uses different modes of systasis in such relationships as male-female, good-evil, and creator-creature. Adam and Eve, opposites capable of a tragic split, join in their bower before the fall in a union of minds and bodies that maintains their concern with both the earthly and the heavenly; after the fall, they exchange union with the good for separation from it, eventually reuniting with it to be redeemed. Though good and evil are opposites, in Milton's poetry they can always be mixed, for Satan remains an agent in God's overall plan. When earth will become heaven and vice versa, creator and creature merge in a synthesis greater than either.

335 Kermode, Frank. "Adam Unparadised." In *The Living Milton*, edited by Frank Kermode, 85-123. London: Routledge and Kegan Paul, 1960. Reprinted in *On Milton's Poetry*, edited by Arnold Stein, 134-50. Greenwich, CT: Fawcett Publications, 1970; reprinted in *Milton: "Paradise Lost," a Casebook*, edited by A. E. Dyson and Julian Lovelock, 179-203. London: Macmillan, 1973; reprinted in *Paradise Lost*, edited by Scott Elledge, 490-507. New York: W. W. Norton and Co., 1975.
Rather than being a monument to any ideas, *Paradise Lost* embodies "life in a great symbolic attitude" (86). Milton chooses an inclusive myth that contains the truth in little, and while omitting his heresies, he takes liberties with the myth to establish its universality.

Poetry, in his view, is counterlogical, appealing to the mind through the senses with its syntax and occasional use of rhyme. Throughout his career, Milton is devoted to the topic of Eden, handled most directly in *Paradise Lost*. Adam and Eve's prelapsarian sexuality is one of the corollaries of Milton's monism. No naturalist or libertine environment, the garden of love is approached through Satan's voyeuristic point of view, which interferes with readers' perceptions of Edenic purity and resembles their perceptions, which contrast innocence and experience. The theme of woe overshadowing joy dominates the epic.

336   Kerrigan, William, and Gordon Braden. "Milton's Coy Eve: *Paradise Lost* and Renaissance Love Poetry." *ELH* 53 (1986): 27-51. Reprinted in *John Milton's "Paradise Lost,"* edited by Harold Bloom, 133-56. New York: Chelsea House, 1987; revised in *The Idea of the Renaissance*, 191-218. Baltimore, MD: Johns Hopkins University Press, 1989.
        Petrarchan poetry exchanges frustration in love for fame and the woman for her image, while libertine poetry comments on the unfulfilling nature of sexual consummation, sometimes calling for anti-fruition in undecaying desire. In *Paradise Lost*, Adam and Eve's sexual connection is a poetically imagined version of the Renaissance's dominant sexual fantasy, in which men aggressively chase, women are coyly ambiguous, and finally the woman gives signs she will yield. Eve's experience at the pool is imitated in Adam's later pursuit and her flight. She knows the erotic value of modesty and withholding, of the "sweet reluctant amorous delay" (4.311) that protects love by incorporating an obstacle to save sexual desire and its object from decay. The game of chase and capture, while it daily reaffirms Eve's worth, leads Adam to abase himself before her as an idol. Since female worth is central to the chase, Eve tempts Adam by making him again calculate her value. The love hunt undergoes a sinister transformation in the last act of eroticism in paradise. See entry 320.

337   Knight, Douglas. "The Dramatic Center of *Paradise Lost*." *South Atlantic Quarterly* 63 (1964): 44-59.
        As the main way to integrate readers into *Paradise Lost*'s "non-naturalistic worlds" (45), Milton's highly allusive similes call for their participation by showing intellectual action existing as a way of comprehension. The similes stand between readers and the narrative events in the early books, creating a focus for descriptions and actions

far removed from the real world. When readers examine these increasingly complex and demanding similes, they must understand them as part of the action and commentaries on it. Not a monolithic entity, *Paradise Lost* requires different points of view and assumptions at different times, such as when Satan appears in hell or God is introduced in heaven. The war in heaven in Book 6 is closely related to other events, presents a kind of dumb show for the epic's central action, and reveals Satan as a character of apparently heroic resistance who has power only over Adam and Eve. Books 11-12 create a fit future for Adam and Eve's descendants as well as a fit past, present, and future for the reader, who is now closely connected to the poem's material and structure as participant and subject. In Adam and Eve's discovery of a character and course of action, readers see *Paradise Lost*'s dramatic center.

338   Knott, John R., Jr. *Milton's Pastoral Vision: An Approach to "Paradise Lost."* Chicago, IL: University of Chicago Press, 1971. xv + 180 pp.

"An epic with a pastoral center" (xii), *Paradise Lost* presents Eden both as a state of being and a place for a harmonious life. Nature in Eden leads one to God, its author and the source of all goodness; after the fall, humanity is alienated from him and so must work to attain an internal paradise. Milton reshapes the tradition of the earthly paradise to create an ordered, idealized scene with sensuous details and a dynamic character. In Eden, life has a well-defined pattern, a rhythm of daily activities and natural cycles in which noon, the time of the fall, is important. By insisting on working alone, Eve lacks an interest in patterns of human behavior; by failing to return at noon, she sins against the order of nature. Milton uses pastoral values to test the epic hero's traditional virtues and destroys "the illusion of an inviolable pastoral world" (122). In his age, the opposition of garden and city has theological significance: Eden and the city cannot coexist on earth, for they symbolize antithetical states of being.

339   Landy, Marcia. "'A Free and Open Encounter': Milton and the Modern Reader." *Milton Studies* 9 (1976): 3-36.

Exploring the importance of communication, Milton elevates reciprocity and views language as the means to create and enhance social solidarity. Satan attacks all tradition and morality without differentiation, while the poet's sense of authority relations is hierarchical, recognizing differences and internalized notions of merit. By dichotomizing women's behavior in terms of virtue and deviancy, Milton's poetry circumscribes their roles. Creativity in *Paradise Lost* affirms meaningful relations and, by setting limits and establishing hierarchies, it is the means to transcend the oppressiveness of the self. Although Adam and Eve must act within limits, his are broader, so the ideas of order and mutuality come into opposition. Eve is portrayed stereotypically in *Paradise Lost*, free only within the social and familial context and identified as a Satanic deviant who violates boundaries. Woman's role must remain in the context of the domestic relations whose principle Milton considers of heroic proportion. While Eve has a limited capacity as a poet, in Milton's work the female muse inspires but the man articulates the poem. The portrayal of the Lady in *Comus*, though she resists temptation, resembles that of Eve, and Dalila's role in *Samson Agonistes* similarly reaffirms Milton's view of women and hierarchy.

340   Landy, Marcia. "Kinship and the Role of Women in *Paradise Lost*." *Milton Studies* 4 (1972): 3-18.
        Not a misogynist, Milton is a representative Protestant poet of his age who believes in the centrality of marriage and defines the man's role as creator and woman's as submissive procreator. As siblings in *Paradise Lost*, Adam is identified with the Father and Eve with nature, the Son as an exalted, obedient offspring and Satan as an aspiring, disobedient one. As marriage partners, Adam and Eve appear to have equal roles, but Adam's speeches echo God's firmness and ultimate intelligence, while Eve's are nonanalytic, nostalgic, and submissive. Although the sibling and marital relationships are not in conflict for Adam and Eve, Satan and Sin's relationships—parent and child, husband and wife—are incestuous and thus perverse and threatening to the sanctity of the nuclear family. Woman is excluded from heaven but appears in hell and on earth to play her main role of mother-wife, receive no authority, and be associated with lust, rape, and incest. The postlapsarian problems between Adam and Eve, including duplicity and subversion of hierarchy, mirror those between God and Satan. To restrain the unnatural, antisocial oppositions to her role, Eve must undergo a transformation of attitude: she learns her place, acts submissive, and is put to sleep while the more intelligent Adam learns from Michael.

341   Lewalski, Barbara Kiefer. "Innocence and Experience in Mil-
       ton's Eden." In *New Essays on "Paradise Lost,"* edited by
       Thomas Kranidas, 86-117. Berkeley: University of California
       Press, 1969.
       Edenic life in *Paradise Lost* involves "radical growth and pro-
cess" as it becomes more complex, challenging, and perfect (88). Just
as everything is made from chaos, so it can regress to that state unless
a creative force continually acts upon it, as the paradisal garden illustrates by tending to profusion and wildness. As gardeners of internal
and external regions, Adam and Eve imitate God's creative act, yet
they are also his fruit or harvest, which requires constant cultivation.
Milton's first couple, unlike traditional portrayals, has sexual relations,
is subject to perturbations, and lives in a monistic universe based on a
fluid hierarchy. Adam and Eve grow by trial and error, particularly
with Raphael's help.

342   Lewalski, Barbara K[iefer]. "Milton on Women—Yet Again."
       In *Problems for Feminist Criticism*, edited by Sally Minogue,
       46-69. London: Routledge, 1990.
       In general, critics view Milton's writing about women in two
ways: as antifeminist because it enforces women's subordination to the
purposes of a patriarchal social structure, and women must respond
with deconstructive or oppositional readings; or as protofeminist because it challenges, modifies, or radically revises the assumptions of
seventeenth-century patriarchy, and these readers historicize Milton's
texts as documents or objects of interpretation. His poems invite a
constructive attention to their complex representations of women and
gender relations, and especially to their recognition of women's worth,
strength, abilities, and freedom. In *Paradise Lost*, Eve's nature is equal
and somehow inferior to Adam's, for ideology and experience sometimes conflict and Milton has an unusually fluid conception of hierarchy. Her role is to share with Adam the entire range of human activities, including education and labor; but the construction of her
identity—indeed, of each identity in the epic—occurs in and through
relationships as well as independent action. Milton insists on Eve's
intellectual capacity and individual moral responsibility, attributes that
undercut patriarchal assumptions. Because he places her at the center
of the separation scene, shows her extensive dramatic dialogue and
soliloquies during the temptation, and has her respond first to prevenient grace, "it is hardly an exaggeration to say that Milton's epic turns

into an Eviad" (58). *Paradise Lost* offers a critique of patriarchy and
traditionally male epic values; Milton honors the traditionally female
qualities displayed by Eve and the Son.

343   Lewalski, Barbara K[iefer]. "Milton on Women—Yet Once
        More." *Milton Studies* 6 (1974): 3-20.
        Distinguished women Miltonists have not written feminist anal-
yses of his work because great art transcends such matters as race,
class, or gender and addresses readers' common humanity; because
such commentary often substitutes sociological for literary analysis,
thus limiting and distorting the framework for examining Milton's re-
creation of the myth of Adam and Eve; and because great artists' visions of human experience are necessarily mediated by the categories
available to them. Few authors of any age have taken women so seriously as Milton does, presenting them as multifaceted human beings
with "impressive intellectual and moral powers and responsibilities"
(6). Before the fall in *Paradise Lost*, Eve participates fully in—and
shares with Adam—the whole range of human activities, including
learning from Raphael, laboring in the garden, conversing with rhetorical skill, and creating poetry. Though she is portrayed as Adam's
inferior in the hierarchy, Milton's presentation of her role as mother of
humanity, like Adam's as father, asserts dignity and honor, not restric-
tion. Her maternal role is neither prior to nor the sanction for her roles
as lover and spouse; rather, Milton emphasizes marriage as human
companionship. Inextricably interdependent, Adam and Eve must still
make their own individual choices.

344   Lieb, Michael. "'Two of Far Nobler Shape': Reading the
        Paradisal Text." In *Literary Milton: Text, Pretext, Context*,
        edited by Diana Treviño Benet and Michael Lieb, 114-32.
        Pittsburgh, PA: Duquesne University Press, 1994.
        When Milton introduces Adam and Eve in Book 4 of *Paradise
Lost*, a Satanic perspective and a language of seeming or indeterminacy
compromise any assertions about the relationship of first man to first
woman based on automatic distinctions of gender. As readers interpret
the paradisal text, they try to transcend such a perspective even as they
install themselves within it. A text within a text, the pronouncement
that Adam and Eve are "Not equal," and all similar claims in this
scene, may be either Satan's discourse or the narrator's. Milton imposes a postlapsarian perspective on his prelapsarian account when the

New Testament views of Paul echo through the passages about gender relationships. *Paradise Lost* thus calls into question both the Pauline paradigm in the Bible and the appropriation of that paradigm to support the sexual politics of *Christian Doctrine*. In *Tetrachordon*, Milton invents his own superior law to counter the gender inequality that Paul advocates. *Paradise Lost* encodes a discourse of conflict and indeterminacy that prevents readers from reaching a final interpretation of sexual politics.

345   Lindenbaum, Peter. "Milton's Paradise." In *Changing Landscapes: Anti-Pastoral Sentiment in the English Renaissance*, 136-79. Athens: University of Georgia Press, 1986.

Milton makes no consistent and definite distinction between human life before and after the fall in *Paradise Lost*. Prelapsarian life in Eden, though complex and filled with educative growth, is a simplified version of fallen life, a correspondence that allows readers to see similarities between themselves and Adam and Eve. Belial may argue for a life of the mind in Book 2, but the narrator denounces it and refuses to give a fair presentation of its superiority, even when portraying Edenic existence. Instead, Adam and Eve need to perform physical labor, which is more toilsome than the poem initially suggests because the garden is profuse and threatening. In Book 9's separation scene, Eve has some justification for arguing that God requires a day's worth of labor, though readers recognize her literal-minded error. The narrator considers prelapsarian sexual love the crown of Eden's blessings, a view that helps readers appreciate Adam's motives when he chooses to fall, yet he also implies that becoming enamored at all and at any time is wrong. When Adam is faced with temptation, Milton distances readers from him by making Eve an unattractive liar and reduces the tension by having Adam treat his decision as a foregone conclusion.

346   McColley, Diane Kelsey. *A Gust for Paradise: Milton's Eden and the Visual Arts*. Urbana: University of Illinois Press, 1993. xviii + 305 pp. 60 illustrations.

Like many contemporary poets, artists, and musicians, Milton sees the creation story as a wellspring of regenerative art. Adam and Eve are primal artists who represent an innocence that leads to intellectual, moral, erotic, and spiritual growth. Milton makes a large contribution to the relation of the sexes when he combines the height of

sensuous delight with the Reformation view of marriage as a divine institution, and when he portrays Eve as "a spiritually equal companion
capable of graceful, earnest conversation and active accomplishment"
(96). Splendid artists, Adam and Eve engage in such acts as poetic
speech, music, and the rudiments of dance and dramatic play that enhance the earth, community, and soul. Eve embodies and performs
many of the properties and processes that Milton also attributes to
poetry itself or to himself as poet. *Paradise Lost*'s account of the fall
detoxifies various motifs associated with Eve and defuses the possibility
that sin brings pleasure, maturity, or civilized arts. Milton develops a
language that keeps the connectedness and wholeness of God's providence before the mind. He writes "eco-verse" (184).

347   McColley, Diane Kelsey. *Milton's Eve*. Urbana: University of
       Illinois Press, 1983. viii + 232 pp. 8 illustrations.
            Unlike the literary and iconographic traditions dealing with
Eve, *Paradise Lost* presents a woman whose virtues and talents encourage readers to reconsider her character and see its relevance to the
process of their regeneration. The portrait of Adam and Eve's original
and regenerate states refutes the stale antifeminist commonplaces of
Milton's age as well as Adam's fallen diatribes against woman. Prelapsarian Edenic life is based on fruitful chastity, free obedience, and rational delight for both sexes; Eve's subordination to Adam, modeled on
the Son's relationship to God, does not imply inferiority. The episode
in which she admires her reflection in the water, like her Satanic
dream, is a good temptation, intended by God to prove the righteous-
ness that prefigures not her fall but her initiating movement toward
reconciliation after it. By showing gardening as part of a creative, productive, responsible, and active life, and as a pattern for regeneration
in the world, Milton departs from most traditional views, though he
develops parts of the classical pastoral, patristic, and Protestant ideas
about humanity's first estate. Far from being sinful before the fall, Eve
is right to seek inward faith and virtue, but Satan deconstructs God's
terms to undermine her faith during the temptation. The judgment of
Adam and Eve restores their original callings and promises a redeemer.

348   Martin, Catherine Gimelli. "Demystifying Disguises: Adam,
       Eve, and the Subject of Desire." In *Renaissance Discourses of
       Desire*, edited by Claude J. Summers and Ted-Larry Peb-
       worth, 237-58. Columbia: University of Missouri Press, 1993.

Although appearances suggest a male-controlled hierarchy, all boundaries in Eden—including gender roles—are determined by individual choice, so Eve's subjection is more apparent than real. The account of Eve's creation does not necessarily prove that differences imply inequality, but by itself it does not disprove the inferiority of her desires. However, when Eve's creation is compared to Adam's, it becomes clear that both humans require divine guidance and that their differences are of degree, not kind. All attempts to subordinate Eve to Adam in a gender hierarchy are undone by role reversals and Adam's repeated habit of following Eve's example. The fall can be seen as both Adam's and Eve's inability to accept the complementarity of each other's gifts—an acceptance that is the basis of both earthly and heavenly union.

349   Peczenik, F[annie]. "Fit Help: The Egalitarian Marriage in *Paradise Lost*." *Mosaic* 17 (1984): 29-48.
        Applying fallen values to Edenic life, readers perceive a hierarchy in which Adam dominates Eve. Milton thus tests readers by stressing conventional views of women that are options for Adam and Eve to consider and reject, and for readers to use in misinterpreting the myth of an ideal past. Before the fall in *Paradise Lost*, marriage has no hierarchy; man and woman live in a divinely ordained state of perfect reciprocity. Adam asks for and receives an equal, Raphael teaches that reciprocity supersedes hierarchy, but Satan invents misogyny and promotes a hierarchical world view. In Milton's epic, equality carries implications not about worth or power but about a spiritual state in God, a point Adam misunderstands when he speaks to Raphael. If Adam too quickly assumes that male superiority is correct, Eve sometimes elevates him too much. After they fall, God's judgment institutes a domestic hierarchy that forces Adam to live without an equal, without the female part of his soul, and Eve to live as the victim of male anger that produces subjection and misogyny.

350   Rosenblatt, Jason P. "Eden, Israel, England: Milton's Spiritual Geography." In *All Before Them: 1660-1780*, edited by John McVeagh, 49-63. Vol. 1 of *English Literature and the Wider World*. General editor Michael Cotsell. London: Ashfield Press, 1990.
        Milton's celebration of the external world is balanced by a sense of its instability and inferiority. In *Paradise Lost*, he creates a

conjunction between Eden and Israel (or paradise and Jerusalem), with England (or London) as the implied final member of the triad of geographic locations and spiritual states. Although Milton acknowledges discontinuities in the religion of Eden, Israel, and contemporary London, he transfers terms between dispensations to emphasize the continuity of God's ways with his creatures. Jerusalem, placed in the triad's center, allows Eden to become intimate with England in *Paradise Lost*. Just as the pagan idols invade Jerusalem, Satan attacks Eden and rioters disrupt Restoration London. An exile, Milton in the end rejects the physical even as he longs for the Eden, Jerusalem, and England of his dreams.

351   Schoenfeldt, Michael C. "Gender and Conduct in *Paradise Lost*." In *Sexuality and Gender in Early Modern Europe: Institutions, Texts, Images*, edited by James Grantham Turner, 310-38. Cambridge: Cambridge University Press, 1993.

Paradise Lost builds on and revises the Renaissance standards of feminine behavior outlined in Castiglione's *Courtier* and Guazzo's *Civile Conversation*. Both works address female empowerment, but carefully avoid disturbing the socially constructed Renaissance gender hierarchy. Although Milton's epic ostensibly embraces a similar ranking of gender, the imagery and language surrounding Adam and Eve suggest a tension between submission and authority that implies equality and even Eve's superiority. In *Paradise Lost*, as in the world of the court, obedience brings power; Eve's submission to Adam provides the model for humanity's redemptive submission before God. Transcending the contemporary social structure, Milton places a creative and socially active Eve at the origin of humanity.

352   Simons, John. "All About Eve: Woman in *Paradise Lost*." In *Jacobean Poetry and Prose: Rhetoric, Representation and the Popular Imagination*, edited by Clive Bloom, 213-25. New York: St. Martin's Press, 1988.

Although Eve's initial perception of herself—as she literally passes through Lacan's mirror stage—is one of completion, she soon discovers that she is a reflection of an Other, Adam, and finds meaning only in him. Unlike Adam, who is created and continues complete, Eve must repress her early feelings of completion and instead find a new unity through the acquisition of a phallus, the serpent. Eve represents Milton's attempt to portray female psychology, but, despite his efforts to treat her fairly, her repeated repression creates a tense undercurrent throughout the epic. Eve threatens *Paradise Lost* because of her clash with the master codes that impose hierarchy and because of the threat she poses as an Other—as a being who seeks re-completion through transgression.

353   Swaim, Kathleen M. "'Hee for God Only, Shee for God in Him': Structural Parallelism in *Paradise Lost*." *Milton Studies* 9 (1976): 121-49.
        Eve's relationship with Adam parallels and provides experiential guidelines for understanding his changing and deepening relationship with a divine agency that must remain mysterious. Just as Eve's love lyric to Adam (4.641-56) parallels and provides material for Adam's conversation with Raphael (8.15-38), so the relationships are analogous. During the separation scene, Adam applies to Eve the angel's advice to "be lowly wise," though when tempted he forgets this very lesson. Adam and Eve's dialogue in Book 9 presents a dramatic adumbration of doctrine, bringing Raphael's narrative into focus and humanizing Book 3's abstract theories of free will. Eve's prayer that Adam not forsake her implies a parallel in God's not forsaking Adam, which occurs with the descent of prevenient grace. With Adam, readers see the self and the world downward through Eve to the concrete and upward through divine agencies to the mysterious realm of faith.

354   Toliver, Harold E. "Milton's Household Epic." *Milton Studies* 9 (1976): 105-20.
        Creating a "household notion of the heroic" (106), Milton in *Paradise Lost* focuses on a married couple who will become archetypal parents, though contemporaries often argue for a connection between heroism and high social class and an alliance of divine and royal modes. But Milton believes civil power should be the executive arm of spiritual reform; the epic is a statement on behalf of a moral revolution in which reformation and heroic dignity work together. In the portrait of Adam and Eve, the poem offers an idyllic dream of dignity for each gender as well as a model, based on labor, pleasure, and order, for restoring honor to contemporary households. Their lives merge the domestic and the divine, as their marriage forms the foundation of spiritual life. Even after the fall, Milton uses Adam and Eve's relationship to refute the heroic tradition by showing that being elevated depends on humility and the awareness of one's lack of dignity.

Book 4 183

355   Toliver, Harold [E.]. "Symbol-Making and the Labors of Milton's Eden." *Texas Studies in Literature and Language* 18 (1976): 433-50.
Symbol-making, Adam and Eve's central preoccupation in *Paradise Lost*, coordinates their other roles, the creation of poetry being an occasional, spontaneous household function modeled on the order and beauty that inspire them. Having part of the Word's creative ordinance, Adam perceives particular things and then the synchronic system of analogies that links them, a progressive, inductive process that is both his linguistic skill and Eden's challenge to him. Because he sees and his songs show that all things express God, Adam, unlike Satan, needs no violent mental activity to place apparently contradictory objects in verbal harmony. He observes the cosmos and then creates a responsive style whose rhythm pleases him. When Adam and Eve are apart, Satan presents a new alliance for Eve, a set of rationalizations for it, and an assault on the principles of order, including hymnal poetic order, on which innocent Adam relies. All aspects of language and perception are redefined after the fall, when they can serve Adam and Eve's illicit urges or help them renew their dialogue with God by petitioning him for redemption.

356   Wilding, Michael. "'Thir Sex Not Equal Seem'd': Equality in *Paradise Lost*." In *Of Poetry and Politics: New Essays on Milton and His World*, edited by P. G. Stanwood, 171-85. Binghamton, NY: Medieval and Renaissance Texts and Studies, 1995.
When Milton introduces Adam and Eve in *Paradise Lost* 4.284-318, "The male supremacist, anti-egalitarian, and absolutist sentiments are proclaimed with an extraordinary brusqueness" (172), yet they lack firmness and clarity. The passage is in fact permeated with uncertainty and equivocation. This description of Adam and Eve also records Satan's interpretive vision or projection, which is the political, hierarchical, and authoritarian perspective that he imports from hell. By negating his negation, readers can deduce the true appearance of paradise. Elsewhere in the epic, absolutism and hierarchies of birth, rank, caste, or class are absent from discussions of Adam and Eve's relationship. But a hierarchy of merit, or moral and spiritual development, with its flowing scale of ascent, subverts fixed political or social or gender roles. Subordination or inequality is a Satanic practice in the fallen world. In *Paradise Lost*, Milton connects gender equality to the

issue of common ownership of all things as part of his revolutionary goal—total human equality.

357   Wittreich, Joseph. "'Inspir'd with Contradiction': Mapping Gender Discourses in *Paradise Lost.*" In *Literary Milton: Text, Pretext, Context*, edited by Diana Treviño Benet and Michael Lieb, 133-60. Pittsburgh, PA: Duquesne University Press, 1994.

As a site from which readers may observe the crevices and contradictions within received myth and ideology, *Paradise Lost* maps misogynous, patriarchal, and feminist discourses with competing but not equally authoritative voices, each of which marks a different state and stage of consciousness. Milton's epic is "mapped by—and a mapping of—debates between the sexes in the seventeenth century" (136). By problematizing Scripture and its interpretive traditions, Milton reminds readers of the incorrect inferences that fallen humans can make. Always partial, truth in *Paradise Lost* is a process, with resolution appearing through gradual revelation. To point to different stages and states of consciousness, Milton accommodates the idealism and mutuality of the sexes in Genesis 1 (Raphael's view) and the unequal relationship of the sexes in Genesis 2 (Adam's view). *Paradise Lost* revises the interpretive traditions that it encodes, negotiating or nullifying human authorities and recuperating divine authority by using the Bible as a sanction for women's rights and sexual equality.

358   Wittreich, Joseph. "'John, John, I Blush for Thee!' Mapping Gender Discourses in *Paradise Lost.*" In *Out of Bounds: Male Writers and Gender(ed) Criticism*, edited by Laura Claridge and Elizabeth Langland, 22-54. Amherst: University of Massachusetts Press, 1990.

In its contradictions, especially concerning sexuality, *Paradise Lost* critiques the traditions and ideologies that inform it. Despite the epic's apparent early agreement with Pauline sexual doctrine, the middle and later books question and then overturn traditional notions of female subjection, leaving Adam and Eve as equals when they depart from paradise. The last two books show Eve using a poetic voice of the kind that vexed seventeenth-century advocates of patriarchal values. Through her song, Eve—much like Miriam, Ruth, and Deborah—exhibits a heroism greater than Adam's, because of its gender neutrality and willingness to elevate Adam as a copartner. Milton's ultimate contribution is the deconstruction of gender conventions, implicit in the confrontation between and consciousness of patriarchal values and feminism.

359   Zimmerman, Shari A. "Milton's *Paradise Lost*: Eve's Struggle for Identity." *American Imago* 38 (1981): 247-67.

Surrendering her identity almost at the start, Eve tries to regain it throughout *Paradise Lost*. She is initially fused with an objective and subjective environment; the reflection in the lake, which she does not recognize, produces pathos in her, but a voice urges her to define the vision as narcissistic. She longs to return to this "positive affirmation of her primary identity" (250). Adam's narcissistic needs force her to relinquish this identity and become his echo, stifling her selfhood and making her uncomfortable in their relationship. In Eve's dream, Satan offers her another perspective beyond Adam's, dividing her from Adam and the landscape in a state of delightful separateness and horrific isolation. Returning to the landscape, Eve affirms her identity by tending to the flowers while Adam and Raphael talk. An interest in autonomy from a restrictive relationship leads her to ask Adam about dividing their labors, even though separation frightens her. The demonic temptation comes at the critical moment when Eve wishes to escape the union with Adam that would smother her identity, and a relationship with Satan—the poem's master isolationist—offers her the opportunity to protect herself from Adam's love. Eve sees the fruit as a way to manage and maintain separateness, or a sense of exclusion that soon becomes a confining problem, leading her to seek reunion with Adam. She can maintain her identity only by balancing union and separation.

Other studies that examine Book 4 are identified in entries 53, 58, 151, and 175.

14. BOOKS 5-8

360   Adamson, J. H. "Milton and the Creation." *JEGP: Journal of English and Germanic Philology* 61 (1962): 756-78. Reprinted in *Bright Essence: Studies in Milton's Theology*, by W. B. Hunter, C. A. Patrides, and J. H. Adamson, 81-102. Salt Lake City: University of Utah Press, 1971.

The power of *Paradise Lost*'s creation scene comes in part from the *ex Deo* theory, according to which God created the world out of himself rather than from nothing or some eternal coexistent matter. Not particularly orthodox, this theory has a long tradition, beginning with Plotinus and including Gregory of Nyssa, and it usually describes the creation in terms of the sun's light flowing out to penetrate all levels of being before returning to its divine source. According to the *ex Deo* theory's tradition, the Logos is not of God's essence but his substance, and it is the first emanation from him—the metaphysical light and first form—in the hierarchy of life. Milton agrees with many parts of the *ex Deo* theory's views: God, though unknowable, can best be understood by describing what he is not (the *via negativa*), often with images of darkness; everything that emanates from him will ultimately return to him; if all life comes from him, no being can be finally annihilated; and a plurality of worlds exists.

361   Allen, Michael. "Divine Instruction: *Of Education* and the Pedagogy of Raphael, Michael, and the Father." *Milton Quarterly* 26 (1992): 113-21.

Raphael and Michael respectively represent mild stimulation of inquiry and firm enforcement of virtuous obedience—opposing elements of Milton's ideal but paradoxical teaching style, as explained in *Of Education*. Only the Father achieves Milton's goal of balancing rather than resolving the polarities. Even Raphael, while able to draw Adam's mind from earthly to higher matters, loses control of the lesson, eventually overcompensating by harshly rebuking Adam's feelings for Eve. Despite the understandably burdensome task of narrating the course of human history in a single afternoon, Michael makes the mistake of taking too much control; he becomes the lecturer who discourages meaningful questioning. By prompting Adam just enough to force him to articulate his thoughts, the Father allows the first human to develop his rational nature. *Paradise Lost*'s teaching methods are part of Milton's social and religious philosophies.

362   Bell, Robert H. "'Blushing Like the Morn': Milton's Human
       Comedy." *Milton Quarterly* 15 (1981): 47-55.
       When Adam in Book 8 describes how he met and was united with Eve, his narrative is comic in conveying mirth and being structured as a miniature romantic comedy: a hero has a desire, faces obstacles, and overcomes them. He is momentarily a self-conscious narrator, for he begins his story by echoing Raphael's introduction to the war in heaven episode. Adam's narrative is not a cosmic epic but a domestic one in which he freely portrays himself as a bewildered and triumphant comic figure. In his comic romance, God is a responsive, playful character who initially blocks the hero's desire and later fulfills it. Eve's first appearance to Adam is quickly followed by her withdrawal, which enhances his sexual anticipation and teaches him the meaning of true loneliness. When Adam tells of the first sexual act, he is transported and curious about whether his intense response to Eve is wrong. That his response is actually only half wrong makes Raphael's high-minded answer appear harsh; Adam turns the tables by inquiring about angelic love, and the self-conscious Raphael hastily concludes the conversation.

363   Bundy, Murray W. "Milton's Prelapsarian Adam." *Research
       Studies of the State College of Washington* 13 (1945): 163-84.
       Reprinted in *Milton: Modern Judgements*, edited by Alan Rudrum, 151-72. London: Macmillan, 1968.
       By dividing Book 7 for the 1674 edition of *Paradise Lost*, Milton clarifies his focus, in the new Book 8, on the human capacity to understand and willingness to accept the creation. Just before the fall, an entire book deals with Adam's moral and intellectual nature, rationality as one made in God's image, and liability to fall. His questions about astronomy show a dangerous inability or unwillingness to accept the philosophy of creation that Raphael just concluded, which emphasized subordination of means to ultimate ends and thus the law of obedience. Merely a hypothesis presented for the sake of argument, Raphael's statement about a heliocentric universe replies to Adam's

superficial reasoning and prepares him for an intellectual and moral test. Unlike Eve, Adam is a healthy extrovert who, in his first moments of existence, infers the creator's existence and has a sense of himself as a thinking subject in relation to objects to be apprehended. His dream is contrasted to Eve's to show that he is not susceptible to the kind of temptation that can influence her. Adam's susceptibility to sin occurs when beauty, fancy, and the appetites are allied, leading him to misrepresent the hierarchical positions of God, Eve, and himself when he tells Raphael about excessive passion. He lacks faith in wisdom.

364   Campbell, Gordon. "Milton's Theological and Literary Treat-
        ments of the Creation." *Journal of Theological Studies* 30
        (1979): 128-37. Translation of "La Creación Según Ideas
        Theológicas y Literarias de Milton." *Káñina* 2 (1978): 99-108.
        Christian Doctrine presents the unorthodox view of creation *ex
Deo*, outlines the creation's formal and final causes, and then considers its efficient and material causes. In this part of the tract, Milton's heterodoxy appears in two assertions: everything has a material cause and the creation's material cause must therefore be God, in whom matter is inherent; and the creation is by the Father but through the Son as the secondary efficient cause or a kind of effect. *Paradise Lost*, on the other hand, does not inquire into the creation's various causes or agree with *Christian Doctrine*'s argument. When he writes of the crea-tion in his epic, Milton uses its final and efficient causes to implement his prophetic aim of interpreting God to his people and the formal cause to fulfill his priestly role by publicly celebrating the creation's goodness. Unlike *Christian Doctrine*, *Paradise Lost* does not depreciate the Son's role in creation. Instead of analyzing the creation for intel-lectual satisfaction, Raphael celebrates it to help Adam and the reader have a worshipful attitude.

365   Champagne, Claudia M. "Adam and His 'Other Self' in *Para-
        dise Lost*: A Lacanian Study in Psychic Development." *Milton
        Quarterly* 25 (1991): 48-59.
        The narcissism that eventually causes Adam to fall originates in his awareness of a void within himself, a void that only his Other—Eve—can fill. Unlike Eve, Adam is denied the identity that accompa-nies Jacques Lacan's mirror stage, but he receives symbolic awareness of himself and his environment by interacting with the authority created by and embodied in the Father. In asking for a mate, Adam attempts

to mirror in himself the completeness he sees in God and animals, but he misinterprets Eve as a loss of himself; thus, she becomes both wounder and healer. Once Eve is created, Adam sees her as he wants to—as the self-completing mirror image he was once denied. But Adam goes too far by making Eve his god. Afraid to admit his need for her, Adam stresses Eve's dependence on him, eventually provoking her assertion of independence that leads to the fall. Far from denying himself, Adam falls with Eve to try to preserve the image of himself that he sees in her. Only by learning to dedicate himself to others and to obey God's authority can Adam break his narcissistic cycle and discover a paradise within.

366   Copeland, Thomas A. "Raphael, the Angelic Virtue." *Milton Quarterly* 24 (1990): 117-28.

Perhaps Milton's most credible portrait of goodness in *Paradise Lost*, Raphael exemplifies the nature of virtue. When he visits Adam and Eve, he seeks to encourage virtue by showing love's part in a universal cycle of creation and adoration. As one who withstood temptation during the rebellion in heaven, Raphael illustrates and explains that love, if it is to become virtue instead of just innocence, must be tested by choice. Obedience, another part of virtue, can open up an angelic state for humans, which is why he reinforces the command to be fruitful with a discussion of the generative force that sustains all living things. Love, Raphael explains, reconciles freedom to obedience. But humility's power produces love's efficacy by directing it toward heaven, and he illustrates this part of virtue with the wings that veil him as well as his lack of pride when he accepts a stalemate at the end of the war's second day. In response to the angel's lessons, Adam displays excessive deference; Raphael strives to teach him new gratitude and respect for his status as a creature, views that form humility's foundation. At the end of his visit, Raphael stumbles by oversimplifying and implying that human sexuality is foolish. Adam protests and clarifies the point, but readers see that no virtue is proof against error—particularly Raphael's error of being trapped within one's own point of view.

367   Freeman, James A. *Milton and the Martial Muse: "Paradise Lost" and European Traditions of War*. Princeton, NJ: Princeton University Press, 1980. xix + 253 pp. 27 illustrations.

While *Paradise Lost* satisfies conventional expectations about war myths, Milton, unlike most contemporaries and authors through the ages, condemns warfare and the idea of desirable conflict. He studies war closely, encounters it frequently in his strife-filled era, and concludes that it is almost always futile, humanity's most vulgar error. Previous writers give arms to the loyal angels, but Milton arms the rebels, who show their ingratitude to God, allegiance to their false god Satan, and hostility to humans with martial obedience and organization. Milton uses the rebels to turn the martial tradition against itself, as it embraces impiety and severs the connection between proper faith and fighting. More exclusively martial in *Paradise Lost* than in any other work, Satan meets contemporary expectations of his role as a warrior even as he parodies epic conventions and debases everything he touches, for he is finally a wily, desperate liar who is defeated at every military activity he chooses. In his critique of warfare, "Milton implies that the communal nightmare of his age is the heroic vision of war . . . [that] centuries of lazy analysis had allowed to grow" (223).

368   Gallagher, Philip J. *Milton, the Bible, and Misogyny*. Edited by Eugene R. Cunnar and Gail L. Mortimer. Columbia: University of Missouri Press, 1990. x + 185 pp.

In *Paradise Lost*'s narrative of the creation, Milton transforms biblical material to suit his rational theodicy, which proposes creation *ex Deo* and clarifies scriptural inconsistencies and contradictions, particularly concerning the creation of the serpent and man. Like Genesis, Raphael's account presents the creation of man and woman as equals, for the epic generally eliminates the programmatic misogyny institutionalized by the patriarchal authors of Genesis 2. The role of deceit in the epic exonerates Eve, who, like Uriel, is its victim, and clears Milton of the charge of misogyny, while pointing to Adam's greater culpability because he falls undeceived. Fallen humanity's rehabilitation begins with God's indictment of Adam, followed by Eve's intervention as "*the* human mediatrix of prevenient grace" (126). In *Paradise Lost*, Raphael's descent is analogous to Samson's marriage to the woman of Timna, because the angel and woman embody prevenient grace sent by God to initiate human regeneration.

369   Greene, Thomas [M.]. "Milton." In *The Descent from Heaven: A Study in Epic Continuity*, 363-418. New Haven, CT: Yale University Press, 1963.

The play of perspective and emphasis on seeing when Raphael descends in Book 5 reveal Milton's expansive cosmic design and fusion of classical and biblical learning. Similarly, *Paradise Lost*'s style is both simple and intervolved, and in different episodes Milton views language as potentially deceptive, an instrument for attaining truth, or divinely inspired. Of all the epics that use the traditional descent from heaven, only *Paradise Lost* incorporates it into a larger pattern of vertical imagery (rising and falling, height and depth), including the paradoxes of pride that abases and abasement that exalts. An instance of divine generosity, Raphael's descent exemplifies the celestial conde-scension that opposes Satanic aspiration. Unlike other celestial visitors in the tradition, Raphael comes not to prod or punish but to lecture, to expound the truth. By internalizing action, questioning the hero's inde-pendence, and detaching heroism from the human community, Milton's epic begins to destroy the genre.

370   Hanford, James Holly. "Milton and the Art of War." *Studies in Philology* 18 (1921): 232-66. Reprinted in *John Milton, Poet and Humanist: Essays by James Holly Hanford*, 185-223. Cleveland, OH: Press of Western Reserve University, 1966.
        Milton includes military study and discipline in *Of Education*'s program, his teaching, and his own reading, though there is no evi-dence that he undergoes military training. *Paradise Lost*, despite its statement of dissatisfaction with purely chivalric matter in Book 9's invocation, mixes romance and science to provide vivid descriptions of military subjects, including an angelic nightwatch, martial preparations, arms, and the war in heaven.

371   Häublein, Ernst. "Milton's Paraphrase of Genesis: A Stylistic Reading of *Paradise Lost*, Book VII." *Milton Studies* 7 (1975): 101-25.
        Three translations of the Bible—the King James, Geneva, and Vulgate—are the most immediate sources for the creation in Book 7 of *Paradise Lost*. Though Milton sometimes presents an introduction to a direct biblical reference, he typically uses the scriptural paraphrase to lead into a creative act, which is followed by an amplification; he quotes additional biblical verses in the middle or, more frequently, at the end of the amplification. Milton portrays the creation as a dynamic process by substituting temporal adverbs and verbs of action or praise. Using synonyms and periphrases, he avoids the biblical account's repe-titions, writes more ornately, eliminates articles, and alters word order. With its preference for participial constructions and complex syntax, the King James Bible is Milton's preferred source. The Geneva Bible provides his logical and temporal conjunctions and possibly his prefer-

ence for subordinate clauses, while the Vulgate mainly contributes vocabulary and zeugma. Milton transforms the biblical account by impos-
ing his own style on its verses.

372   Hughes, Merritt Y. "Milton's Celestial Battle and the Theog-
        onies." In *Studies in Honor of T. W. Baldwin*, edited by Don
        Cameron Allen, 237-53. Urbana: University of Illinois Press,
        1958. Reprinted in *Ten Perspectives on Milton*, 196-219. New
        Haven, CT: Yale University Press, 1965.
        Classical accounts of the Titans and giants assaulting the gods
of Olympus give Milton evidence for the occurrence of the war in
heaven and a model by which he represents it in corporal forms. However sketchy, scriptural passages also record the battle and Satan's
motive, the exaltation of the Son. Early readers find Book 6 powerful,
some arguing for its aesthetic validity because it deals with a tradition
about an event in cosmic history. In Milton's view, classical myths of
the titanomachia, particularly Hesiod's, contain both fraudulent material
and recognizable pieces of biblical history, and they are interpreted as
history, allegory, and ethical lessons.

373   Hunter, W[illia]m B., Jr. "Eve's Demonic Dream." *ELH* 13
        (1946): 255-65. Reprinted in *The Descent of Urania: Studies
        in Milton, 1946-1988*, 46-55. Lewisburg, PA: Bucknell Uni-
        versity Press, 1989.
        Eve's dream, conceived in terms of contemporary dream and
demon lore, presents a dramatic foreshadowing of the temptation and
fall. When Satan causes the dream, he wants to raise Eve's pride by
attacking the fancy or confusing the animal spirits, but Milton does not
believe demons can possess a human by operating on the reason.

374   Hunter, William B., Jr. "Milton on the Exaltation of the Son:
        The War in Heaven in *Paradise Lost*." *ELH* 36 (1969): 215-
        31. Reprinted in *Bright Essence: Studies in Milton's Theology*,
        by W. B. Hunter, C. A. Patrides, and J. H. Adamson, 115-
        30. Salt Lake City: University of Utah Press, 1971.
        Though the newly begotten Son must have been antecedent to
the angels, for Abdiel explains that the Son created them, the angels
witness the begetting of the Son. The exaltation, according to *Christian
Doctrine*, occurs at the Resurrection, when Christ triumphs over death
and receives immortality and glory from God. In *Paradise Lost*, these
changes are applied to the Son with his introduction in Book 3. When

Milton narrates the begetting of the Son and the war in heaven, he tells
of the angels' fall before the creation of the world, the demons' defeat
at the end of time as described in Revelation, and the Son's exaltation,
which occur concomitantly with his resurrection as incarnate God-man.
Unified by the theme of the Son's victorious exaltation, these events are
simultaneously and metaphorically present in a single narrative framework. The Son is begotten virtually (or metaphorically) when he offers
himself as sacrifice and actually at the Incarnation.

375   Hunter, William B., Jr. "Prophetic Dreams and Visions in
        Paradise Lost." *Modern Language Quarterly* 9 (1948): 277-
        85. Reprinted in *The Descent of Urania: Studies in Milton,
        1946-1988*, 21-30. Lewisburg, PA: Bucknell University Press,
        1989.
        Rabbinical and Neoplatonic traditions suggest that prophecy is
a psychological phenomenon related to true dreams. If prophecy comes
through the active intellect via the reason and imagination, only for
Moses is imagination (and thus dreams) unnecessary because he receives the highest, direct revelation, as do Adam and Eve when God
addresses them in *Paradise Lost*. God's words pass directly to their
intellect with no intermediary or simulacra. When Eve calls his sole
prohibition the "Daughter of his voice," she underestimates its status,
for her term applies to the lowest form of prophecy rather than an un-
alterable statement of the divine will. Raphael and Michael communicate through the level of prophecy that is just below the Mosaic. During the two dreams Adam relates in Book 8, the outer senses and common sense do not function (though Jewish authorities believe reason
should be involved), but the imagination or fancy remains active.

376   Ide, Richard S. "On the Begetting of the Son in *Paradise
        Lost.*" *Studies in English Literature, 1500-1900* 24 (1984):
        141-55.
        Despite Raphael's claim that earth is heaven's shadow, he nar-
rates heavenly events as if they were temporally determined and causally connected—indeed, as a representation of Christian history on earth
from the Incarnation to the Resurrection. Heavenly and earthly time in
Books 5-6 are analogous and continuous, combining to encapsulate all
time and to form a revelation, to the angels and then men, of God in
the Son. In *Paradise Lost*, the begetting of the Son in heaven refers
principally to his generation in his divine nature, analogically to his
generation in his human nature at the Incarnation, and metaphorically

to his exaltation on the third day, in heaven and on earth, when he fulfills the purpose of his begetting.

377   Kuester, Martin. "The End of Monolithic Language: Rapha-
       el's Sematology in *Paradise Lost.*" *English Studies in Canada*
       15 (1989): 263-76.
       Not only is Raphael powerless to prevent the fall, but his linguistic techniques cause Adam and Eve to cease believing in the monolithic state of language, a loss Milton feels can be overcome only by faith. Basing his theory on Augustinian semiotics, Milton rejects the notion of an ideal language in which every word embodies an aspect of reality and instead stresses the process of language as a path toward truth. Unlike God, who deviates from but does not shatter Adam's faith in the relationship between signifier and signified, the archangel intro-duces ambiguity and arbitrariness, which produce, yet are not sufficient causes of, the fall. Raphael's reliance on analogy may not even be nec-essary; he repeatedly admits that, while heaven may differ from earth in degree, in many respects their innate qualities are the same. In effect, he creates an artificial barrier. Raphael's confusion and limita-tions make him the mouthpiece of God's irony, which stresses the im-portance of faith and asks Adam to weigh what he is told.

378   Labriola, Albert C. "'Thy Humiliation Shall Exalt': The
       Christology of *Paradise Lost.*" *Milton Studies* 15 (1981): 29-
       42.
       Milton uses the interrelation of Moses, the Son, and Satan to elaborate a basic concept of *Paradise Lost*'s Christology. Each charac-ter is associated with light and dark imagery and the cycle of humili-ation and exaltation, which present a typological relationship between Moses and Christ, while revealing Satan to be an idol or parody of them. The Son is humiliated twice, when begotten as an angel and when incarnated as a man, with each event also producing an exalta-tion. Satan refuses to recognize that the begetting acts as a model by which all angels can be exalted; rather than imitate the Son's humili-ation, Satan seeks to exalt himself from the role of governor to become a deity. The rebels end up being not elevated but degraded, imbruted. Throughout *Paradise Lost*, the Son's humiliation and exaltation are bal-anced and contrasted with Satan's parodic enactments of them.

379   Langford, Larry L. "Adam and the Subversion of Paradise."
       Studies in English Literature, 1500-1900 34 (1994): 119-34.

Various characters, including Raphael and God, conduct a type of social, not biological, engineering that dictates certain roles for Adam and Eve to fulfill. Revealing a developmental pattern that is the opposite of Eve's, Adam in his first moments of life moves from feeling peaceful sufficiency to anxiety, as he grows increasingly discontent with his existence and searches for alternatives that disrupt the existing mode of being. Adam initially looks up and stands up. Unfettered by any experience of hierarchy, he demonstrates independence, self-confidence, and self-reliance; he shows "the possibility of independent will and action in a world hierarchically structured by an omniscient and omnipotent creator" (122). The effect is a sense of vastness, which diminishes his presence and makes him feel isolated. If God uses his first intervention in Eve's life to create a crisis, for Adam he resolves one by lifting his despondency, which produces spontaneous, independent responses that do not account for God and shape a subjectivity that knows nothing of submission and hierarchy. More deliberately than Eve's, Adam's narcissism follows Satan's pattern and manifests itself in self-absorption and the search for a companion who is another Adam. God imposes on Adam the status of benign master in the patriarchal order.

380   Le Comte, Edward. "Dubious Battle: Saving the Appearances." *English Language Notes* 19 (1982): 177-93.

Many early readers of *Paradise Lost* praise the war in heaven primarily because it has a long line of literary precedents and it surpasses them, but some find the episode ridiculous. Though recent criticism views the war as an ironic, mock-heroic event, it is so only from God's point of view; the loyal angels see the war as truly heroic, and for the rebels it is ultimately tragic. In the invocation to Book 9 and Raphael's remark that such a war seems strange, Milton may be conveying doubts about the success of Book 6.

381   Lieb, Michael. "The Book of M: *Paradise Lost* as Revisionary Text." *Cithara* 31 (1991): 28-35.

Milton's interpretation of the biblical text which underlies his epic, especially the description of Eve as a "help meet" for Adam, is colored by his position as what Harold Bloom calls a *Gevurah* or "great lady." Despite repeated translations which denote an inferior position, the Hebrew phrase *'ezer keneghdo* (often rendered "help meet") actually conveys a sense of empowerment and correspondence to another.

In *Paradise Lost*, Adam captures the meaning of '*ezer* by asking for a counterpart who, complete of herself, can both give and receive companionship. Recognizing his lack of the completion inherent in God, Adam seeks a collateral relationship—one that involves a partner who is not only by him but part of him. By infusing his description of "help meet" with the copartnership inherent in the original Hebrew, Milton is a kind of *Gevurah* who is able to transform and revise the biblical text.

382   Lim, Walter S. H. "Adam, Eve, and Biblical Analogy in *Paradise Lost*." *Studies in English Literature, 1500-1900* 30 (1990): 115-31.

In *Paradise Lost*, Milton uses biblical allusions, parallels, and echoes to define Adam's and Eve's personalities and experiences through theological and dramatic contexts. When Adam entertains Raphael, the scene has parallels with Genesis 18, where Abraham encounters three heavenly visitors, and Eve's role as hostess recalls Sarah's similar activity in Genesis. The Bible's Samson and Solomon, beguiled and idolatrous men, are analogues of the movement from innocence to experience through disobedience or fornication, a pattern Adam and Eve follow by disrupting the hierarchical order of God's universe. In the temptation and fall, Satan, not Eve, is the Dalila figure; allusions to the Virgin Mary, Ruth, and Mary Magdalene point to Eve's act of beginning the processes of regeneration and reconciliation after the fall. In the epic's conclusion, she is linked to Ruth and Sarah in allusions that prevent closure and encourage hope.

383   Loewenstein, David. "'An Ambiguous Monster': Representing Rebellion in Milton's Polemics and *Paradise Lost*." *Huntington Library Quarterly* 55 (1992): 295-315.

In the seventeenth century, people of all political sympathies are deeply anxious about rebellion, which writers represent as "a kind of monstrous, demonic, threatening Other" (296). Milton's early prose tracts, sonnet on Fairfax, and depiction of Satan in *Paradise Lost* configure political rebellion in images of the monstrous and unnatural. But Milton's complex relationship to the various monstrous and ambiguous forms of rebellion in the 1640s and 1650s stimulates the mythic representation of political rebellion in his epic. Just as Milton simultaneously attacks and promotes forms of rebellion during the Civil Wars, so *Paradise Lost* offers a paradoxical portrait of Satan as raging tyrant and political rebel. Assuming new shapes and transforming rebellion into an art, Satan uses an artful self-presentation and powerful words to appropriate the language and gestures of seventeenth-century political revolution and resistance. Milton makes him an equivocal monster who usurps and manipulates the language of political resistance and impersonates contradictory kinds of radical revolutionaries.

384   Low, Anthony. "Angels and Food in *Paradise Lost*." *Milton Studies* 1 (1969): 135-45.
    Milton invents the scene in which Adam and Eve eat with Raphael to emphasize the relationship between host and guest or the giving and receiving of hospitality. The choice of foods reveals a careful balance among tastes and the ease with which nature feeds humans before the fall. Connecting different levels of the creation with ease, the meal shows the lower order of nature innocently providing for Adam and Eve, as well as the familiar intercourse between earth and heaven. With the fall, these relationships change, though the meal, along with the banquet of saints in heaven, prefigures the communion service, particularly as contrasted to the pomp of the mass. Once Adam and Eve eat the forbidden meal, God and humans are distant and meet on different terms.

385   McColgan, Kristin Pruitt. "'God Is Also in Sleep': Dreams Satanic and Divine in *Paradise Lost*." *Milton Studies* 30 (1993): 135-48.
    In *Paradise Lost*, dreams represent either divinely sanctioned relationship with an "other self" or Satanic exaltation of the self. Adam's two dreams are divinely inspired, but Eve's first dream has Satanic origins. In her demonic dream, Satan "produces the drama of self on the stage of Eve's imagination" (138). He borrows material from what he has heard and seen in Eden and from his experiences in heaven. The perverse joining of Eve and himself that Satan creates in the dream is a parody of relationship. Inverse parallels exist between this dream and Adam's divinely inspired ones. Although Eve's demonic dream presents Satan's wish-fulfillment rather than her anxiety or hope, it still foreshadows the fall. The poem's last spoken words, in which Eve discusses her second, divinely inspired dream without revealing its precise contents, testify to God's presence in sleep and confidently proclaim restoration.

386   Madsen, William G. "Neoplatonic and Christian Symbols in
        Paradise Lost" and "The Eye and the Ear." In *From Shadowy
        Types to Truth: Studies in Milton's Symbolism*, 85-144 and
        145-80. New Haven, CT: Yale University Press, 1968.
        When Raphael suggests that earth may be the shadow of heav-
en, he defines their relationship not in terms of a Neoplatonic analogy
but of a Christian foreshadowing. He is the spokesman for other aspects of Neoplatonism, such as the vertical ascent, a perspective undercut and finally made irrelevant because he addresses only prelapsarian
conditions. With sin comes the human perception of typological meaning, and Christ in turn abolishes all types. Unless they use Scripture as
their guide, fallen humans cannot read the book of nature.
        Raphael's description of the ladder of love is a Neoplatonic
view in which love refines and leads upward. For Adam, however, the
love of Eve produces a descent. During the temptation, she is attacked
mainly through the ear, while he is tempted through the eye, though his
regeneration is accomplished primarily through the ear. Milton follows
the Puritan beliefs that Christ gives meaning to the Old Testament's
types and his word enters the heart by images created from the types
he abolishes and by the Holy Spirit's symbolic language.

387   Mengert, James G. "Styling the Strife of Glory: The War in
        Heaven." *Milton Studies* 14 (1980): 95-115.
        Because human wars have not occurred when Raphael narrates
the war in heaven, Milton uses paradoxical strategies in Book 6: language and incident suggest classical epic and history, which must be
excluded for Adam and Eve. Thus the battle's significance is reduced
because, while it invites many imaginative associations with numerous
military events, it necessarily contains no explicit reference to them. By
putting great pressure on the literal level, Milton depreciates the spiritual level of the war narrative and refuses to accept its allegorical implications. The event is true, he insists, yet he will not affirm that it
directly conveys spiritual significance. His narrative strategy signals the
end of the heroic and allegorical traditions. When Satan's moral depravity is associated with physical bestiality in Book 6, traces appear
of an allegorical tradition containing similar representations, but, as in
the war narrative, Milton uses the association only with considerable
indirection and diminished spiritual significance. Throughout this book,
he depreciates the significance of signs or vehicles, refusing to treat his

literary material as a representation of something else. Satan, on the other hand, engages in the opposite enterprise, affirming the battle's significance and realizing that this affirmation is a product of style.

388   Miller, George E[ric]. "'Images of Matter': Narrative Manipulation in Book VI of *Paradise Lost*." *Ariel: A Review of International English Literature* 11 (1980): 5-13.

In the war in heaven episode, Milton uses narrative techniques involving language and perspective to define part of Book 6's lesson. The war's terms and struggle grow increasingly literal, becoming separated from moral or spiritual significance and thus permitting Satan's illusion. Though Raphael narrates this episode, the point of view is that of the disloyal angels, who begin to lose comprehension of the spiritual and focus on the material. Inverting the structure of sacred metaphor, Satan's puns operate on a literal level with a physical referent rather than a moral one behind them. Near the end of Book 6, readers finally return to a perspective that is broader than Satan's: God has permitted and limited the war, and Satan's epic aspirations collapse when the war's literal meaning assumes moral significance. Portraying an evil attempt to redress a moral disparity by physical means, Raphael's reductive narrative reveals this lesson even as it confines the reading experience.

389   Nyquist, Mary. "The Genesis of Gendered Subjectivity in the Divorce Tracts and in *Paradise Lost*." In *Re-membering Milton: Essays on the Texts and Traditions*, edited by Mary Nyquist and Margaret W. Ferguson, 99-127. New York: Methuen, 1987.

Milton's divorce tracts contain an exegesis that results from an ideologically overdetermined desire to unify the two creation accounts in Genesis. His reading of Genesis is masculinist, as are the assumptions in his articulation of a radically bourgeois view of marriage. Although she was created after Adam, Eve narrates her first experiences in Book 4, while Adam relates his in Book 8. Milton's narrative distribution of these two events is ideologically motivated in *Paradise Lost*. When Raphael presents the two accounts of creation, he joins them, leaving the impression that they have always been unified. Yet he barely alludes to Eve's creation, leaving Adam to disjoin the two accounts when he relates this episode in a second telling of or commentary on the first. By privileging the male voice, Milton ensures that the doctrine of marriage is produced and comprehended by the person for whom it is ordained. If Eve had told her story after Adam told his, the poem may have made her appear necessary and superior because she was set in motion to satisfy a lonely Adam's one imperfection. The poem subverts this logic. Eve recalls a time when she believed she was autonomous, with no knowledge of or commitment to Adam, but she is informed that this belief was false. She must submit desire to paternal law.

390   Peczenik, Fannie. "Milton on the Creation of Eve: Adam's Dream and the Hieroglyphic of the Rib." In *A Fine Tuning: Studies of the Religious Poetry of Herbert and Milton*, edited by Mary A. Maleski, 249-72. Binghamton, NY: Medieval and Renaissance Texts and Studies, 1989.
       In Adam's story of Eve's creation, based on Genesis 2.21-24, Milton offers a critique of prevailing contemporary interpretations, which feature harshness and embarrassment, unlike *Paradise Lost*'s secular treatment of the subject. That Eve is formed from a rib makes her, according to commentators, derivative and subordinate, an origin that thus accounts for her defects and union with man. When Adam describes Eve's creation, the dream circumvents naturalistic questions about a superfluous or surgically removed rib, and Milton turns instead to the secular tradition of Renaissance erotic verse. The second half of Adam's dream-vision emphasizes Eve's creation as the first metamorphosis in a cycle that will end in humanity's attaining angelic nature. Exchange and transformation, not hierarchy, characterize the true relation of man and woman. After Adam attempts to make a literal, naturalistic exegesis of Eve's creation and a fleshly definition of love, Raphael rebukes him because these views diminish her status. The dream-vision of the hieroglyphic of human love is emended by Michael's lesson, which argues that Eve's creation is meaningful only in the light of Christ's Atonement.

391   Revard, Stella Purce. *The War in Heaven: "Paradise Lost" and the Tradition of Satan's Rebellion*. Ithaca, NY: Cornell University Press, 1980. 315 pp.
       Unlike their modern counterparts, Milton's eighteenth-century critics often admire his depiction of the war in heaven, which comes out of an extensive literary and theological tradition. The intellective sin of pride, according to the Bible and patristic commentators, causes

Satan to choose to rebel against God. Through Raphael's narrative of the war in *Paradise Lost*, Adam must relive Satan's struggle, learn why he refused to obey, and see the oneness of total creation. If the Book of Revelation speaks of the Civil Wars for many in the Parliamentary party, Milton sees the struggle in Revelation as atemporal and perhaps as an archetype. His contemporaries agree that Satan is the father of war, and only Renaissance authors, particularly in hexameral poems, provide detailed descriptions of the heavenly war. *Paradise Lost* is unique in dividing the war into three stages and three consecutive days, each with its own kind of warfare. Books 5-6 offer a critique of war as Satanic in essence and based on a classical ethic in which strength and skill, not faith, determine victory. With the Son's appearance on the third day, however, Milton defines a new view of the heroic: a hero of faith's spiritual and martial values oppose Satan's stance as a militaristic general in the glory of battle, a role the poem exposes as illusory.

392   Rosenblatt, Jason P. "Structural Unity and Temporal Concordance: The War in Heaven in *Paradise Lost*." *PMLA* 87 (1972): 31-41.

Occurring at the beginning of time, the middle of *Paradise Lost*, and the end of the Bible, Milton's war in heaven is linked by typology to the exodus, an event referred to in Books 1, 6, and 12 to provide a temporal concordance of beginning, middle, and end. Pharaoh, the hard-hearted tyrant swallowed by the Red Sea, is a type of Satan when he is forced to plunge into hell's depths. Both evil characters ultimately bring glory to God in battle, and Milton's war in heaven echoes God's fight against the Egyptians. The climax of the exodus provides structural unity in *Paradise Lost*, for the event has figurative significance as a type of baptism and a foreshadowing of the Messiah's advent. Because Milton's dream of the imminent establishing of God's kingdom on earth was ruined, however, he subscribes to an Old Testament view of the exodus. The war in heaven shows that he believes a future redemption will occur in God's own time.

393   Schiffhorst, Gerald J. "Patience and the Humbly Exalted Heroism of Milton's Messiah: Typological and Iconographic Background." *Milton Studies* 16 (1982): 97-113. 2 illustrations.

As part of the patience tradition, the Son's victory in the war in heaven shows that his triumph over sin prefigures the Redemption and that his exaltation and humiliation on the cross are inseparable. His victory conflates his roles as judge and savior by beginning the fulfill- ment of his exaltation as the obedient Messiah and prepares for the def- inition of patience that applies to Adam near *Paradise Lost*'s con- clusion. Defined as both passive and active by many commentaries, pa- tience is considered Godlike and synonymous with spiritual fortitude because it follows Christ's example of humbly enduring present afflic- tions in the hope of future fulfillment. In Book 6, Milton associates the Son with images of victorious kingship, majestic soldier, and future judge; allusions to David; and overtones of his status as the heroically patient victor. Milton's concept of heroism includes obedience, humil- ity, and the active readiness of patience.

394   Swaim, Kathleen M. *Before and After the Fall: Contrasting Modes in "Paradise Lost."* Amherst: University of Massachu- setts Press, 1986. xiv + 291 pp.

Raphael's and Michael's descents, lessons, and pedagogical methods in *Paradise Lost* illustrate the contrasts between pre- and postlapsarian life. Seeking to lead Adam toward a kind of humanistic improvement, Raphael uses lectures about unity and hierarchy, while Michael uses a discussion format and prophecy to promote something like Christian amendment. Raphael wants to share wisdom and the facts of history or the book of God's works; Michael trains his pupil in an exegetical technique in the book of God's Word, with which he can transcend postlapsarian multiplicity and regain unity through Christ. If Raphael's main interest is ontology, shown in his ascending spatial analogies, Michael's is teleology, explained in typology or temporal analogies. In terms of Ramist logic, Raphael is the master of argument, distribution, and invention, and Michael of disposition, method, and memory. Before the fall, Adam receives a creative poetic from the Platonic Raphael; later, the Christian Michael provides a critical poetic.

395   Tung, Mason. "The Abdiel Episode: A Contextual Reading." *Studies in Philology* 62 (1965): 595-609.

As one example in Raphael's lesson for Adam and Eve, Abdiel illustrates the positive alternative that angels, like humans, can take when faced with the pressure to disobey. Abdiel acts as a foil to Satan by recognizing and opposing his fraud and revolt. When Abdiel pre- dicts the demons' defeat and fall, the reader and Adam already know this to be true; the angel's prophetic power thus functions less to warn

Adam about disobedience than to testify to the lone Abdiel's fearlessness and faith in divine justice. If Adam displays too much curiosity and too little faith in reason, Abdiel's example reminds him of reason's ultimate triumph and the importance of loving God. Central to *Paradise Lost*'s plot is the idea that Adam and Eve's fall is evitable, a point Raphael's various lessons emphasize, thus making Abdiel a foil to Adam and Eve. When Milton portrays examples of the one just man, including Abdiel, this character knows evil's true nature even under great duress. Abdiel resembles the person in *Areopagitica* whose virtue is not cloistered but who apprehends vice and chooses to abstain.

396   Williams, Arnold. "The Motivation of Satan's Rebellion in *Paradise Lost*." *Studies in Philology* 42 (1945): 253-68. Reprinted in *Milton: Modern Judgements*, edited by Alan Rudrum, 136-50. London: Macmillan, 1968.

A key action that introduces evil to the world and eventually leads to humanity's creation and fall, Satan's rebellion receives scant attention in the Bible and commentaries on Genesis. Isaiah 14.12-15, containing the most influential account of Lucifer's rebellion and motivation, attributes his fall to pride and the ambition to equal or surpass God. Yet this view leaves only abstract vices and no explanation of Satan's opportunity to translate an innate moral perversion into an overt act, problems Milton solves by replacing the Trinity manuscript's dramatic form with the epic form and, by beginning *in medias res*, having more time to develop Satan's proud character before defining his motivation. When God announces the Son's exaltation (not his generation), Satan begins his rebellion, which is motivated by envy rather than pride because he refuses to perform the act of obedience that God has commanded. Many contemporaries argue that the rebel angels would not accept God's announcement of the Incarnation and the exaltation it gives human nature, through Christ, as the means of salvation. To fit *Paradise Lost*'s chronology, however, Milton's God announces the Son's begetting, which produces Satan's motivation of envy.

397   Williamson, George. "The Education of Adam." *Modern Philology* 61 (1963): 96-109. Reprinted in *Milton: Modern Essays in Criticism*, edited by Arthur E. Barker, 284-307. London: Oxford University Press, 1965.

Adam's education prepares him for a trial and readers for its significance. While the didactic element motivates and amplifies the fall's tragic consequences, it still leaves humanity with hope. Raphael teaches Adam that contemplating created things can lead to God as well as to prideful aspiration. Various events narrated by the angel teach Adam about important issues in Eden—obedience and disobedience, love, curiosity and its limits, temperance, and the greatest human need, relief from solitude, which is Adam's basic weakness. If the fall brings alienation, Adam and Eve's moral drama prepares them for divine reconciliation. Michael gives Adam a historical perspective on his sin by teaching him the heroic lesson of Christ and suffering for truth, necessary wisdom for the world and a hopeful conclusion.

398   Wooten, John. "The Poet's War: Violence and Virtue in *Paradise Lost*." *Studies in English Literature, 1500-1900* 30 (1990): 133-50.

The war in heaven in *Paradise Lost*, a parable of large-scale physical harm directed at one group by another, produces discordant effects because of God's curious responses to it (including a grin and a lie), the compromising of the loyal angels' action, the fallen angels' extremely grotesque conduct, the split between the angelic narrator and his narrative, and the confusing intrusion of the Son. Milton's presentation is incoherent, in part articulating the theory of just war and in part undercutting the entire episode, because of his temperamental anger and disappointment about the Puritan Revolution's collapse. Using art to sublimate hostile feelings in Book 7's invocation to Urania, Milton is both vulnerable and combative, isolated and "yet not alone." His limited control over this invocation's discordant emotions impels him into the violent lines about Orpheus. He responds to the violence in his world and himself in complex and contradictory ways.

Other studies that examine Books 5-8 are identified in entries 46, 50, 118, 120, 151, 164, 168, 181, 183, 200, and 205.

15. BOOKS 9-10

399   Bell, Millicent. "The Fallacy of the Fall in *Paradise Lost*."
        PMLA 68 (1953): 863-83.
        Milton's source material indicates that the fall is causeless, yet
the reader can accept Adam and Eve's first sin only by denying their
absolute perfection. What the reader usually considers the fall's cause,
disobedience, is in fact the result of a prelapsarian Eden that has already been infected with fallen nature's symptoms. *Paradise Lost* thus
presents no sharp division between pre- and postlapsarian life. Susceptible to sin from the moment of Eve's Satanic dream and Adam's feeling the force of passion, the couple cannot fall because they have
already done so. At the tree, Adam and Eve experience not the onset
of sin but the climax of self-realization by two imperfect humans. The
fall is inevitable and necessary, particularly in a universe and souls
where the existence of good requires the existence of evil.

400   Bennett, Joan S. "'Go': Milton's Antinomianism and the Sep-
        aration Scene in *Paradise Lost*, Book 9." *PMLA* 98 (1983):
        388-404. Reprinted in *Reviving Liberty: Radical Christian
        Humanism in Milton's Great Poems*, 94-118. Cambridge, MA:
        Harvard University Press, 1989.
        Antinomianism, which holds that the Mosaic law is abrogated
for Christians by the coming of Christ, who dwells in the believer's
heart and acts as a moral guide, raises the question of how one can
know whether a decision is based on the internal spirit or personal
desire. As the separation scene in Book 9 of *Paradise Lost* illustrates,
unfallen Adam and Eve are the first humans to face the dilemma of
total spiritual liberty. Milton's humanist antinomian view states that the
Christian, released from positive law and with Christ in the self to
rectify reason, must build moral judgment or inner authority by recognizing the valid hierarchy of natural laws applicable to ethical situa-
tions. In Book 9's separation scene, Adam and Eve's moral decisions
are not concerned with obeying a code of laws that expresses God's

will; they work to discern his meaning, growing "through the steady exercise of the inner light within a dynamic moral context" (397). Eve begins the scene by seeking advice from Adam, who reasons that they should not separate, a decision she must make freely, according to Milton's antinomianism. Because the inner light is right reason, Adam fails as Eve's governor when he later lets her go, for this act substitutes his authority for her truly free choice. Adam, with his quicker axiomatic mind, should have continued to help Eve work toward attaining the genuine imitation of the divine nature he has.

401   Bowers, Fredson. "Adam, Eve, and the Fall in *Paradise Lost*." *PMLA* 84 (1969): 264-73.
        Through dramatic representation, Milton makes the fall credible, even inevitable, at the level of the reader's postlapsarian understanding. Thus God creates humans perfect but free, with love playing the paradoxical role of imperfection—a search for potential or a lack within one's state of being—within perfection. Complementing each other, Adam and Eve form a relationship that creates a complete, fulfilled state. When the stronger element, Adam or reason, relinquishes its sovereignty over Eve or passion, the fall occurs. Adam and Eve are contrasted even in their creations, which foreshadow their falls, as do Eve's dream and Adam's confession to Raphael that his reason falls in her presence. In the dream, Satan successfully poisons Eve's animal spirits and rouses discontented thoughts, creating a latent, unconscious infection that leads to pride and the fall. After demanding her obedience, Adam in Book 9 then reverses the hierarchical order by allowing her to make the crucial decision that will determine humankind's fate. Adam is not deceived when he gives Eve permission to depart or when he falls; on both occasions, passion affects but does not obscure his reason. He knows the truth and chooses not to follow it.

402   Chambers, A. B. "The Falls of Adam and Eve in *Paradise Lost*." In *New Essays on "Paradise Lost,"* edited by Thomas Kranidas, 118-30. Berkeley: University of California Press, 1969.
        When he explains that Adam falls without being deceived, Milton adopts Augustine's exegesis of Genesis. His prelapsarian Adam and Eve experience "motions" of flesh and appetite, but they are not inordinate and therefore not signs of sin. In their innocent state, Adam and Eve have finite reason and will, both liable to change and error, as

Michael states. According to moral theology, one can sin out of affected ignorance, from deception (as with Eve), or against one's knowledge (as Adam does). The psychology of sin states that temptation leads
to sin by a threefold process—suggestion, delight, and consent—which
Satan, Eve, and Adam traditionally represent. This interpretation must
have had allegorical overtones for Milton's readers.

403   Farwell, Marilyn R. "Eve, the Separation Scene, and the Re-
       naissance Idea of Androgyny." *Milton Studies* 16 (1982): 3-
       20.
       Many critics believe Adam and Eve are united in an ontologi-
cal whole that readers can call androgyny, which points to egalitarian
views and a fatalistic interpretation of the fall. But Renaissance philosophies of androgyny argue that the male Adam is both a part and the
whole of the androgyne. The female Eve is subsumed by the male principle in an attempt to appropriate her power of creation and reproduc-
tion. Though Milton appears to adopt this theory in *Paradise Lost*, in
fact he presents Adam and Eve as an ontological whole and as separate
individuals, with a healthy tension emerging from their two roles in the
relationship. As the separation scene makes clear, Adam and Eve's
strength is based not on androgynous, ontological fusion but on responsibility and existential support. Never a misogynist, Milton allows Eve
the possibilities of separateness, individuality, and independence.

404   Fresch, Cheryl H. "Human and Divine Reconciliation in *Par-
       adise Lost*, X-XI: The Strategy of Milton's Structure." In
       *Praise Disjoined: Changing Patterns of Salvation in
       Seventeenth-Century English Literature*, edited by William P.
       Shaw, 259-71. Frankfurt am Main: Peter Lang, 1991.
       While Adam and Eve's dramatic human reconciliation does not
cause or model divine reconciliation, the two events do not exist in
isolation. Building on Lucan and Pauline theology, Milton stresses the
importance of penitence, of moving from the earthly to the heavenly,
and of reciprocal forgiveness in human reconciliation. Eve mirrors the
weeping woman of Luke who falls at Jesus's feet. However, initially
Eve is not truly repentant, and Adam is not truly forgiving. Once he
sees the sin in himself, Adam follows the pattern of conditional
forgiveness; when Adam forgives Eve, God forgives him. By accepting
God's grace through faith, Adam and Eve find divine reconciliation and
look forward to the promised seed.

405   Fresch, Cheryl H. "Milton's Eve and the Problem of the Additions to the Command." *Milton Quarterly* 12 (1978): 83-90.

As in the Bible, Eve in *Paradise Lost* adds to God's sole command by mentioning that she cannot touch the fruit and that violating his order would lead only to the possibility of death. Biblical commentators argue about who adds to God's prohibition—Adam, after receiving it from God (Genesis 2.17), or a wavering Eve (Genesis 3.3), as many Protestant writers believe—and thus about culpability for the fall. To prevent any consideration of blame from arising when these additions are acknowledged, Milton has Adam and the narrator state them. *Paradise Lost* dramatizes Eve's wavering to show the completely human nature of the middle of a tripartite temptation, whose stages are *suggestio*, *delectatio*, and *consensus*. In the final part, she stops wavering and commits the first sin.

406   Howison, Patricia M. "Memory and Will: Selective Amnesia in *Paradise Lost*." *University of Toronto Quarterly* 56 (1987): 523-39.

The narrator implies that Adam and Eve fall because they willfully disjoin knowledge from memory. Yet the forbidden tree provokes their specific memory of the prohibition revealed by God. While memory should help knowledge lead to obedience, however, the prohibition concerns abstract ideas that are not sensible but intelligible. Adam and Eve rely on more than the tree as a thing or sensory evidence; they must also recall God's words concerning the tree as a sign. Satan dissociates signs from their signified truth. When he ignores the tree's status as a memorial and asserts the primacy of sense knowledge and immediate experience, he successfully convinces Eve that the tree has its own inherent power. Eve and Adam fall when they move away from the claims of memory and toward trust in the immediate. Like the tree of knowledge, the tree of life is a symbol with a historical reality; both trees demonstrate that an accurate perception of creation, and the obedience that accompanies it, depends on understanding the relationship between sense-based knowledge and revelation-based knowledge. God banishes Adam and Eve from the garden to show that, while they are free to remember what they will, they ought to remember the quality of God's relation to them.

407   Kerrigan, William. "Gender and Confusion in Milton and Everyone Else." *Hellas* 2 (1991): 195-220.

Milton's account of the fall attempts to resolve the biblical paradoxes that emphasize equality and Yahwistic subordination. Gender differences probably do exist but are confused by biological and cultural obstacles. However, this perplexity is ultimately productive. Although *Paradise Lost* favors patriarchal authority, Milton presents a countercase of gender differences, creating useful confusion that can teach without impairing. His own identification with the female role influences his treatment of the sexes. The poem's language and imagery are flexible, hinting at the gender confusion (and possibility for improvement) in both Adam and Eve. The gender hierarchy turns out to be self-subverting; Adam's fear of inferiority and Eve's longing to be superior cause them to fall. Milton's greatest contribution to gender studies is to admit that gender is not, and never will be, immutable.

408   Klemp, P. J. "Milton's Pastourelle Vision in *Paradise Lost*." *Études Anglaises* 46 (1993): 257-71.
        When Satan sees Eve alone for the first time in *Paradise Lost* 9.445-54, Milton appropriates the popular pastourelle genre as the basis for an extended simile. The traditional pastourelle poem describes an urban knight's chance meeting with a shepherdess whom he seduces or rapes. Because the narrator of a pastourelle draws no conclusion about such episodes, the genre appears to be amoral. But Milton's reconstruction of the genre in Book 9 shows how the pastourelle simile clashes with the events in Eden. Milton locates the genre's origins in Genesis 3.1-6 and thus defines the medieval pastourelle as Satan's distorted, immoral version of the first conflict between male and female, city and country. While reconstructing the genre's origins and moral assumptions, the embedded pastourelle simile in *Paradise Lost* emphasizes Satan's and Eve's motives and methods in the temptation scene.

409   Low, Anthony. "The Parting in the Garden in *Paradise Lost*." *Philological Quarterly* 47 (1968): 30-35.
        When Adam and Eve discuss working separately, his rhetoric does not convince her, so he tries reverse psychology: instead of presenting Eve with a prohibition, Adam surrenders, hoping she will also surrender. Given the centrality of freedom in Milton's ethical principles, Adam does the only right thing when he allows her to go, an action for which he is never authoritatively exonerated or blamed in *Paradise Lost*. Readers still feel his action is a mistake, yet it seems he could not have done otherwise without violating Eve's freedom of

choice. According to God's single prohibition and evidence in *Samson Agonistes*, however, commanding is not the same as forcing because the former does not necessarily deprive others of free choice. By allowing Eve to go, Adam abdicates his position of loving and natural authority. Had he commanded Eve to work with him, as she seems to have expected him to do, she still would have had the freedom to disobey.

410   Nyquist, Mary. "Fallen Differences, Phallogocentric Discourses: Losing *Paradise Lost* to History." In *Post-Structuralism and the Question of History*, edited by Derek Attridge, Geoff Bennington, and Robert Young, 212-43. Cambridge: Cambridge University Press, 1987.

When Adam and Eve awaken after their first experience of postlapsarian sex, both are compared with Samson and his betrayal by Dalila (9.1059-62). Modern critics misread this simile by seeing a misogynistic Milton in the background, acting as an injured husband who wants to exact revenge. But he does not here associate Eve with Dalila or privilege the personal; as in *Samson Agonistes*, he uses the Samson story in heterogeneous ways. Adam and Eve's fallen lovemaking is, in Aristotle's terms, the probable means that leads to discovery (*anagnorisis*) of loss, which in the epic's logocentric discourse is far greater than the reversal (*peripeteia*) or loss itself. To pair Adam and Samson, and thus Eve and Dalila, in Milton's simile is to misread by focusing on an atemporal form of proportional analogy and by drawing on a patriarchal symbolic order and phallogocentric discourse. If the simile shows that Adam's and Eve's eyes have been opened, the context indicates that only Adam's guilt truly counts.

411   Ogden, H. V. S. "The Crisis of *Paradise Lost* Reconsidered." *Philological Quarterly* 36 (1957): 1-19. Reprinted in *Milton: Modern Essays in Criticism*, edited by Arthur E. Barker, 308-27. London: Oxford University Press, 1965.

Though not perfect, Adam and Eve are not fallen before the fall, which is the climax of *Paradise Lost*'s narrative. The fall is causeless, but Milton still presents a plausible description of the psychological change from innocence to sin in such episodes as Eve's staring at the reflection in the water, her Satanic dream, Adam's confession of inordinate love for Eve, and the separation scene. These events show merely the liability to sin rather than the commission of sin. With the fall, Adam and Eve choose to sin; everything before Book 9 points to this moment and every subsequent event proceeds from it. Milton constructs the climactic scene by evoking fear when Eve is tempted, dismay when she eats the apple, and pity when Adam sins. The fall in *Paradise Lost* is not fortunate.

412   Patrick, J. Max. "A Reconsideration of the Fall of Eve." *Études Anglaises* 28 (1975): 15-21.

Not a narcissistic character, Milton's Eve uses experience and received information to make judgments and act responsibly. Perfection, as applied to Eve and everything in Eden, implies completeness rather than infallibility. Her Satanic dream does nothing to impair the ability to make free choices, though it does provide her with an awareness of evil and an experience of being tempted. When Adam and Eve discuss working separately, they trade roles: he is susceptible to her beauty, while she develops into a subtle debater. Dismissing many of Satan's arguments during the temptation, Eve provides her own reasons to fall by exercising free will and not making good use of her faculties, particularly memory and reason. She is not forced to fall because of her nature, preconditioning, or inferiority.

413   Revard, Stella P[urce]. "Eve and the Doctrine of Responsibility in *Paradise Lost*." *PMLA* 88 (1973): 69-78.

Milton's God makes no distinction between Adam's guilt and Eve's. When the first sinners quarrel, the concept of divided responsibility enters *Paradise Lost*, and they locate the turning point in the morning debate about laboring individually. The Son's judgment, however, focuses not on the events preceding the crime or the sinners' motivation but on the act itself. Judging each individually, he is far more favorable to Eve's admission of guilt and acceptance of responsibility, though of course he finds her blameworthy and assigns a punishment. Adam tries to avoid responsibility by blaming Eve, earning him a rebuke from the Son for being evasive but not for allowing Eve to work alone. The separation of Adam and Eve is neither the turning point nor a matter over which Adam should exercise control. Concerning her sin, his worst failure is as a provider of effective advice. Because inferiority does not predispose one to sin, Eve is created sufficient to stand. Her intellect falters only when faith and love of God fail her during the temptation. In *Paradise Lost*, Milton focuses on the individual's freely chosen commitment to God.

214 *Paradise Lost*: An Annotated Bibliography

414   Safer, Elaine B. "'Sufficient to Have Stood': Eve's Responsibility in Book IX." *Milton Quarterly* 6.3 (1972): 10-14.
        The hierarchical structure of relationships in *Paradise Lost* is clear: Adam depends on God, Eve on Adam. Despite her inferiority to Adam, Eve is sufficient and responsible for her fall. To believe otherwise is to make her inadequate, immune from guilt, and incapable of performing a meaningful repentance.

415   Savage, J. B. "Freedom and Necessity in *Paradise Lost*." *ELH* 44 (1977): 286-311.
        Milton believes freedom is a moral act that subsumes all moral thought and values. In *Paradise Lost*, the premise of free will requires readers to dismiss the notion of causation because it defines actions in terms of necessity. But readers are faced throughout the poem with the contradiction of believing in free will and thinking in terms of causality or necessity. If readers try to view the developing action as a noncausal sequence of events, it becomes incomprehensible; if readers say Adam's actions are not caused but free, then they must occur by chance. Humans possess a provisional freedom, Milton argues, a moral freedom relative to the circumstances in which it is first given. Adam's freedom is limited by and dependent on the scope of his true stature as a rational creature, and he is rational only to the degree that he chooses the good. To do evil is to act in contravention to one's freedom and rationality. Milton leaves readers with an ambiguity—Adam, in one sense, is free to sin or not to sin, but in another sense he is not free if he sins—that leads critics to define events before the fall as devoid of implication and morally distinguishable from the fall or as portents and pre-falls. The fall, almost as a condition of its happening, has the effect of altering readers' ideas about preceding events, a revisionary process Milton reproduces by manipulating perspectives. When Adam confesses that he is entranced by Eve, the fall is morally inevitable.

416   Smith, Russell E., Jr. "Adam's Fall." *ELH* 35 (1968): 527-39. Reprinted in *Critical Essays on Milton from "ELH,"* 182-94. Baltimore, MD: Johns Hopkins Press, 1969.
        According to traditional views, Eve falls by aspiring to a higher place in the hierarchy, and Adam falls by failing to maintain his place. But he also suffers from intellectual ambition and pride; like Eve, he is tempted by forbidden knowledge. Because Adam is suddenly in the unfamiliar role of an inferior, his equilibrium and sense of self-

worth are disturbed when he converses with Raphael. The questions he directs at the angel reveal an increasingly ambitious curiosity that seeks to elevate the self and is less and less controlled by reason. Structurally parallel, Adam's speeches to Raphael are self-conscious, uncertain, clumsy, and intemperately curious. He has a split personality: the Adam in him knows the danger of dissatisfaction; the Eve in him aspires to angelic status.

417   Thickstun, Margaret Olofson. "Effeminate Slackness Substantially Expressed: Woman as Scapegoat in *Paradise Lost*." In *Fictions of the Feminine: Puritan Doctrine and the Representation of Women*, 60-86. Ithaca, NY: Cornell University Press, 1988.

While Adam's temptation comes from within, his other self (Eve) is the immediate cause of his disobedience: his "effeminate slackness," that aspect of human nature embodied by woman, creates his woe when he does not maintain control of his "female" half. Eve is punished for this. In a parody of Adam and Eve's marriage, Satan and Sin's relationship shows unfit partners engaging in sinful mutuality. These characters undercut their own argument in a burlesque of domestic rhetoric that corrects the reader's possibly inappropriate response to the first couple's discussion during the separation scene. Adam and Eve part innocently yet deliberately, for Milton is committed to portraying woman as morally independent and responsible for her own rectitude. But he sends conflicting signals by also making Eve Adam's subordinate and the embodiment of his temptation. After the fall, Eve becomes an idolater of marriage, displaying possessive love that makes her an unfit wife because she does not contribute to her husband's spiritual welfare. At the end of *Paradise Lost*, Eve is left humbled and aware of her own inadequacy.

418   Ulreich, John C. [Jr.]. "'Sufficient to Have Stood': Adam's Responsibility in Book IX." *Milton Quarterly* 5 (1971): 38-42.

Disobedience is a violation of being, one's God-given nature, which leads to a loss of free choice, while rational obedience is choice and the source of love. By failing to realize their capacity for love, humanity falls. When Eve suggests working independently, Adam responds badly because his self-love produces idolatry. He receives primary responsibility for the fall because he destroys their love by failing to protect or restrain Eve. Adam merely pretends to unite with Eve when he chooses to join her in sin; abandoning her to self-love and pride, he increases their separation. Like most readers, Adam thinks he has only two choices: to die with Eve or to give her up. If he trusted God and knew the real meaning of love, however, he would see that a new Eve might be a restoration of the prelapsarian one. Adam could thus redeem Eve by dying for her, not with her.

Other studies that examine Books 9-10 are identified in entries 24, 38, 48, 62, 66, 87, 100, 219, 345, and 382.

16. BOOKS 11-12

419   Amorose, Thomas. "Milton the Apocalyptic Historian: Competing Genres in *Paradise Lost*, Books XI-XII." *Milton Studies*
17 (1983): 141-62.

Paradise Lost's closing books combine suffering and error
with hope for the future to show God producing his desired results by
destroying patterns of behavior that obstruct his freeing humanity from
fallen history. Rejecting the Greco-Roman cyclic conception of history,
Milton does not unquestioningly accept the Judeo-Christian linear
model. Rather, his apocalyptic vision proceeds according to a tripartite
dialectic that subverts the two dominant historical models along with the
behavior they praise and encourage. Books 11-12 subvert inaccurate
views of historical events through the interplay of epic, history, and
prophecy. While cyclic and linear configurations of history appear to
act in a dialectic, they produce only a cycle of destruction; above them,
as Michael teaches Adam, God acts as a guiding force in history, and
his chosen people participate in a progressive tripartite dialectic in
which an age of conscience (Book 11) and an age of law (Book 12) are
synthesized by an age of inward law initiated by Christ's sacrifice.

420   Blackburn, Thomas H. "Paradises Lost and Found: The
Meaning and Function of the 'Paradise Within' in *Paradise
Lost*." *Milton Studies* 5 (1973): 191-211.

Three paradises structure humankind's history: Eden in the
beginning, a paradise within in the middle, and God's eternal kingdom
at the end. *Paradise Lost* is itself an image of the internal paradise and
a means by which the individual may achieve it. Neither eternal nor the
highest state many may attain, according to Raphael (who relates God's
words), the earthly paradise is a conditional state destined to end, even
if humans remain innocent, when many of them are united with God.
A new conditional status appears after the fall, as Michael explains, for
Christ's sacrifice restores the possibility of eternal life for the faithful—but this existence is no higher than that which unfallen humans

could have achieved by resisting temptation. Even in a hellish world of sin, Michael suggests, Adam's mind may become a paradise if he recovers something of the inner state of innocence. The faithful may thus have virtual, if not yet actual, possession of eternal life in heavenly paradises that are "happier far" than was Eden.

421   Bryan, Robert A. "Adam's Tragic Vision in *Paradise Lost*." *Studies in Philology* 62 (1965): 197-214.

In Adam's vision (11.385-411), Milton makes ironic use of the traditional idea that humane learning and civilization move westward, originating in China and later reaching Europe and the new world. The last two books invert this concept to show the movement of sin, not empire and learning, from east to west, the tragic history of human frailty, and the propensity to sin. While Milton omits some geographical sites that are seats of empire and learning, he presents many associated with decay, opulence, and the tyranny of the individual leader. Far from being exotic, many places Michael identifies are connected to destruction, inhumanity, and tragedy. By recording humanity's failure to let reason control passion, Michael uses these locations to reenact the fall.

422   Cavanagh, Michael. "A Meeting of Epic and History: Books XI and XII of *Paradise Lost*." *ELH* 38 (1971): 206-22.

Unlike Virgil, Milton segregates prophetic history from the rest of the poem and makes it explicit and vitally important to the protagonist. He follows Augustine in reflecting the pagan scheme of history as circular and viewing history as God's providential Christocentric plan that culminates in a final salvation outside history. Based on this definition of history, Books 11-12 show the essential process of using one's active virtue to understand God's justice and present a new drama imposed on the previous framework, including demonic conduct, heavenly war, and human weakness. By connecting Adam with the rest of the human race in these books, Milton merges biblical fable into history. Michael's lesson makes Adam heroic by teaching him why he lost paradise and what consequences this loss brings, consequences Adam must be courageous enough to call just as he accepts responsibility for the fall and his descendants. His final optimism gains meaning because he now bears the burden of knowledge and responsibility.

423   Chambers, Douglas. "'Improv'd by Tract of Time': Art's Synopticon in *Paradise Lost*, Book 12." In *Of Poetry and Pol-*

itics: New Essays on Milton and His World, edited by P. G. Stanwood, 79-93. Binghamton, NY: Medieval and Renaissance Texts and Studies, 1995. 4 illustrations.

In Books 11-12 of *Paradise Lost*, not only is Adam's visual and auditory experience identified with the reader's, but his visions "are of the selves that we discover. Our experience becomes like Adam's as his becomes like ours" (79). Michael's revelation to Adam shows the narrative manifestations of synoptica or depictions of all sacred history in one work of art, including the disjunction between the orders of occurrence, telling, and reading. In the Renaissance, secular and sacred tapestries taught that providence rules history, that history's significance is found by observing the workings of eternity in time, and that the viewer has a part in the historical narration.

424   Coiro, Ann Baynes. "'To Repair the Ruins of Our First Parents': *Of Education* and Fallen Adam." *Studies in English Literature, 1500-1900* 28 (1988): 133-47.

Raphael's lessons for Adam correspond to the learning that Milton's *Of Education* proposes for younger students. In Books 11-12 of *Paradise Lost*, Michael leads Adam through a series of lessons that exactly parallels the course Milton outlines in the prose tract, moving from the mere receiving of practical knowledge to self-education about abstract matters. *Of Education* briefly touches on *proairesis*, the ability to make moral judgments, but it is "the cornerstone of Michael's pedagogy" (139). In the tract, part of the second, contemplative stage of education deals with politics, and in *Paradise Lost* this is central to Adam's instruction. Adam's experience follows the plan described in *Of Education*, as he next learns about theology, logic, and rhetoric, but in the epic each lesson contains a darker vision of the human capacity for corruption and failure, as well as the admission that knowledge can lead to good, but also to evil. When the narrator concludes the epic, he teaches readers the final lesson from *Of Education*: what religious and glorious use might be made of poetry.

425   Durkin, Sister Mary Brian. "Iterative Figures and Images in *Paradise Lost*, XI-XII." *Milton Studies* 3 (1971): 139-58.

The instructional emphasis of Books 11-12, in which Adam and Eve learn the rules for living outside of paradise, is intensified by the skillful use of rhetorical figures, which also heighten the auditory and visual beauty of many lines. Fruit and seed images point toward the hope of fertility and a redeemer, and Milton's use of metaphor and color adds to the poetic force of *Paradise Lost*'s final books. See entries 24 and 311.

426   Fitter, Christopher. "'Native Soil': The Rhetoric of Exile Lament and Exile Consolation in *Paradise Lost*." *Milton Studies* 20 (1984): 147-62.

Although Adam and Eve initially respond with paralysis and grief when Michael says they must leave paradise, the angel soon provides comfort based on the topos of exile consolation. Eve's plaint (11.268-73) draws poignancy as an established literary pathos and a contemporary reality concerning the love of one's native grounds. While she fears the separation from an environment where gods visit, Adam fears the separation from God himself and, in an idolatrous perception, holy ground. Using exile consolations outlined by Plutarch, Michael consoles Eve by showing her how to remake adverse fortune and appealing to her corrective values; he consoles Adam by presenting the argument of the universal home. The couple also learns about the lover as a homeland, about the sufficiency of happiness in the beloved's company. Spiritual contentment, as *Paradise Lost* repeatedly argues, transcends physical, historical circumstances. Milton emphasizes the primacy of universal goodness over geographical sentiment.

427   Knoespel, Kenneth J. "Milton and the Hermeneutics of Time: Seventeenth-Century Chronologies and the Science of History." *Studies in the Literary Imagination* 22 (1989): 17-35.

Confronting history as a hermeneutic practice, Books 11-12 are not integrated into *Paradise Lost* because Milton wants readers to complete the work of using those books to negotiate the entire poem. Contemporary universal chronologies provide a visual scheme of metaphysical order, and their blank spaces urge readers to conduct further research. Similarly, Books 11-12 are not the objects but the vehicles of historical inquiry as they challenge Adam and the audience to become readers of chronologies. While Book 11 describes an evolutionary pattern of turning away from God and Book 12 a series of divine revelations promising guidance, the various stages are marked by "a recurrent attraction to the place of technology in the transmission of culture" (24). By showing how historical interpretation is related to the progression of technology, the final books register Milton's response to his society's technological transformation.

428   Loewenstein, David. "*Paradise Lost* and the Configurations of
       History." In *Milton and the Drama of History: Historical
       Vision, Iconoclasm, and the Literary Imagination*, 92-125.
       Cambridge: Cambridge University Press, 1990.
   In Books 11-12, Milton places his poetics of history in the
service of rendering "truth naked" as he struggles with his imaginative
responses to history as a tragic process. These books present conflicting
historical configurations—"degenerative, cyclical, apocalyptic, typological" (93)—that respond imaginatively to Milton's revolutionary writings
and years. The poem posits consolation in the internal paradise and
future apocalypse, but the author's responses to the drama of human
history are deeply divided. Like the revolutionary prose works, *Paradise Lost*'s historiographical enterprise is a search for causes and explanations, with Michael focusing initially on tragic human history and
then on the just men who try to reshape it through prophecy. God, in
the angel's view, is an iconoclast in the drama of history, which vacil-
lates between periods of decline and progress. In *Paradise Lost*'s closing books, Milton never resolves the conflict between a view of history
as degenerative and cyclic or as progressive and apocalyptic. The typological configuration, which attempts to move beyond history's cycles
into an eternal pattern of promise and fulfillment, remains in tension
with the more pessimistic configurations.

429   Lovejoy, Arthur O. "Milton and the Paradox of the Fortunate
       Fall." *ELH* 4 (1937): 161-79. Reprinted in *Essays in the
       History of Ideas*, 277-95. Baltimore, MD: Johns Hopkins
       Press, 1948; reprinted in *Milton's Epic Poetry: Essays on
       "Paradise Lost" and "Paradise Regained,"* edited by C. A.
       Patrides, 55-73. Harmondsworth: Penguin Books, 1967; re-
       printed in *Critical Essays on Milton from "ELH,"* 163-81.
       Baltimore, MD: Johns Hopkins Press, 1969.
   Milton's assertion of the paradox of the fortunate fall (12.469-
78), that the first sin can neither be sufficiently condemned because it
contained all other sins nor rejoiced over because without it the Incarnation and Redemption would never have occurred, includes the view
that the final state of the redeemed will far surpass the first couple's
prelapsarian condition. Human history is thus structured as a divine
comedy. The fortunate fall's long tradition extends back perhaps to the
Gallican sacramentary, which was adopted by the Roman church.

430   MacCallum, H[ugh] R. "Milton and Sacred History: Books XI
       and XII of *Paradise Lost*." In *Essays in English Literature
       from the Renaissance to the Victorian Age*, edited by Millar
       MacLure and F. W. Watt, 149-68. Toronto: University of To-
       ronto Press, 1964.
       Books 11-12 of *Paradise Lost* are structured according to the
traditional Christian chronology of six ages that correspond to the creation's six days. By emphasizing the Mosaic law as a watershed in history, Milton lets readers see the ages' tripartite organization into an age
of patriarchs, an age of law, and an age of gospel. All the ages are
linked by typology, repeated motifs and character types, and a common
cyclic pattern of fall, judgment, regeneration, and renewal. Milton's typology shows his Puritanism and rationalism, however, for he does not
stress the prefigurative function of objects, avoids external or allegorical analogies, and evokes associations by indirect means. Michael's
lesson is arranged in a dialectical pattern of ascent that leads Adam
from type to truth. Like Christ the teacher, the angel proceeds by indirection, leaves each stage of Adam's education inconclusive (except
the last), and misleads so Adam can formulate the false interpretations
he must reject. Michael's teaching has two main movements—a thesis
and an antithesis—the first using natural theology to expose natural
humanity's spiritual bankruptcy, the second using Christianity's revealed truths to present points about spiritual regeneration through
grace.

431   Miller, George [Eric]. "Archetype and History: Narrative
       Technique in *Paradise Lost*, Books XI and XII." *Modern Lan-
       guage Studies* 10 (1980): 12-21.
       Paradise Lost's last two books shift from nonhistorical or
archetypal to historical narration. If Milton uses suggestive terms to
portray the limitless prelapsarian world, Michael describes the limited
world of history with specific, concrete words and signs. During the
angel's lessons, Adam learns to move from his fallen, literal perspective back to a moral, metaphoric one. Spiritual value, according to the
dialectical structure of Book 11, does not guarantee physical reward or
safety, though the internal and external correspond before the fall. With
the flood, language and perspective change: abstraction and personification signal "a momentary return to a more sacred perspective" (18), as
nature becomes animated when it works God's will. The simpler narrative style of Book 12 presents more difficult and abstract lessons, leav-

ing Adam in a choric role. Moving beyond a mere recognition of the effects of Adam and Eve's disobedience, the final book examines the fall's cause and the possible compensation for humans. The Son's entrance into history brings a final metaphoric and moral understanding, while Michael's entire narrative reveals the limitations of the very history it contains and emphasizes the significance of what readers lost after the fall.

432   Miller, Timothy C. "Milton's Religion of the Spirit and 'The State of the Church' in Book XII of *Paradise Lost.*" *Restoration: Studies in English Literary Culture, 1660-1700* 13 (1989): 7-16.
Michael's denunciation of post-apostolic churches in Book 12 does not exempt the Reformation because Milton believes salvation is given through the Spirit's direct guidance, apart from the distracting influence of any institutional church. Milton undercuts some orthodox justifications of a church by stressing the validity of every believer's inner scripture, illuminated by the Spirit, and asserting that no church official is more qualified to administer sacraments than any believer. He goes on in *Treatise of Civil Power* to denounce all imposed religious forms, emphasizing instead the individual and private nature of salvation guided by the Spirit. In *Paradise Lost*, Michael stresses that worldly clergy can never usurp the Spirit's teaching role. Living by the Spirit turns out to be a type of rebellion, whereby believers learn to rely on inner understanding even when it contradicts church doctrine. Ultimately, Michael and Milton reject all possibilities of church reformation, and instead look to the individual conscience and its ability to prefer the Spirit over the world as the only true route to salvation.

433   Miner, Earl. "*Felix Culpa* in the Redemptive Order of *Paradise Lost.*" *Philological Quarterly* 47 (1968): 43-54.
The fall is fortunate because it shows God's glory in absolute terms and his mercy for the few who will be saved during the final days, points that God carefully explains in Book 3 and Abdiel's example illustrates. To the damned, however, the fall brings God's just wrath. Michael's silence when Adam presents his statement of the fortunate fall may suggest that Adam is overenthusiastic and applies this doctrine too broadly, as he should recognize from the visions of human sin that establish the terms for understanding the paradox of the fortunate fall. Like the poem's closing lines, an awareness of the fortunate

fall should be expressed in a mixed tone of joy and tragedy. Books 11-12 narrate the redemptive process in human history, emphasizing those who will be saved and when they will receive their eternal reward. The redemptive order is consistent throughout *Paradise Lost*.

434   Mollenkott, Virginia R. "Milton's Rejection of the Fortunate Fall." *Milton Quarterly* 6.1 (1972): 1-5.

If Adam and Eve had not fallen, they would have progressed, without interference from evil, toward the magnificent goal of heavenly bliss. In *Paradise Lost*, Adam voices the concept of the fortunate fall, yet even he doubts its validity. Milton insists on a vision of a glorious, unfallen future and the magnitude of its loss; thus *Paradise Lost*, instead of concluding with joy, mixes resignation and hope. Michael mentions the happier internal paradise to encourage Adam and Eve to accept the fall's reality and consequences: living in godliness outside Eden will be better than living dishonestly in a paradise where they no longer belong. Adam and Eve would have been better off if they had not fallen, as God states.

435   Moore, C. A. "The Conclusion of *Paradise Lost*." *PMLA* 36 (1921): 1-34.

Neoclassical criticism of *Paradise Lost*'s conclusion as too bleak is answered by eighteenth-century commentators, who note how the final lines balance sorrow for the loss of innocence with hope for future redemption. Concerned not only with sin and its effects, Milton's poem is primarily interested in the remedy—the defeat of Satan, redemption, and salvation. The Judeo-Christian system of mythology produces the epic's inconsistent treatment of death, God, and Satan. From the start, Milton knows he must make the story more logically consistent and conclude by showing Adam and Eve's mixed feelings.

436   Pecheux, Mother Mary Christopher, O.S.U. "Abraham, Adam, and the Theme of Exile in *Paradise Lost*." *PMLA* 80 (1965): 365-71.

Michael presents Abraham as a biblical type who, like Adam, sees distant promises. Called to leave his country, Abraham must respond with faith in God as he departs, just as Adam faces an important test, his first after the fall, in which his obedience and faith will determine whether he goes forth "sorrowing" but "in peace." By acknowledging God's supremacy and accepting his decree, Adam passes the test in a tone that mixes resignation and confidence in the face of exile. His apparent state of wandering is, like the Israelites' journey through the desert, in fact a sure path marked by providence. Instructed in various virtues, he understands the redemptive plan as well as the demands it places on his cooperation. Adam learns about the detachment from, not the repudiation of, earthly things. Just as Abraham is the father of the chosen people, Adam expresses joy at being the father of the race that will produce the Savior. Milton uses the typology of Abraham to universalize the theme of exile and its requirements of obedience, faith, patience, and fortitude. He also presents parallels between Sarah and Eve.

437   Prince, F. T. "On the Last Two Books of *Paradise Lost*." *Essays and Studies* n.s. 11 (1958): 38-52. Reprinted in *Milton's Epic Poetry: Essays on "Paradise Lost" and "Paradise Regained,"* edited by C. A. Patrides, 233-48. Harmondsworth: Penguin Books, 1967.

     Because *Paradise Lost* is both historical and prophetic, the vision of the future in Books 11-12 is necessary, though it is also the epic's most sustained statement of dogma. Milton does not change his usual dramatic technique here, instead continuing to narrate the evolution of Adam's consciousness. Sharing the goal of classical epics, *Paradise Lost* shows human destiny working out through history, with repeated examples of adversity and disaster reaching into the future. Near the end of Book 10, Milton begins to integrate his subject matter with the inevitable weariness readers experience: in Books 11-12, readers meet humans and a world that they know.

438   Radzinowicz, Mary Ann. "'Man as a Probationer of Immortality': *Paradise Lost* XI-XII." In *Approaches to "Paradise Lost,"* edited by C. A. Patrides, 31-51. London: Edward Arnold, 1968.

     Books 11-12 deal with the theme of Adam and everyman receiving an education in liberty, learning within time what God knows in eternity and recognizing that action based on free will is an essential condition for a peaceful existence. Adam sees that patience and heroic martyrdom contribute not just to an inner condition but to a species of ethical conduct that makes one a probationer of immortality. According to these final books, human behavior matters—it affects history—because each virtuous or loving act marks a triumph of good over evil. Michael reveals the growth of Christian liberty and the accompanying increase in the possibility of regeneration, even as human affairs in

politics grow darker. Through typology, all of history is made to serve
the education of Adam and his descendants. In *Paradise Lost*'s concluding books, Michael teaches Adam that heroic virtue is the lesson
of charity that fulfills all Christian virtues.

439   Rajan, Balachandra. "*Paradise Lost*: The Hill of History." In
       The Lofty Rhyme: A Study of Milton's Major Poetry, 79-99.
       Coral Gables, FL: University of Miami Press, 1970.
       Not dominated by a wrathful tone, Books 11-12 prepare for
the idea of a paradise within by indicating that the battle between God
and Satan now occurs in the human mind and history is "the collective
result of the individual struggle for moral transformation" (80). Humanity covenants with sin again and again, but the good makes a
mounting commitment to the movement of history. Unlike readers,
Adam gains serenity not woe from Michael's lessons.

440   Reesing, John. "The Rhythm of *Paradise Lost*, Books XI and
       XII." In *Milton's Poetic Art: "A Mask," "Lycidas," and "Par-
       adise Lost,"* 89-104. Cambridge, MA: Harvard University
       Press, 1968.
       Book 11 begins with three speeches in contrasting tones or
rhythms—God is regretful but firm, Adam livelier, and Eve burdened
with shame. In Books 11-12, the narrator speaks in a rapid rhythm that
is replaced with the efficient, pedagogic style of Michael, who becomes
more and more involved and excited. The rhythms of these books create a sense of order restored.

441   Rogers, John. "Milton and the Mysterious Terms of History."
       ELH 57 (1990): 281-305.
       When considering one issue of history and causation—"what
cause" moved Adam and Eve to sin—*Paradise Lost* engages the discourses of psychology, theology, philosophy, and physiology. Milton's
God, explaining to the Son why Adam and Eve may no longer live in
paradise, appeals to the impersonal justice of nature's laws, which
require the expulsion to preserve the garden's purity. But God then
presents a contradictory rationale to the heavenly community: through
Michael, he must intervene in the realm of nature to prevent the couple
from indulging in the tree of life, a stern act of retributive justice by an
anthropomorphic deity. Divine causation in *Paradise Lost* is thus based
on either an impersonal, natural force or a personal, transcendental
force, yet it can be both only through a monistic union. Human free-

dom and divine necessity are interdependent until Michael presents his theocentric theory, in which God intervenes in history, now a forum for divine retributive justice. The conflict between rationalistic and anthropomorphic deities receives a poetic resolution because Michael's description of the movement from law to grace implies the obsolescence of his own historical discourse. In the expulsion scene, causation is a supernatural force, a material one, or both—that is, the poem concludes with irreconcilable versions of providence to show historical transformation.

442   Sasek, Lawrence A. "The Drama of *Paradise Lost*, Books XI and XII." In *Studies in English Renaissance Literature*, edited by Waldo F. McNeir, 181-96. Louisiana State University Studies, Humanities Series, no. 12. Baton Rouge: Louisiana State University Press, 1962. Reprinted in *Milton: Modern Essays in Criticism*, edited by Arthur E. Barker, 342-56. London: Oxford University Press, 1965; reprinted in *Milton: Modern Judgements*, edited by Alan Rudrum, 205-18. London: Macmillan, 1968.

Modifying the epic convention of describing history's movement, Milton, like Du Bartas, uses the final books to enlarge the scope of the action and present a narrative sequence. He also shows Adam and Michael engaging in a dialogue, shifting the focus of Books 11-12 from biblical events to a study of Adam's developing responses, conscience, and Christian fortitude. Besides being theologically necessary, Adam and Eve's removal from paradise is dramatically necessary because God finds that Adam's postlapsarian behavior makes him unfit to stay. Michael must help Adam and Eve achieve stability, understand their sin, and recognize their hopes. The angel's vision and narrative—the latter used for instruction in theological doctrine—present dramatic events to fulfill a dramatic purpose. Though Milton never endorses the idea of a fortunate fall, Adam moves from despair to hopes and fears, and finally to an awareness of good's victory over evil.

443   Schwartz, Regina. "From Shadowy Types to Shadowy Types: The Unendings of *Paradise Lost*." *Milton Studies* 24 (1988): 123-39.

The movement from the Old to the New Testament, and of Michael's education of Adam, is usually described as a transition from flesh to spirit and law to grace, but these phrases are inappropriate for

Milton's work. Adam's new-found confidence and clarity of vision are both false, for the angel manipulates typology to lead from shadowy types not to truth but to unfinished conclusions and incomplete revelations, producing frustration or deferral rather than fulfillment. *Paradise Lost*'s narrator allows Michael to reach the world's end only in his inset narrative; this final rest becomes a mere pause when the narrator copies the angel's technique and returns to his own story of Adam. The biblical text is embedded within Michael's narrative, which is embedded in the narrator's poem. By shifting among these three narratives, Milton subverts the biblical plot: he concludes—actually, he breaks off—not with Revelation but with the expulsion scene in Genesis. In the final two books, Michael offers Adam the temptation to possess the entire story of biblical history, to know rather than to decide his future.

444   Shullenberger, William. "Sorting the Seeds: The Regeneration of Love in *Paradise Lost*." *Milton Studies* 28 (1992): 163-84.
     The sorting of good knowledge from evil involves removing Eros from Thanatos, a task that Adam and Eve begin in *Paradise Lost*'s final books and that marks the first significant postlapsarian differentiation in gender roles. In Milton's epic, characters discover who they are when their lives are offered as an image of an other. By using the recognition of the other to reactivate their capacity to love and by struggling to understand the enigma of the seed, which is stated in the *protevangelium* (10.179-81), Adam and Eve initiate the regeneration of their love. When Eve tells Adam of her dream (12.610-23), she suggests that her knowledge may now exceed his. The dream describes her delivery to the future intact, but Adam is "the body knowledge of human life which is destined for suffering and death" (173). In Books 11-12, Adam becomes a student of Protestant poetics who demystifies forms of spiritual and temporal authority, uses his sharpened recognition of fallen ambiguities to read providential signs typologically, and interiorizes the process of regeneration. A countermovement in those books, the alienation effect makes spiritual complacency impossible. Fallen existence brings human solitude as both numinous consolation and loneliness.

445   Tayler, Edward W. "*Paradise Lost*: From Shadows to Truth." In *Milton's Poetry: Its Development in Time*, 60-104. Pittsburgh, PA: Duquesne University Press, 1979.

Milton writes highly proleptic verse that ties and unties the workings of the eternal in time. Using such stylistic devices as repetition and enjambment, *Paradise Lost* presents progressive revelation in and through time with a typological pattern of promise and fulfillment, as is particularly evident in Books 11-12. While God writes the allegory of human history that Michael explains to Adam, the poet's muse uses the same "mysterious terms" throughout. Adam slowly learns to comprehend typological thinking—that is, to be an exegete—but Satan remains "a kind of fundamentalist of the imagination" (82). By using the theory of types to transmute history, Milton shows how Adam's education is analogous to the muse's method and God's grand design. The idea of wandering takes on many connotations in *Paradise Lost*, ranging from the innocent to the pejorative, as language moves from a univocal vehicle of expression before the fall to an ambiguous and ironic medium in the postlapsarian cosmos.

446   Thompson, Elbert N. S. "For *Paradise Lost*, XI-XII." *Philological Quarterly* 22 (1943): 376-82.

In *Paradise Lost*'s final books, Milton effectively selects and orders his material and writes in a style much like that of the preceding ten books. The concluding two books are also necessary, for Adam lacks extensive experience and must learn the full effects of his sin. Michael teaches him about obedience as his ethical inheritance and history as a direct expression of God's will. The divine council scene in Book 11, unlike the one in Book 3, carefully conveys both God's mercy and justice, as the heavenly and earthly worlds readjust their relationship. When Michael shifts from vision to narration, the poem's style may be more compact and difficult, for the social and political problems he explains are more complex. With his guidance, Adam reaches a calm and confident acceptance of the facts of life.

447   Ulreich, John C., Jr. "A Paradise Within: The Fortunate Fall in *Paradise Lost*." *Journal of the History of Ideas* 32 (1971): 351-66.

Michael's assurance that Adam and Eve will possess a paradise within seems to contradict the poem's basic assumption that the loss of Eden causes all our woe. When they account for the paradox of the fortunate fall, some critics deny God's providence and thus impugn his integrity and wisdom, while others deny human freedom and thus deny that the fall is fortunate. But Milton's justification of God's ways depends on the premises that humanity falls of their own free will and receives that will in order to choose. The fall is fortunate only because humans may still gain infinitely more than they lost. Michael teaches Adam and Eve that they would have been happier if they had not fallen, and that they may yet become happier than they were in Eden.

448   Waddington, Raymond B. "The Death of Adam: Vision and Voice in Books XI and XII of *Paradise Lost.*" *Modern Philology* 70 (1972): 9-21.

The dominant typological pattern of Books 11-12 is that of the first and second Adam, the sinner and the redeemer. While the images and themes of Book 11 point to a descent into evil, the heroes of faith who emerge keep alive the paradox of good emerging from evil as well as the possibility of redemption. Correspondences between Adam's six visions of the first age of humanity (11.429-901) and the remaining six ages (12.1-551) reveal a symmetry between the two books that compensates for the asymmetrical structure that the book division imposes on the week of sacred history. Michael shifts from vision in Book 11 to narration in Book 12 because Adam's death occurs in the fifth vision, before the recession of the flood, and thus he cannot be permitted to see the final book's events.

449   Walker, William. "Typology and *Paradise Lost*, Books XI and XII." *Milton Studies* 25 (1989): 245-64.

Typological or figural thinking dissolves temporal connections and disrupts the concept of history as a sequence of causally linked events that unfolds like a narrative. This way of thinking is accompanied by a new vocabulary and syntax, as appears in the fragmented narration, flat style, and denial of definitiveness to the events in Books 11-12. The typological paradigm posits not an opposition between shadowy type (model or signifier) and truth (copy or signified) but a shaded continuum between type and antitype. Even the nature of a type's fulfillment in the antitype is called into question when both are ultimately fulfilled in the apocalypse, a complication that renders figural thinking incoherent by turning the antitype into another type awaiting completion. Insisting on the difficulties of articulating the typological view of history, Books 11-12 indicate that the fulfillment of the type matters less than "the human engagement with the type as law which disciplines man to the point of allowing him to accept the new covenant" (261).

Paradise Lost interrogates both the fulfillment that seems to come with the Nativity and Crucifixion, as well as the complete fulfillment to be achieved by the apocalypse. History contains types that are fulfilled in some sense yet remain signs of what utterly transcends them.

450   Wilkes, G. A. "'Full of Doubt I Stand': The Final Implications of *Paradise Lost.*" In *English Renaissance Studies*, edited by John Carey, 271-78. Oxford: Clarendon Press, 1980.

According to the reader's total experience, *Paradise Lost*'s positive movement of a providential design based on the fortunate fall is too faint and theoretical, while the loss of paradise is conveyed quite powerfully. If Books 11-12 leave a weaker impression, that is their purpose because Milton intends to offer a "disturbing vision" (273). A new, superior Eden is a remote promise to be fulfilled beyond the poem's scheme; before the reader in the final books loom the fallen world and postlapsarian humanity's experience. Grace will be ultimately victorious, but the fall itself is irreversible.

Other studies that examine Books 11-12 are identified in entries 57, 93, 100, 118, 148, 151, 178, 211, 271, 394, and 404.

INDEX OF SCHOLARS

All references are to entry numbers

Bundy, Murray W., 363
Burden, Dennis H., 110
Bush, Douglas, 1, 111

Campbell, Gordon, 364
Carey, John, 6, 450
Carnes, Valerie, 112
Carrithers, Gale H., Jr., 113-14
Cavanagh, Michael, 422
Chambers, A. B., 231, 259, 402
Chambers, Douglas, 423
Champagne, Claudia M., 365
Cirillo, Albert R., 115, 232
Claridge, Laura, 358
Clark, Ira, 116, 323
Coffin, Charles Monroe, 324
Coiro, Ann Baynes, 424
Colie, Rosalie L., 117
Collett, Jonathan H., 45
Cook, Eleanor, 293
Cooley, Ronald W., 118
Cope, Jackson I., 119
Cope, Kevin L., 114
Copeland, Thomas A., 366
Corns, Thomas N., 25
Corthell, Ronald J., 92
Cotsell, Michael, 350
Cox, Catherine I., 120
Crosman, Robert, 121
Crump, Galbraith M., 122
Cunnar, Eugene R., 368
Curry, Walter Clyde, 123

Damrosch, Leopold, Jr., 124
Daniells, Roy, 125, 325
Danielson, Dennis Richard, 294

Darbishire, Helen, 2, 10, 126
Davies, Stevie, 127-28, 240, 326
Davis, Walter R., 26
Demaray, John G., 129-30
Di Cesare, Mario A., 27, 92, 134, 316
Diekhoff, John S., 131, 219
Dillon, Steven C., 132
Dobbins, Austin C., 46
Duncan, Joseph E., 327
Durham, Charles W., 274
Durkin, Sister Mary Brian, 425
DuRocher, Richard J., 47
Dyson, A. E., 28, 36, 80, 133, 137, 167, 192, 219, 335

Eliot, T. S., 28, 80
Elledge, Scott, 3, 36, 107, 137, 140, 172, 295, 315, 335
Emma, Ronald David, 12, 27, 33, 41
Empson, William, 295
Engel, William E., 260
Engle, Lars, 134
Entzminger, Robert L., 135
Evans, G. Blakemore, 299
Evans, J. M., 48

Fallon, Stephen M., 136, 296
Farwell, Marilyn R., 403
Ferguson, Margaret W., 106, 156, 293, 389
Ferry, Anne Davidson, 233, 328
Fiore, Amadeus P., O.F.M., 70, 261, 269, 303
Fiore, Peter A., 49
Fish, Stanley Eugene, 93, 137

INDEX OF SUBJECTS

All references are to entry numbers

Moseley, Edwin M., 248
Murry, John Middleton, 91
Myth, 160, 172, 212, 335

Narrator, 43, 47, 67, 81, 105,
113, 118-19, 121, 135, 137,
147, 160, 163, 165-66, 168,
171, 174-75, 178-80, 184,
196, 199, 202, 205-207, 210,
220, 229-30, 233, 235, 242,
244-45, 247, 250-52, 262,
309, 326, 443
Nativity Ode, 102, 205
Newton, Isaac, 427
Newton, Thomas, 88, 94-95
Numerology, 6, 210, 249

O'Brien, Mary, 88
Of Education, 67, 118, 147,
361, 394, 397, 424
Of Reformation, 147
Ontology, 123, 207, 263
Origen, 327
Orthography, 2, 9-12, 22, 40,
126
Ovid, 47, 52-53, 55, 57, 60,
63, 68, 166, 201

Palingenius, Marcellus, 54
Palmer, Samuel, 83
Paradise Regained, 22, 25, 40-
41, 56, 71-73, 76, 79, 88,
102, 113, 119, 135, 140-41,
159, 169, 179, 183, 193, 198,
214-15, 219, 222, 224, 236,
242, 247, 250, 269, 310, 330,
354
Paterson, James, 95
Pearce, Zachary, 94-95
Peck, Francis, 95

Pedagogy, 122
Penseroso, Il, 113, 330
Peter, John, 36
Petrarch, Francis, 320
Peyton, Thomas, 54
Phillips, Edward, 9, 12, 75
Philo Judaeus, 75, 327
Philostratus, 219
Physics, 123, 155
Pichot, Amédée, 96
Plato, 165, 231, 234, 259,
303, 375, 386, 410
Platonism (and Neoplatonism),
67, 123, 136, 267, 386
Plotinus, 386
Plutarch, 426
Poems (1645), 113, 170
Point of view, 117, 121, 128,
175, 206, 233, 335, 388
Pongerville, J. B. Sanson de,
96
Pope, Alexander, 81, 369
Pordage, Samuel, 54
Prolusions, 147
Psalm Paraphrases, 292
Publication history, 17, 170
Punctuation, 10-11, 40
Purchas, Samuel, 130
Puritanism, 87
Pushkin, Aleksandr
Sergeyevich, 79

Radzinowicz, Mary Ann, 92
Rajan, Balachandra, 163, 261
Ramism, 119, 155, 394
Ramsey, Andrew, 54
Reader, 137, 163, 248, 316
Ready and Easy Way, 109
Reason of Church-Government,
147

ABOUT THE AUTHOR

An Associate Editor of *Milton Quarterly*, P. J. Klemp teaches at the University of Wisconsin, Oshkosh. His publications include such works as *Fulke Greville and Sir John Davies: A Reference Guide* and *The Essential Milton: An Annotated Bibliography of Major Modern Studies*, and he is the Associate Editor of Calvin Huckabay's *John Milton: An Annotated Bibliography, 1968-1988*. He has edited Samuel Sheppard's *The Faerie King* (c. 1650) and published articles about Milton, Donne, Spenser, Jonson, Dante, Petrarch, and Lancelot Andrewes.